CULTURAL HERITAGE OF BUDDHISM

Cultural Heritage of Buddhism

Manohar Bhardwaj

CYBER TECH PUBLICATIONS
4264/3, Ansari Road, Daryaganj, New Delhi-110002 (India)
Ph.: 011-23244078, Fax: 011-23280028
E-Mail: cyberpublicationsdelhi@yahoo.com

CULTURAL HERITAGE OF BUDDHISM

Manohar Bhardwaj

First Edition 2009

Published by :

G.S. Rawat for **Cyber Tech Publications**
4264/3, Ansari Road, Daryaganj, New Delhi-110002 (India)
Ph.: 011-23244078. Fax: 011-23280028
E-Mail: cyberpublicationsdelhi@yahoo.com

Printed at : Asian Offset Printers

Preface

Over thousands of years of national building and defense, the Indian people have made untold sacrifices to gain the fundamental human rights, namely the right to live in independence and freedom, the right to food, clothing, housing, education and dignity. All the nations on the earth are equal from birth, all the nations have a right to live, to be happy and free.

It is the Indian policy to respect and protect human rights. The State has also done its utmost to ensure the realization of human rights through the building and constant improvement of the legal system and the undertaking of concrete measures aimed at promoting economic, social and cultural development so that every citizen can enjoy a better life both materially and spiritually in an equal, democratic and civilised society.

To help the world public better understand the Indian tradition in protecting and promoting human rights and the current human rights implementation in India, the Ministry of Foreign Affairs.

This book is a sincere attempt of the undersigned to bring the masses near to the cultural of Buddhism.

—*Author*

CONTENTS

1

The Origin and Characteristics of Buddhism

Religion is a social phenomenon and studying it with a view to understanding its historical development has special significance today. We can see similar trends in other countries where the rapid developments of science and technology do not in any significant way lessen the people's sense of, nor interests in, religion. Even the people of China, for some reason or other, show similar interests in the development of religion. This phenomenon is enough to raise several theoretical questions concerning the need for a better understanding of religion: what is the nature of religion? Does the human psyche require a religious faith? Is religion synonymous with religious belief? Is religious belief beneficial to social life? Is science complementary to, or inconsistent with, religious belief? Can religion be a modernizing agent? and so forth. This paper does not pretend to deal specifically with these questions, But, why do we study the history of religions? Should an ideal history of religions be time-conscious? Can such an history help people think seriously about the problems of religion that exist in the world today? All historians of religions need to address themselves to these kinds of problems.

The religions which had been popular in Chinese history include Buddhism, Buddhism, Islam, Christianity and animism. However, of all these religious traditions, only Buddhism is indigenous to China. To be sure, Buddhism is a Chinese religion; it has characteristics peculiar to the Chinese. Besides, it has exercised considerable influence on the development of Chinese culture and psychology, customs and habits, science and technology, philosophy and thought, medicine and hygiene, and even political life. Can our investigation into one of the more influential religions--the origin of Buddhism, its development and characteristics--help us deepen our understanding of Chinese culture, personality and way of thinking? Can it indirectly help us understand, more intimately, the theoretical and practical problems of religion in the world today? I think it can and toward this end the present discussion is an attempt to analyze and discuss the following issues.

General Background

The development of Buddhism was an attempt to orientate the Han Chinese to their social, political, economic, moral and psychological lives at the end of the Eastern Han.

Why did Buddhism develop only at the end of the Eastern Han period? Historically, such Daoist ideas, as `immortality' and `sanctification of the bodies' had already existed during the time of the Warring States (Zhanguo). They became even more popular during the Qin and Han dynasties--why? We know that not just any kind of superstition can be called religion, although religion often embodies a good deal of superstitious elements. Neither can we say that any theistic discourse can become a religion, even if it is capable of extending its influence over a sizeable cross-section of the population. Its growth and development were directly related to the social life of the people, their history, and other objective facts. The development of Buddhism during the Eastern Han may be attributed to the following factors.

First, the reality of social life at the end of the Eastern Han had laid fertile grounds for the growth of Buddhism. The social and political conditions, since Shundi of the Eastern Han, had begun to deteriorate. There was outside interference in the day-to-day administration and the administrative machinery was in the hands of a bureaucracy. Debauchery, unruly behavior and social strife, both from within and without, were the order of the day. Finally there were crop failures due to severe drought, and large numbers of people died in ditches

(Chong Zhangdong, Changyuan). Undue economic exploitations and political pressure at that time had made it impossible for the populace to lead a decent life; bankruptcy and emigration were common. The conflict between the ruling class and the ruled was intense and acute. According to historical records, from Shundi's time, peasant uprisings were rampant. At that time, apart from the common class-interest that united them in social movements, their leaders resorted to magic and superstitions as organizing agents. That is why, in history books, the rebels after Shundi's time were often called yaozei, or `the goblin thieves'.

Two conclusions may be drawn from the above discussion. First, a period of economic and political unrest, as well as spiritual and moral decay, provided an objective vantage for the development of religion. Second, as the leaders of the peasantry had used magic and superstitions to rally support in their movements, they knew that these could be used as tools for mobilizing the people, thus paving the way for the widespread development of religion. As is always the case, social turbulence often caused great hardship and suffering to the lower class. Thus, when people became desperate they tended to hinge their hopes upon some kind of spiritual power, or shenling. This was one of the most common avenues through which people, in antiquity, reconciled themselves with their social reality. This also explains why a majority of the early Daoist believers were members of the lower social strata.

Second, the social conditions at the end of the Eastern Han had provided useful material for the founding of Buddhism. Since the time of Han Wudi, when Dong Zhongshu pointed out that "of the hundred schools, only Confucianism is the most revered," Confucian thought had adapted itself to the needs of building a unified feudal society and serving as an ideology for the ruling class. From then on the development of Confucianism depended primarily on the teaching of a reciprocal relationship between heaven and man, followed by an increased interest in the development of theology and metaphysics. Though ideally a religion is theistic, not any form of theism is adequate or sufficiently meaningful to become a religion. This is because such a religion (namely, the religion of the masses) must include not only the worship of spiritual beings, but also possess a body of canon together with an endurable form of church organization, doctrines and dogmas, and an historical medium for the dissemination of religious knowledge. Generally, religion must see the world in two forms: the real and the supernatural. Based on this premise, human beings feel that they can only disengage themselves from the problems of social life in a supernatural world--believing that an ideal life can manifest itself only in the yonder shore of the supernatural world.

Despite the fact that Confucianism acknowledged the existence of Shen or God, especially during the Han dynasty, it had never thought it necessary that its ideals be fulfilled outside the world, but required rather that the ideals of "governing the state and pacifying the world" (zhi guo ping tianxia) be actualized in the real world, even though this were merely an illusion. Although religion had played a very important role in feudal China, it had never become a force to reckon with. Instead it had, many a time, occupied a secondary position, which state of affairs clearly bespoke as well the dominance of Confucian ideology.

From the developmental point of view, after the Eastern Han Confucianism could very well have become a religion, because its metaphysics together with the conception of the sacred could be easily converted into religion. However, Confucianism did not become a religion during the Han dynasty for the simple reason that it attempted to materialize the ideals of "governing the state and pacifying the world" in the real world. Thus, following the decay of the Han dynasty, Confucian ideology not only fell short of becoming a religion but its position as an ideology of the ruling class continued to decline. Because of this decline, Confucian thought had given way to the growth of Buddhism. History shows that, whenever the dominant ideology of the ruling class lost its power, it often signalled the growth and dominance of a countervailing religion.

Even though Confucianism had declined at the end of the Eastern Han, certain facets of its ideology could still be absorbed and put to good use by an ongoing religion. The fact that

Confucian ideas are found in Buddhism is clear proof that such assimilation did take place. For example, the idea of "the ultimate peace in the unity of the three (heaven, earth and man) in one" (tian-di-ren san heyi zhi taiping) shows that the Confucianists were concerned about political reality and the notion of sancai (three endowments) mentioned in Yi Zhuan2. The idea that the sky and the universe were formed by breath (qi) could have derived from the knowledge of world creation as well as the yin-yang principles and the five elements mentioned in the apocryphal texts. All these ideas were closely connected to Han Confucian thought. That most of the scholars who studied the development of Buddhism focused their attention on its relationship with Daoist sources and overlooked the nexus between Daoist and Confucianist ideas is a bias.

Buddhism could have another source in its gradual mingling with the tradition of the saints. Although there was a connection between the Daoists and the saints of the early Qin, both seem to belong to quite different schools of thought. Until the beginning of the Western Han, the popular Huang-Lao learning was essentially Daoist. It frequently emphasized the exemplary qualities of the sage and was thus deemed capable of exercising its power over the state and the cosmos. That is why Sima Qian, in his preface, commented that the importance of the Huang-Lao learning lies in the doctrine of "self-actualization through non-action, and self-correction through expiation" (wuwei zihua, qingjing zizheng).

The Huang-Lao Daoist learning underwent a change during the Eastern Han: part of its adherents sought the help of the gods installed in shrines, thus becoming unified with the saints. Huandi, for example, made sacrifices to Laozi (Lao Tzu) at the latter's shrine with the aim to "preserve shen for the uplift of character and the ultimate ascent to heaven," thus signalling the initial transformation of Huang-Lao's Daoist teaching. Also, as early as the end of the Western Han, there was already in existence what was known as "Huang-lao's Dao" (the Way of Huang-Lao) and, later on, the "Fangxian's Dao" (the Way of the Saints), all of which actually belonged to the immortalist sects. Further, the saints' underlying objective was to attain `eternal life' (changsheng busi) and to cause the bodies to be sanctified (routi chengxian). Thus, once it merged with the Daoist ideas of "attaining peace through inaction, and remaining in peace through abstinence" (qingjing wuwei, tiandan guayu), it increasingly began to attract the masses and became a powerful social force. Lastly, the basic tenets of Buddhism, such as "immortality" and "the sanctification of the bodies," although derived from the Way of the Saints, became part of the Daoist system. Hence, its transformation also represents an important factor contributing to the growth of Buddhism.

From the above viewpoints, Buddhism as a religion may be said to have deviated from the Confucianists' and Daoist' schools of thought. However, its source of ideas was inseparable from both. Hence, from the beginning, it had distinguished itself as a religious system in which Confucian and Daoist ideas supplemented each other. This system represents some of the characteristics typical of Chinese culture, psychology and way of thinking.

Third, the introduction of Buddhism into China had greatly stimulated the development of Chinese religion. From the time Buddhism spread to China during the Western Han till after the middle of the Eastern Han, it maintained a steady level of propagation. Buddhism, acting like a catalyst, escalated the development of Buddhism. Actually, the school of the saints was already popular during the Western Han, and disciples frequently had given tributes to Huang-Lao. This was evidenced in the existing learnings of "Huang-Lao's Dao" and "Fangxian's Dao." The former sanctified Huangdi and worshipped him in shrines dedicated to him; the latter talked about "non-death and everlasting life" (zhongshen busi). Shiji3 records that the teacher of the river elder, Le Jigong, learned about Huangdi.

The book of Fengchan records that Huangdi became an immortal because of Fengchan. Yujie (more appropriately, Ganjie), who compiled the Daoist scripture Taiping Jing, suggested that the book was originally by Laozi (Lao Tzu). During Han Mingdi, Chu Wangying had already worshipped Huangdi and Foutu. Chu Wangying recited Huang-Lao's words and honored Foutu's shrine. Huandi erected Huang-Lao's and

Foutu's shrines in his palace. The fact that Huang-Lao and Foutu were worshiped manifestly shows that Huangdi was at that time regarded as a deity or a Buddha. Sainthood was in fact a form of sagehood. Living the life of an immortal is but a human discipline. There was no formal, nor endurable form of organization to be used as a base for the interaction of the religious community. But after the spread of Buddhism to China, it became an organized form of religion, possessing not only a set of teaching which differed from that of traditional China, but also an organized church, with a religious canon and a spiritual community, all of which served as a blueprint for the founding of Buddhism.

It is true that Buddhism had served as a model for the establishment of Buddhism. Of even greater importance is that Buddhism was alien to Chinese culture, and its propagation in China was greeted with protests by the bearers of Xia's cultural tradition. This defensive attitude acted as a stimulus spurring the Chinese to strive even harder towards establishing an indigenous religion. When an ethnic culture encountered an alien culture it often gave rise to mutual absorption or rejection.

This situation was particularly marked in the case of the Chinese response to Indian Buddhism. We can provide evidence to show how it was actually reflected in the earliest Daoist scripture, Taiping Jing. In this scripture, we see how some Buddhist ideas, like benqi (the primal beginning) and sanjie (the three worlds), had their origins in the Buddhist canon. On the other hand, there were criticisms about Buddhism, for example, the talks that "the conduct of the four destructions collectively denigrates the spiritual way of heaven" (Shihui zhi xing, gong wuru huangtian zhi shendao). Moreover, upon the establishment of Buddhism, its adherents circulated the story about Laozi (Lao Tzu)'s role in bringing about a renaissance among the northern Chinese (Laozi [Lao Tzu] huahu). This was designed not only as a blow to Buddhism but also as an attempt to boost the image of Buddhism. All this suggests a kind of antagonistic reaction against the entry of the alien culture.

Therefore, it is not at all surprising that the end of the Eastern Han period saw the need for the development of an indigenous religion. The founding of this religion could be traced to the existing tradition of the saints. The fact that it adopted Confucian and Daoist ideas as a basis for the development of Buddhism is even less surprising. Once it emerged, it immediately became charged with an intense ethnic fervor and came into direct conflict with the alien Buddhist religion. The outcome is, precisely, a manifestation of an indigenously endowed Chinese culture.

THE DEVELOPMENT OF BUDDHISM

The Process through which Buddhism developed into an organized religion also a clear manifestation of how a religious community came into being.

What is the nature of religion? It can be defined in a great number of ways. Even in Marx's writings, religion is conceived differently under different circumstances. He said, "religion is the opiate of the people," which is interpreted in terms of the use of religion as a way of hypnotising the masses. This statement came not from Marx but Feuerbach. It means that the purveyors of religion who claimed that it could bring comfort to humankind were not being honest. Lenin conceived of "religion as the workers' groaning sound," which is interpreted as relating to the agony of the proletariat. Brezhnev said, "Religion has a countless number of definitions. . . . It may be interpreted as a form of relationship that helps to realize the existence of the mystical superhuman power, for humans believe that they can depend on this power." Brezhnev's definition seems to be more relevant and practical, but is there such a mystical power? How do we adjust to the existence of such a power? Why do people find it necessary to believe in such a power? Is belief in a mystical superhuman power superstitious? This raises some philosophical problems, viz., the problems of religion vis-a-vis superstition and belief.

Is religion a superstition? This question can be debated for a long time and no one knows when it will end, but devout believers most certainly will reject the pronouncement that "religion is superstition." Why? It is because believers frequently rely upon certain ideal principles to interpret what often is called the "mystical superhuman power" in the form of ultimate "truth, goodness, and beauty" (zhen, shan, mei), or else they often look upon the ideals of "truth, goodness, and beauty" as a form of "mystical superhuman power." They sincerely believe it to be true and try very hard to apply these ideals in their social life. Probably the belief in, and dependence upon, this ultimate "truth, goodness and beauty" in the guise of a "mystical superhuman power" is a matter of the human psyche's response to specific social conditions. But believers of the "mystical superhuman power" assume superstition and religion to be two different things. To them, `superstition' can only be a trick played upon those who lack scientific knowledge, i.e. a manifestation of spiritual poverty due to a lack of ideals. Devotees who believe that the "mystical superhuman power" is a manifestation of "truth, goodness, and beauty" may perhaps accept the idea that "religion is synonymous with belief" but certainly will not accept that "religion is superstition." According to them people should have faith: even the agnostics believe in agnosticism.

Religion and belief are undoubtedly related. Religion is based on belief, but whether belief is based on religion, in the classical sense, is a different matter. As a matter of illustration we can say that "we believe in the scientific explanation of atheism" or even accept that "we believe in Confucian philosophy." Nonetheless, there is no doubt that atheism is not a religion, but a scientific doctrine. Even Confucianism may be said to have embodied certain religious elements, although it is not a religion. Therefore, we should distinguish not only between `religion' and `belief,' but also between `religion' and `religious thought.' Otherwise, almost any kind of philosophical discourse could be regarded as a religion, and if that be the case, it would be as good as abnegating the existence of religion.

Based on our understanding of the human psyche, we may postulate that human beings really need a certain kind of belief. The question is whether there is the need for a religious belief. If we could divide religion into two categories--one a scientific belief--and another a non-scientific belief - religion may be said, generally, to belong to the latter category. What follows immediately will be questions like whether human spiritual life requires a certain kind of self-satisfaction obtained from a non-scientific discipline, or whether social life looks upon religious belief itself as a psychological need. This is too gigantic a problem to be discussed here. We can only postulate that for a non-scientific belief to become an organized religion, it must offer some kind of theoretical bases or support. Also, these arguments must be able to reflect the spirit of the time. If there were no religious teachings to be used as a theoretical system, non-scientific beliefs could become an established religion. Besides, as an established religion, especially one that had colored the history of the social masses, there must be a perduring church organization, a religious canon, a community of devotees, and a history of religion.

In Chinese history, there were thousands of the so-called "religious sects," but not all of them could be regarded strictly as "religious organizations." In fact, a number of them could only be looked upon as "superstitious cults." If that be the case, what then may be thought to be an organized religion? We shall analyze the growth of Buddhism first before illuminating the really meaningful form of religious organization.

An organized religion must have a canon with a philosophical base of its own. The religious teachings should not be nonsensical, but must contain a well-organized system of ideas for the advancement of humankind. The reason why Indian Buddhism has become an influential world religion is that it provides an impressive system of thought which is capable of enlightening the human mind. If Buddhism merely confined itself to a haphazard way of thinking, as is represented in the Taiping Jing, it would have been difficult to become an established religion in China.

Thus, from the end of the Han dynasty, through the Three Kingdoms, till after the Western and Eastern Jin, there emerged Daoists like Ge Hong, Lu Xiujing, Kou Qianzhi, Tao Hongjing and others who, in an attempt to fulfill the requirement of the time, not only integrated some of the Daoist and Confucian ideas but also absorbed some of the Buddhist elements to enrich Buddhism.

A really meaningful and influential religious community must have a formal or more serious form of church organization. Even though the ideas of `immortality' and `the sanctification of the bodies' were subsequently incorporated into the Daoist religion, the saints relied heavily on personal devotion without developing a distinctive church, and so they failed to develop a religion. It was not until the end of the Han dynasty that Buddhism became an established religion with a permanent membership of disciples, together with a body of clergy and church leaders. However, the regimes of the Three Kingdoms and the Western Jin banned this organization, subjecting it to dissolution until the Eastern Jin when Du Zhigong and others revived it and once again set it on course.

An organized religion must also have a more permanent set of religious teaching and canon. Although Buddhism had its own precepts and canon when it was first instituted at the end of the Eastern Han, they were rather simple and impermanent in nature. From the Eastern Han onward, Buddhism gradually became more firmly established under the impact of Buddhism and with the tireless efforts of Lu Xiujing, Kou Qianzhi and others.

An organized religion must have its own canon and scriptures for the guidance of its believers. Although there were a number of Daoist books, like the Laozi (Lao Tzu) and the Zhuangzi, before the Wei and the Jin dynasties, these books came to be accepted as scriptures only after being popularized by the devotees. All these books were written by Daoist philosophers of the early Qin, and they had hardly any connection with Daoist religion. It was due to the believers' attempt to look for historical evidences that they decided to upgrade them as scriptures. Taiping Jing, for example, was written before the inception of the Daoist religion. Hence, it served only as a groundwork for the development of Buddhism. However, by the time of the Eastern Jin and the Northern and Southern dynasties, when Buddhism was firmly rooted and a church was organized, a large quantity of scriptures expounding the Daoist canon began to appear (Ge Hong's Pao Pozi, This period saw the appearance of three distinctive categories of scriptures: Sanhuangjing (the Three Emperors Scripture), Shangqingjing (the High Pure Scripture), and Lingbaojing, (the Spirit Protected Scripture). All these scriptures subsequently combined to form the `three caves' (sandong) of the Dizhangjing, namely: the cave of the real (dongzhen), the cave of the gods (dongshen), and the cave of the occult (dongxuan).

An established religion must have a spirit being, or shenling, as a specific object of worship and a history of its own. When Buddhism was first instituted it had inherited part of the saints' tradition. The Daoist disciples claimed that it was imparted to them by the immortals, mostly with Laozi (Lao Tzu)'s assistance. Until the Northern and the Southern dynasties, Daoist disciples created the "rank of the real being" based on the conception of the social hierarchy prevailing at the time.

Tao Hongjing's Zhenlin Yueweitu (Real Spirit's Occupational Status Chart) divided the immortals into seven classes, the highest of which was occupied by the first three: the Primal Lord of Heaven (Yuanshi Tianzun), the Daoist Lord on High (Gaoshang Daojun), and the First Divine Daoist Lord (Yuanhuang Daojun). From then on, these three deities became the most honored in the objects of worship in the Daoist temples (daoguan). Since a religion always finds it necessary to undermine the existence of other competing religions, it has to create a history of its own in order to raise its own status. Thus, being an indigenous Chinese religion, Buddhism had to tackle the entry of alien Buddhism. Besides emphasizing the differences between `Chinese' and `non-Chinese' (huayi zhi bian) to undermine Buddhism, Daoists also spread the story of "Laozi (Lao Tzu) huahu" and elevated Laozi (Lao Tzu)'s position to that of Buddha Sakyamuni's teacher. Consequently, both Buddhism and Buddhism remained in conflict for a long time.

However, it was not until the Eastern Jin and the Northern and Southern dynasties that Buddhism finally became an established religion. The various stages of its development may be summarized as follows. First, from the Eastern Jin onward, the Daoists began to revive their religion by reorganizing the Daoist community which had become scattered and unstable. At the same time, in order to overcome the inadequacy of Daoist teaching and theoretical formulations, Ge Hong and others had provided a body of Daoist canon and precepts. Thereafter, as an attempt to consolidate the founding of the Daoist church, a set of religious teaching was formulated; and in order to propagate Daoist teaching the required scriptures were made available. Lastly, so as to set the religion on a proper footing, a compendium of fairy tales and legendary stories was kept alive. The various phases involved in the development of Buddhism may thus be said to be characteristic of the circumstances under which a religious body came into existence. One of our aims of studying the history of religion is to use it as a source for illuminating the various phases of its development so as to enable us to assess, more accurately, the role it played in society.

CHARACTERISTICS OF DAOISM

As a form of religious philosophy Buddhism has special characteristics which can be illuminated only through comparison with other religions.

An established religion has characteristics which are distinctively different from those of other religions. Besides such external forms, as church organization, religious doctrines and canon, as well as its conception of the sacred, its characteristics should be reflected in the theoretical system which forms the core of the religion. This theoretical system usually contains a body of basic ideals and conceptual schema. For instance, the ultimate reality of the Buddhist belief, as embodied in the concepts of self-denial, transcendentalism and nirvana, is the insignia which distinguishes it from other religions. The three doctrines of the medieval Christianity--namely, "the existence of God," "the resurrection of the soul" and "free will"--form its religious philosophy and conceptual schema.

If that be the case, does Daoist philosophy contain any doctrines and tenets which differ from those of other religions?

I think it does, especially in the earlier form of Buddhism. Whilst almost all religions ask the question, "what happens after the demise of a person?" Buddhism wanted to know "why humans don't die?" This basic question serves as the key to the theoretical system of Buddhism. All this shows that it has characteristics different from those of other religions. The early form of Buddhism held that its body of belief was made up of the tenet of "the ascent of the three in one," that is, "the unity of heaven, earth, and man for the attainment of the Great Peace" (tian-di-ren, sanzhe heyi yi zhi taiping); "the blending of the essence, breath, and shen to become a saint" (jing-qi-shen, sanzhe hunyi er cheng shenxian). From this it evolves into "non-death and eternal life" (zhongshen busi), "resurrection of the bodies" (routi feisheng), and "transformation of the breath into the three pure ones" (qihua sanqing), thus forming the basis of Buddhism.

To understand the tenets of the Buddhist philosophy, one must know the meaning of nirvana. Hence, a Russian Buddhist scholar wrote a book analyzing the meaning of nirvana. In Mou zhongsan's book, he analyzed the concept of nirvana from the Chinese Buddhist viewpoint. In studying Christianity, one should analyze the concept of "God." Thus, Aurelius Augustinus (354-430) in his The City of God, formulated his thesis regarding the `godliness' of the `Almighty'. In his Shenxue Dazhuan, Thomas Aquinas (1225-1274) put forward five parameters to prove that "God exists." In Daoist philosophy, the basic concept is breath (qi), the existence of which may be proved by the following.

First, the unity of the three in one refers to the unity of heaven, earth and man, and the reason why "heaven, earth and man" can be unified is due to the fact that the breaths of Tian-di-ren are the same. The three Jing-qi-shen (essence, breath, and god) blend to become one, and the reason why Jingqishen can be fused in one is due to the fact that the breaths of the Jingqishen are the same.

Second, the so-called one breath giving birth to the three pure ones means the three most respected worthies of Buddhism were the manifestations of the breath, or the three layers of the most sacred heaven were manifested by breath, or qi. This also shows how the basic concept of Buddhism came to be formed.

Third, although dao (the way) is the highest form of Daoist doctrine. its early period identified three circumstances under which the relationship between dao and qi was highlighted. The first circumstance was that dao is more basic than qi, but dao cannot be isolated from qi. Another circumstance showed that qi is more basic than dao, because Buddhism used qi as its prime mover--for example, Liu Xie in his Mie Huo Lun (On the Extinction of Illusion), while citing Sampolun (The Three Breakthroughs), said "qi is the prime mover of dao." The third circumstance was the synthesis that dao is qi--for example, Tao Hongjing in his Yangsheng Yanminglu cited Fuqijing (Breathtaking Scripture) that "dao is qi." In studying the philosophical basis of the Daoist canon, if one could analyze the meaning of qi and the conceptual base upon which it is built, one would be able to gain further insight into the various salient features of Buddhism.

Hegel in his Lectures on the History of Philosophy said, "the difference in cultures is due to the difference in the systems of ideas." If we compare Buddhism with other religious systems, the doctrines formulated by Daoist ideas, and the school of thought which formed the basis of these doctrines, we would be able to understand more clearly the characteristics of Buddhism. Although Buddhism is indigenous to the Chinese, it actually owes its development to the inspiration of Buddhism when the latter spread to China. Thus, we are able to identify the rival relationship between Buddhism and Buddhism as one of its special characteristics.

The earliest Daoist scripture, Taiping Jing, on the one hand, shows that it was influenced by Buddhism. For example, it relates to the question of conformity, a concept which was already in use in traditional Chinese thought. But in Taiping Jing this was discussed in such a detailed and outstanding manner that it became obvious that it was influenced by the Hinayanist Zen Buddhist concept of "mind control" or "control of desire." On the other hand, the scripture also shows that it was antagonistic to Buddhism. For example, Taiping Jing's satirical expression, "the way of the four destructions" (sihui zhi xing), was clearly aimed at Buddhism. It also put forward the argument that "one's burden is one's responsibility" (chengfu) as a direct confrontation to the Buddhist concept of "reincarnation" (laishi baoying). After the Eastern Jin, Buddhism gradually developed into a full-fledged religion. It had a theoretical system of its own, and consequently its differentiation from Buddhism became more and more pronounced. At that time, the differences between Buddhism and Buddhism might be related to the following problems: (i) life and death and the form of god; (ii) the cause and effect of one's deeds and misdeeds (yinguo baoying); and (iii) this-worldly and other-worldly orientations. By analyzing of all these issues, we would be able to appreciate the special characteristics of Buddhism as a religion.

In comparing Buddhism and Buddhism, we may encounter yet another question: why does not Buddhism become a world religion as did Buddhism rather than remaining merely a Chinese religion? From the historical point of view, it is possible that Buddhism could have spread to Korea at the end of the Northern and the Southern dynasties.

Sanguo Shiji (The History of the Three Kingdoms) recorded how Buddhism spread to Korea at the beginning of the Tang dynasty but, shortly afterwards, Buddhism became popular in Korea and very soon it outran Buddhism, which thence forward ceased to retain its foothold there. During the same period, Buddhism passed through Korea to Japan, where it might have exercised some influence on Japan's Shinto, though this does not mean that the development of Shinto was due to the Daoist influence. Unlike Buddhism, however, Buddhism also failed to spread its wing over Japan. In history Buddhism had even less influence on other countries (notwithstanding its continuing impact on Chinese devotees who made their homes outside China).

In my opinion, the main reason why Buddhism could not become a world religion is that it not only contains defects in its system of beliefs and practices, but also carries a heavy load of sentiments which are peculiarly Chinese. The goal Buddhism seeks to achieve is "non-death and eternal life" and "the sanctification of bodies." All this differs from the monotheistic doctrine that "the soul does not die." On the one hand, its theoretical arguments, such as "the sanctification of bodies" and "non-death and eternal life" are too crude and difficult to be absorbed. Consequently, Buddhism had no alternative but to take in some Buddhist ideas, such as "when the form ceases, its spirit remains" (xingjin shen bu mie) and "the three kalpas' wheel of karma" (somshi lunhui).

Thus, the spread of Buddhism has been seriously restricted, whereas wherever it goes Buddhism has been able to take the place of Buddhism wherever the latter goes. On the other hand, Buddhism is too closely related to science. For the sake of preserving life, ensuring "non-death and eternal life" and sanctifying the dead it emphasizes a great deal of physical conditioning for lifting the breath (qi) of material reality to the highest level. Consequently, China's science and technology, especially medicine, came to be developed alongside Buddhism. Buddhism's use of science was bound to curtail its dynamism as a religion.

Thus, the "non-science" and "anti-science" components, in conjunction with the basic qualities of science, began to contradict each other. Religion usually emphasizes "other-worldly orientations," but Buddhism seems to insist instead on "this-worldly orientations" instead. Its adherents believe that they could blend "the three (jing, qi, shen) to become saints" (sanzhe heyi er cheng xian). But as a religious system Buddhism also advocates the unity of the three (tian, di, ren) in one to ensure the Great Peace (sanzhe heyi er zhi taiping) and for this reason can be a potent disruptive force in the political process. In thus fabricating the supernatural world of the saints, Buddhism hopes to translate the real world into an ideal one--this undeniably is a conflict of ideas.

The study of the characteristics of Buddhism is of great importance for it enables us to understand the difference between Buddhism and other religions. By analyzing its characteristics we are able to illuminate the salient features of Chinese culture, psychology and philosophy, as well as the direction of developments in science and technology, medicine and hygiene, and the ensuing shortcomings hidden therein. For a people to succeed in development, they must know not only the present and the future, but also the past. They must come to grips not only with the reality of political life and economic exigencies, but also with their traditional culture, religious belief and pattern of thought. Herein lies the reason why serious research must be conducted on Buddhism so as to enable us to understand its role as a Chinese religion.

THE DAOIST RELIGION OF CHINA

In Chinese history there have been various religions such as Buddhism, Buddhism, Islam and Christianity, both Catholic and Protestant, but among them only Buddhism is the religion of the Chinese people.* To be more precise, Buddhism is a religion of the Han people and has certain concrete features that come from this association. It has had a large influence on Chinese culture, psychology, customs, science and technology, medicine and hygiene, philosophy and even on Chinese politics and economics. How did the Daoist religion arise and what are its particular characteristics relative to other religions?

Daoist religion was born at the time of the Han Emperor Shun-di at the end of the first century A.D. At this time China already had a written history of about 2,000 years. At the end of the Warring States period (that is, the third and second centuries B.C.) there had existed people called "immortals" who claimed that by certain practices they could `extend their lives and not die.' These `immortals' were only individuals practicing by themselves; they never formed any kind of religious organization. However, at the end of the Western Han period (at the beginning of the first century A.D.) Buddhism came to China from India. The entry of Buddhism had a transformative effect and sped up the foundation of a Chinese religion. Because Buddhism was a foreign culture entering China, however, it elicited a strong reaction among the Chinese people.

The interaction of Chinese culture with a foreign culture led to both borrowing and criticizing. We can see both of these in the earliest of the Daoist religious writings, the Taiping Jing. In this work Daoists borrowed such Buddhist terms as the `three realms', but also criticized Buddhists for their so-called `four practices.' (These were the unfilial abandonment of father and mother to become a monk, the abandoning of wife and therefore the cutting off of future generations, the practice of begging, and the practice of eating excrement). The Daoists said that this was contravening the spiritual way of heaven. In particular, once established the Daoist religion set forth the doctrine of `Laozi (Lao Tzu) converting the barbarians' in order to criticize Buddhism. They said that Laozi (Lao Tzu), the original teacher of Buddhism in the Zhou period (the sixth century B.C.), had left China through the Hangu Pass and gone to India, where he had taught Shakyamuni, the historical Buddha. Therefore, the Buddha was the disciple of Laozi (Lao Tzu).

The founder of the Daoist religion is generally recognized to be Zhang Daoling. There are two views in the Chinese scholarly community as to where the Daoist religion originated. The scholar Chen Yinge claims that the Daoist religion originated in Shandong, Jiangsu and other coastal areas. Another scholar, Meng Wentong, claims that it originated in Sichuan and was influenced by the customs and practices of minority peoples there. I think that the Daoist religion originated in the coastal areas because the immortals were active in this area. Further, Zhang Daoling himself was from Feng County in Jiangsu and only later went to Sichuan, where he formally established the organization of the Daoist religion. It is quite possible that certain elements of minority peoples' customs were absorbed into his teachings at that time.

The Daoist religion that later developed in Sichuan and the Han River area is called Five Pecks of Rice Buddhism because people on entering the sect made an offering of five pecks of rice. It is also called Heavenly Teacher Buddhism because the leader of this sect, Zhang Daoling, was called the Heavenly Teacher. Heavenly Teacher Buddhism was passed on from Zhang to his son, Zhang Heng, and again transmitted to Zhang Lu, the latter's son. Zhang Lu established a Daoist kingdom in the Han River area, which he ruled for thirty years. Eventually he was defeated by Cao, to whom he surrendered. Zhang Lu's son, Zhang Sheng, fled to Longhu Mountain in Jiangxi where he became the fourth generation Heavenly Teacher. At the present time this sect of Buddhism has already been transmitted to its sixty-fifth generation. The sixty-fourth generation Heavenly Teacher is in Taiwan. His nephew is on the Chinese mainland continuing the tradition as the sixty-fifth generation Heavenly Teacher. This young Heavenly Teacher, a man in his twenties, came to my home to study the Daoist religion.

After the Five Pecks of Rich school, in Yan (Hebei), Qi (Shandong), Jiang (Jiangsu), and Huai (Huaihe, Anhui), another sect of the Daoist religion was founded by Zhang Jiao called Taiping Buddhism. Zhang Jiao used the Daoist religion to organize an extremely large-scale peasant uprising. When this was put down, Taiping Buddhism largely disappeared.

In the Three Kingdoms and Western Jin periods (the third century A.D.) the Daoist religion was hemmed in by imperial rulers and developed very little. However, in the Eastern Jin period (fourth century A.D.) the Daoist religion began to develop speedily and many nobles adhered to it. For example, the most famous aristocratic families of the time for generations believed in Buddhism. The most famous calligrapher in Chinese history, Wang Xizhi, was also a follower of the Daoist religion. One story recounts that Wang Xizhi particularly loved geese and wanted to buy the dozen or so geese raised by a Daoist priest. The priest would not sell, and Wang asked a second and a third time. Finally the priest said that if Wang would copy out for the whole Dao De Jing (Tao Te Ching) he would give him the geese. So Wang copied the entire work.

An interesting development occurred in the Tang period (618-907), whose rulers had the surname Li. At this time the leaders of the Daoist religion were looking for a mythological figure they could venerate as the founder of the religion, and they came upon Laozi (Lao Tzu), who was also named Li. This was not a coincidence. First of all, even before the Daoist religion was formally established, Laozi (Lao Tzu) had been mythologized. Second, the Han dynasty had venerated Confucian thought as orthodoxy, which, of course, honored Confucius. The Daoists claimed that Laozi (Lao Tzu) was Confucius's teacher, thus hoping to overcome the Confucianists. Now, according to the Shiji, Laozi (Lao Tzu) was surnamed Li with a given name of Erh. Since the Tang emperors were also surnamed Li, in order to increase their own importance they said that they were descendants of Laozi (Lao Tzu). Because of this, the Tang emperors took the Daoist religion relatively seriously: emperor Xuanzong even wrote his own commentary on the Dao De Jing (Tao Te Ching).

After the Daoist religion was established, on the one hand, it struggled with Buddhism and, on the other, it absorbed Buddhist thought. But the Daoist religion also has its own definite characteristics. Many religions seek to understand or answer such questions as What happens to human beings after death? For example, Buddhists seek to answer the question: What can people do after death to keep from being reborn into this world? The Daoists, however, seek to answer this question: How can people keep from dying? The ideal in the Daoist religion is for people to `extend their lives and not die,' to `fly up in this very body'--that is, to become an immortal.

Regarding this question the Daoist religion has certain theories. Daoists claim that people have both a spirit or soul and a body, both of which are constructed from qi. The qi that makes up the spirit or soul is called soul-qi. The qi that makes up the body is called form-qi. Only when the soul-qi and the body-qi are joined together in a single person do we have life. People should seek two things--to live forever and to obtain good fortune. If you die, everything is finished, so in order to seek to extend life, first, you must get a body that does not decay so that the spirit or soul will have a place to abide. Then seek a method for the soul to stay with the body, otherwise you will be dead and not be able to achieve any kind of good fortune.

Because of this Daoists seek ways to keep body and soul together, and Buddhism has various methods to accomplish this purpose. The most basic of these are of two sorts: the outer pill and the inner pill. The outer pill consists of using various minerals, especially mercury, in order to concoct a potion. It is hoped that by ingesting various potions one can keep one's body from decaying, and then the soul can continue forever in its midst. They claim that if you put a bronze mud on your feet and soak your feet in water for a very long time, you will not decay. If you can find the so-called golden pill, once you eat it your whole body will be able to live forever without decaying.

The inner pill is a series of practices that cause the qi within the human body to circulate through certain channels. This is called "working on your qi' and is the same kind of thing that is known these days as qigong. If the qi continually circulates in the human body, the whole body will be suffused with the light of an extremely fine qi. The body itself will become as light as qi and the person will be able to ascend to heaven, which is called "to fly up in this very body."

When Buddhism became a religion it had to have its own deities to venerate. At first the deity most venerated was the mythologized Laozi (Lao Tzu), called `Laojun' or 'Taishang Laojun.' Afterwards, under the influence of Buddhism, very many other deities were added. Originally Buddhism had only Shakyamuni as the Buddha, but afterwards they said that before Shakyamuni there had been seven other Buddhas. Towards the end of the Northern and Southern Dynasties a Daoist priest named Tao Hongjing wrote a book called Zhenling Weiye Tu in which he divided Daoist deities into seven levels. The highest level contained three deities. In the center was one called Yuanshi Tiandao. On his left was Gaoshang Daojun and on his right was Yuanhuang Daojun. Laozi (Lao Tzu), or Taishang Laojun, was placed below on the fourth level. Today in Daoist temples the formal hall is called the Hall of the Three Pure Ones, and most sects worship these three deities. However, not all Daoist sects are alike. Some still claim Taishang Laojun as the highest deity, saying that he existed before Heaven and Earth were dreaded and that in different times he has different causes. Originally he was Pan'gu Xiansheng. Heaven and Earth were separated by him, and he has various spiritual powers.

The Daoist religion has one female deity of particular power who is named Xiwang Mu (Queen Mother of the West).

Xiwang Mu existed as a deity before the founding of the Daoist religion. In the Shanhaijing (from the fourth to the second century B.C.) Xiwang Mu is not yet a female deity, but either of undifferentiated sex or male. Only after the Mutianzi Zhuan does Xiwang Mu become a female deity. This book recounts the story of the Zhou King Mu (of about 1000 B.C.) who went to the Kunlun Mountains to seek Xiwang Mu. In the earliest Daoist scriptures, however, where it is said there that the character `Mu' indicates the proof of the longevity of the deity Xiwang Mu is merely a deity of long life. Thus `Mu' here does not necessarily mean a female deity. Only in the Jin and Northern and Southern Dynasties, when the Daoist religion set up Dongwang Gong as a counterpart to Xiwang Mu, did Xi-Wang Mu emerge as an important female deity.

The Daoist religion took the human body and its cultivation very seriously, as in such matters as exilers, the inner and outer pill, and qigong. Because of this it has had a great influence on ancient medicine, pharmacology, chemistry and the nourishment of the human body. Many great Daoist leaders such as Ge Hong, Tao Hongjing and Sun Simiao were important scientists of Old China. Because of this, people today who research the history and development of Chinese science and technology cannot but study the history of the Daoist religion. The English historian of science, Joseph Needham, in his Science and Civilization in China, has relied extensively on the writings of the Daoist religion.

Daoists have written many works. The earliest collection of Daoist works, called the Zhengtong Daozang, has five thousand volumes. It was compiled in 1445 in the tenth year of the Zhengtong Emperor of the Ming. Later, in the Wanli period, a supplement appeared. These are important resources for the study of the history of Chinese religion.

In China today Daoism (Taoism) is one of the important religions. About three thousand people who have formally become Daoist priests, and several important Daoist temples have been restored. In Beijing there is a Daoist temple, called the Temple of the White Clouds (Baiyun Guan), which was established in the Yuan dynasty (the thirteenth century) and belongs to the Guanzhen sect of Daoism (Taoism). Its Hall of the Three Pure Ones is very fine; it also has two areas for the display of historical objects of the Daoist religion. In Chengdu, Sichuan there is the Green Goat palace and in Wuahn the Temple of Eternal Spring, both of which have been very well restored and belong to the Guanzhen Daoist sect. In Xian a Daoist temple called Louguan Tai belongs to the Northern sect of Daoism (Taoism). It was first built in the Northern Zhou dynasty (fifth century A.D.), but what exists now was rebuilt in the Ming (fifteenth and sixteenth centuries). It is said that in the Louguan Tai, Laozi (Lao Tzu), before he left for the West, dictated the Dao De Jing (Tao Te Ching) to the gatekeeper, named Yixi.

Longhu Mountain in Jiangxi is the birthplace of the Zhengyi sect of Daoism (Taoism). Maoshan in Jiangsu is the birthplace of Tao Hongjing's Maoshan sect. Hangzhou has a Daoist temple in Geling where, it is said, Ge Hong refined the pill. At each of these Daoist temples are Daoist priests, young and old, male and female. At Beijing's Temple of the White Clouds a school of Daoist religion teaches priests how to read Daoist scriptures. Beijing also has a Daoist Association, a national organization publishing the Journal of the Chinese Daoist Association. At Sichuan University the Institute for the Study of Religion is dedicated solely to the Daoist religion and is editing a Daoist dictionary. Beijing University has established an Institute for the Study of the History of the Daoist Religion, where I teach. The Institute for the Study of World Religions at the Chinese Academy of Social Sciences in Beijing is doing a synopsis of the five thousand volumes of the Daoist canon. Two national conferences have been devoted to the study of the Daoist religion, one at Beijing University. Thus the study of Daoist currently is developing very quickly.

2

The Introduction of Indian Buddhism into China

THE BEGINNINGS OF BUDDHISM IN CHINA

There are diverse theories regarding the timing of the introduction of Buddhism from India to China. There is, however, a general consensus that the introduction of Buddhism commenced with the dispatching of an envoy to the lands of the west by Emperor Mingdi of the Eastern Han dynasty during his reign of Yongping (58-75 A.D.) to seek the Buddhist teachings. According to even earlier legends the emissary Zhang Xian, who had been sent to the Western lands, "heard of the teachings of foutu (Buddha) and had been commissioned by the monarch of Da-rou-zhi to preserve and transmit the teachings of the futu jing (Buddha's classic, or sutra). Even disregarding this, I am convinced that the introduction of Buddhism into China predated the dispatch of the imperial envoy during the Yongping reign to seek out Buddhist teachings. In the eighth year of the reign of Yongping, Emperor Mingdi decreed that those criminals who had incurred the death penalty might atone for their crimes by offering jian cloth to the state and thus escape the execution of their sentences. Prince Ying, a brother to Mingdi, sent in thirty bales of jian, whereupon the emperor issued the following explanatory edict:

Prince Ying of Chu has been reciting the refined teachings of Huang and Lao [Huangdi, or the Yellow Emperor, and Laozi (Lao Tzu) are together revered as the founders of the Daoist school of philosophy, and particularly of its so-called Esoteric or Immortal school--Tr.] and has worshiped at the benevolent shrine of Buddha. He has undertaken to cleanse himself and has fasted for three months, observing his vows to the gods. [In the Chinese Buddhist contexts, fasting does not necessarily mean abstinence from food altogether but usually refers to the assumption of an exacting vegetarian diet avoiding the taking of life, which is known as zaijie--Tr.] He has repented and should be considered to have expiated any crime he may have perpetrated or any suspicions he may have provoked. He is now, by way of atonement, submitting his property to add to the grand fete of the Upasaka [Buddhist disciples] and to the glory of the temples of Buddha.

The fact that Prince Ying worshiped Huangdi, Laozi (Lao Tzu), and Buddha at the same time and in the same fashion tells us that Buddhism certainly already had been introduced into China for quite some time prior to the eighth year of the Yongping reign. Therefore, it would be quite late to take the sending of the imperial envoy to seek out Buddhist teachings during the reign of Yongping to be the point of beginning of the introduction of Buddhism into China. Still, although Buddhism was not introduced into China after that event, it would perhaps be generally correct to say that it was only during, or even after, the reign of Yongping that Buddhism became a religion of some influence in China. After its introduction into China, Buddhism did not attain the height of its influence until the Eastern Jin dynasty, meanwhile undergoing several significant stages of propagation and evolution.

During the Eastern Han dynasty, Buddhism was propagated in China as one of several Daoist practices [daoshu] popular at the time. Daoist teachings and practices had gained great currency since the beginning of the Western Han dynasty and remained in vogue throughout the two Han dynasties. At that time all Daoist practices, whether the [philosophical] teachings of Huangdi and Laozi (Lao Tzu) or the sorcerous practices of the magicians, were indifferently known as daoshu [Daoist practices or techniques]. The techniques practiced and taught by the magicians covered a very wide area: worshiping at shrines and temples, ancestral worship, ways to immortality and longevity, and such methods as jiushi [long vision] According to the Fangshu zhuan [Biographies of the Magi] in Hou Han shu [History of the Later Han Dynasty], at that time, many people studied diverse things and the teachings of many schools such as "Numbers of Steps according to the Yin and Yang," "The Writings of He and Luo" [Huang He, or Yellow River, and the Luo River], "The Tortoise and Dragon Graphs," "The Methods of Ji Zi," "The Book of Wei [Latitudes] and Hou [Seasons]," "The Talismanic Graphs of the Decision of the Bells," and "The Book of Shi Kuang," as well as such techniques as "Wind Horn," "Transmutation and Transportation," "The Seven Ways," "Cardinal and Primal Breathing," "The Seven Divisions of the Six Days," "Divination for Chance Encounters," "Omen of the Day," "Firmness and Singularity," "Instantaneity," "Solitude and Emptiness," and so on. The following passage explains the reason for this proliferation of these Daoist practices and methods at that time:

In the Han dynasty, since Emperor Wudi turned his favor toward the methods and crafts of the Daoists, scholars throughout the land who possessed the least learning on those subjects could not afford to miss taking advantage of the situation; they converged upon the royal court, each with his books and with his hands clasped together [in the sign of salutation]. Thereafter, Wang Mang [The 'usurper' who dethroned the Han emperor and founded the short-lived Xin dynasty from 8 to 23 A.D.--Tr.] usurped the throne by falsely assuming the mandate under the guise of receiving talismans for that effect secretly. Later on, Emperor Guangwudi [25-57 A.D.] was found to be fond of portents and oracles and believed in them. Thus the scholars who had learned to be attentive to the fashions and ways of the times strove to compete with one another on the field of these techniques and practices and ideas. Whenever they could, they would bring their crafts to the attention of His Majesty and would debate about the validity and relative virtues of these things whenever they could.

According to the records of the day, "Huang-Lao" and Buddha were equally regarded as Daoist techniques. In the ninth year of the reign of Yanxi of Emperor Huandi (166), Xiang Kai memorialized the emperor, saying:

We hear that shrines for Huang-Lao and for Buddha have been erected in the palace. These teachings exhort people to purity of mind and tranquillity of the soul; they place inaction and quietude at the top of their list of values; they emphasize the value of life and abhor killing; they exhort people to restrain their desires and purge themselves of extravagant ways. But Your Majesty is shorn neither of desire nor extravagance, and your habits of killing and punishing people have extended beyond the bounds of reason. Since you violated their way, how can you expect to receive their mandate?

Even the disciples of Buddhism referred to their own teachings as the craft of the dao (tao) [Way]. In Li Huo Lun [Discourse on the Disposition of Error] Mouzi wrote, "There are ninety-six types of people adhering to the teaching of Dao; of these, none is as great as or is more exalted than the teachings of Buddha. The Sishi'er Zhang Jing [Sutra of Forty-two Chapters] [a sutra often attributed to Kasyapa Matanga and Gobharana, the first Indian monks to "officially" arrive in China as envoys from a Buddhist state--Tr.] also referred to its own teachings as fodao [or, Way of Buddha]. Furthermore, the Buddhist teachings at that time contained elements which coincided with, or bore resemblances to, the Chinese Daoist teachings--for example, when it taught:

Arhan [worthy men, or saints] are beings which can fly and are capable of transformation; their longevity is the kalpa [age] that is past, and they live and move throughout the heaven and the earth (Chapter 1 of the Sishi'er Zhang Jing) and: those who have learned the Way should purge their minds of impurities and they shall instantly become pure and clean. (Chapter 35)

At such times, the Buddhist sutra came very close to the "immortality teachings" of the Huang-Lao school of Daoism (Taoism).

At that time, the principle contents of Buddhist teachings were such things as "the imperishability of the spirit, or soul," yin-guo [causes and effects as the basic method of understanding the development of things] and baoying [retribution]. For example, in the book Hou Han Ji [The Chronicles of the Later Han Dynasty] Yuan Hong wrote,

> [Buddhism] also posits that when the person dies the spirit does not perish but would subsequently take on new form. For all one's deeds in life, whether good or evil, there will be retribution. For that reason one must value the performance of good actions and the cultivation of the dao, so as to persist, and continue to persist, in the tempering of the soulspirit, until it arrives at the realm of wuwei [inaction or quietude], and at that point one would become Buddha.

This was an idea that existed previously in China. In the Chinese form, the idea of the imperishability of the soul was expressed in the long held you guei lun [theory of the existence of ghosts]. The poem Wen Wang [King Wen] in the Da ya section of Shi Jing [Classic of Odes] described the "presence of the three hou [secondary, or humane sovereign spirit] in Heaven" and the ascension to that realm of the refined spirits and ghosts [jing ling] [of mortals]. In the chapter Yang sheng zhu [Lord Nurturer of Life] in the book Zhuangzi, there was a parable which spoke of the "continuation of the flame even though the tinder has expired," and in the chapter Jing shen xun [Exhortation on the Spirit] in Huai Nan Zi the idea was posited that "the form indeed has its limitations, but the spirit does not dissolve. Therefore, [the relationship between spirit and form is one in which] something that is incapable of dissolving is adapted to something that does dissolve; the result is that there can be myriad such adaptations; one cannot in any way see these ways of changing and permutation as finite." It was precisely because of the prevalence of this thought, and in response to it, that opponents such as Huan Tan argued for the theory of "the simultaneous destruction of the form and the spirit," and Wang Chong suggested that "when a man dies he is not transformed into a ghost." These latter were all critiques of the idea of the "imperishability of the soul." The idea that the imperishability of the spirit or soul itself depended on the exercises of tempering and cultivation [in mystical or metaphysical ways] was a concept which also already existed in the tradition of China. As for the ideas of causes and effects and retribution, although these theories of Buddhism in general were not entirely similar to previously existing Chinese theories, the popular forms that they assumed during the Han dynasty corresponded to certain ideas which the Chinese already held at the time, such as the idea in the Kun Gua [Changes through the Feminine Symbol] section of Yi Jing (I Ching) [Book of Changes] which held that "good fortune would come to those who performed good deeds, and ill fortune to those who are evil," or that "the family which accumulates good actions will be rewarded with exceedingly great causes for celebration, whereas households which pile up evil deeds will have much cause for suffering."

By the time of the transition between the Han and the Wei dynasties, owing to the gradual expansion of Buddhism, more and more Buddhist sutras were translated into Chinese. Translations at the time included both Hinayana [Theravedic, known in Chinese as xiao cheng] and Mahayana [da cheng] sutras. Consequently, the processes by which Buddhism was popularized in China fell into two main channels: the history of the An Shigao school, which belonged to the Hinayana category, and that of the Zhi-lou-jiacan school, which belonged to the Mahayana and emphasized the teaching of prajna [wisdom].

The An Shigao of Hinayana School

This emphasized the teachings of dhyana [meditation exercises, in Chinese, chan]. In the first year of the reign of Jianhe of Emperor Huandi of the Han dynasty [147 A.D.], an Shigao arrived at Luoyang and began a prolific career in translating sutras. [An Shigao was the Chinese name of the Buddhist pandit who went to China from Parthia or Persia. The name An translates as tranquillity and may have derived from the monk's Persian identity, since Parthia was, at the time, and for much of Chinese history, known to the Chinese as Anshiguo, or land of tranquillity. We have no knowledge of the monk's Persian name--Tr.]

The most influential of his translations were the An Ban Shou Yi Jing [Sutra on the Maintenance of Thought by the Practice of Anapana] and the Yin Chi Ru Jing [Sutra on Entrance to Truth by Covert Maintenance]. The first described a method for practicing chan, or meditation exercises; it was a book on breathing methods designed to "keep one's thoughts in place," which methods were in some ways similar to the breathing and respiration exercises and techniques espoused by the Daoists, and particularly by the School of Immortals. The latter sutra was an exposition of the esoteric significance of names and numbers in the Buddhist canons and bore some resemblance to the line-by-line and phrase-by-phrase exposition of the classics, a method of scholarship known as zhangju xue. This was practiced in general by many Han Confucianist scholars in their various annotations and exegeses of the Confucianist classics, often attempting to find "true" meanings that were camouflaged by the words of the scriptures.

This methodology in the studying of the Hinayana scriptures continued in the An Shigao school until at least the third generation of his disciples, chief among whom was Kang Hui the Monk [Kang Zeng Hui], who lived during the time of the Kingdom of Wu [222-280]. This school's theory of life was fundamentally based on the concept of yuanqi [original breath]. It maintained that "original breath" was the same as what the Chinese have called the wu xing [Five Elements, or Five Agents] or the wu yin [Five Negatives, of Five Feminine Qualities] [later this was translated into Buddhist terminology as the wu yin, or Five Inward Contents, similar in meaning and identity to the Sanskrit term skandhas, of which there were also five-Tr.]. The Sutra on Entrance to Truth by Covert Maintenance explained the wu yin zhong [five yin species] thus:

> The five yin species make up the body . . . this is similar to the original breath [yuanqi] . . . the original breath contains the escalation and demotion of all things, as well as their establishment and ruin. When it reaches its end it will begin again and will continue to go on through the triloka [Three Realms]; it does not end, but is infinite; that is why it is called the zhong [species, or seed].

This brand of Buddhism believed that in the beginning the human being was made up of the accumulation and aggregation of the five yin [elements]; thus the Sutra on Entrance to Truth by Covert Maintenance translated by An Shigao posited that "yin was the accumulation of all appearances." The theory of yuanqi [original breath] had been popular in China since pre-Qin times, and it flourished in the two Han dynasties. Moreover, there was an intimate connection between the idea of original breath and the issue of the form-spirit relationship for it was maintained that whereas form was made up of the chuqi [crude breath] the spirit was the jingqi [refined breath]. Such a theory had a great deal of connection with the teachings of yangsheng [the cultivation and nourishment of life essence] as espoused by the School of Immortality.

In the book Lü Shi Chunqiu [Spring and Autumn Classic by Master Lu] the point was made that in order to become immortal and to achieve jiu shi [long vision] the qi, or breath, must circulate without impediment of any kind in the body; only then will the "refined breath [spirit] be rejuvenated everyday and the evil breath be daily abated," so that "the spirit shall reside at peace within the form and one's days and years shall be stretched to everlasting." At that time, the adherents of the An Shigao school of Buddhism also learned to bring together the ideas of the five yin and yuanqi and claimed that, if one were able to coordinate one's original breath well, one's mind would be tranquil, at ease, and the body would be also free of sicknesses, whereas if the original breath were not well coordinated and if the yin and the yang in a person, and the five elements [wuxing], were not properly blended, the body would succumb to illness. The Fo Yi Jing [Buddha's Medical Sutra], translated in the time of the kingdom of Wu by Zhu Luyan and Zhi Yue, said,

In the human body there are four illnesses: one is related to Earth, another to Water, a third to Fire, and a fourth to Wind. As the Wind increases, the qi [breath] arises; as the Fire increases, the heat arises; as the Water increases, the cold would rise; as the Earth increases, the strength [of the person] would wax. It is from these four [basic] illnesses that the four hundred and four illnesses have arisen. Earth belongs to the body, Water to the mouth, Fire to the eyes, and Wind to the ear.

Such sayings bore much resemblance to the medical theories popular during the Han dynasty, in which emphasis was given to the methods of creating a balance or coordination system within the body for the yuanqi. This was seen in terms of the need to orientate the development of the yuanqi in a good or correct direction and away from the evil or wrong direction. It was felt that, if the mind and the spirit were tranquil, the person would be able not to generate or create any desires or worries, and that it was only because the mind and spirit moved or acted, thereby generating thoughts, that all sorts of worries and troubles were created. As to how all these various worries may be eliminated, the Hinayana school of chan or meditation believed that one simply had to nourish the mind and cultivate the spirit, in which the main thing was to "keep thoughts [yi] in their proper place" [namely, in the state of non-being, or the state prior to when thoughts were created]. The meditation exercises were therefore intended to prevent the generation of thoughts or ideas by means of concentrating. The An Ban Shou Yi Jing said, "One must maintain one's mind and keep it in place--i.e., before any thoughts have been generated. Once thoughts are generated the maintenance will have been broken." The Chu Jing [Sutra on Abiding in That Which is Fixed] translated by An Shigao told the following story:

Buddha said to the gathered bhiksu [mendicant disciples]: You must learn to understand all things by sitting in meditation, but you must also learn to be able to speak the words of the Law. Those who cannot do so must block out their vision and screen sounds and learn to keep their minds in place and be good at listening only within themselves. In this way they may find their way [to Enlightenment or Buddhahood]. When the congregated bhiksu heard Buddha make this proclamation, their hearts were glad and understood Buddha's words, and immediately they found the way to becoming Arhat [saints].

The method of keeping one's mind in place was known as an ban [anapana], in which ana referred to inhalation and pana referred to exhalation. This was similar to the tu na breathing exercises espoused by both the Huang-Lao school and the Immortality school of Daoism (Taoism), both of which were popular in the Han dynasty. Thus, the An Ban Zhu Xu [Preface to the Annotations on Anapana] written by [the monk] Dao An explained: "By anapana we mean exhalation [externalization] and inhalation [internalization]" and "One can entrust one's breath to anapana and maintain, or preserve, simply that which is achieved already." If one could keep one's mind in place, so the argument went, one's mind and spirit would become clear and serene, and if one's mind and spirit were clear and tranquil, one would become Buddha. Thus also Kang Hui the Monk said in the An ban xu [Preface to Anapana]:

> He who cultivates anapana has a totally clear mind; if he should raise his eyes, there is no darkness or gloom within the scope of his vision which he may not pierce . . . there is nothing so far away in the distance that he cannot see, no sound so obscure that he cannot hear. His understanding shall encompass the uncertain, the ambiguous appearances, and the false impressions and resemblances; he shall be completely free in his existence; he shall be big enough to contain within himself all that is within the bounds of the Eight Extremes and yet also small enough to penetrate the stem of a hair or a quill. He shall control the heavens and the earth, and stay the progress of time and longevity. His godly characteristics and powers shall be so fierce as to destroy Heaven's own arms, and he shall have the power to remove the trisahasra [the Three Thousand Things, or All Things] and all the temples on earth. The Eight Unthinking [Non-Thoughts] are unfathomable by even the Brahman, and the Virtuous Character of the God knows no limitations. This is the origin of the six paramitas [methods].

From the above, it is clear that the Hinayana chan [dhyana, or meditative] techniques espoused by the An Shigao school were certain ideas which had already gained popularity in China before that time through the espousal of the Huang-Lao school and the Immortality school in Daoism (Taoism) and that what we have seen was an obvious attempt to use prevalent Daoist techniques [daoshu] to explain and popularize Buddhism.

The Zhi-lou-jia-qian of Mahayana School

This system of thought was quite different as its Mahayana teachings emphasized prajna [wisdom]. Zhi-lou-jia-qian had a disciple called Zhi Liang and a third-generation disciple called Zhi Qian; together they were known as the "Three Zhi's." Zhi-lou-jia-qian arrived in Luoyang in the last year of the reign of Emperor Huandi [167] and, in 169, translated the Daoxing Banruo Boluomi Jing [Prajnaparamita Sutra on the Cultivation of the Truth]. Later, Zhi Qian retranslated this sutra as the Da ming Du Wuji Jing [Sutra on the Transition by Way of the Great Enlightenment to Infinite Endlessness]. This system of thought, espoused originally by Zhi Qian, emphasized that the fundamental principle of life was to make the spirit revert to its original, virginal truth or reality and that life would then conform to the dao [or the Way of Natural Things]. With this postulate the ideas of Laozi (Lao Tzu) and Zhuangzi exerted a profound influence over this particular school of Buddhism.

It becomes even more obvious that Zhi Qian's purpose was to make Buddhism conform to the school of Chinese metaphysics which at the time had as its core the ideas of Laozi (Lao Tzu) and Zhuangzi when in the title of his new translation of the Prajnaparamita sutra "The Great Enlightenment" or "The Great Light" for "prajna". [Technically, the Sanskrit for the Chinese term ming, meaning brightness or enlightenment, is vidya, and not prajna--Tr.]. This reflects the idea contained in the saying in Laozi (Lao Tzu) [or Dao De jing]: "Zhi chang yue ming" [To know the constant is Enlightenment]. Also, the translation of "paramita" as du wu ji [ferrying across to infinite endlessness] appears to refer to the arrival at the realm of oneness or unity with the dao. [Actually the term du, meaning to make a crossing or transition, is contained in the Sanskrit term paramita itself, which means ferrying across, and hence saving--Tr.] Therefore, in the annotations which Zhi Qian made for the first pin [folio] of the Sutra on the Transition by Way of Great Enlightenment to Infinite Endlessness we find the following passage:

The teacher [Zhi Qian's mentor Zhi Liang] said: The Bodhisattva's mind treads on the Great Way in order to be able to understand and empathize with the Way. The mind became one with the dao [Way]. This takes no form; that is why it is simply described as the Void.

Here, the idea of mind "being one with the Way" seemed to be the same notion as that expressed in Daoism (Taoism) as "[having the spirit] revert no more to the yin corpus [i.e., the dead body], but join the dao (tao) in oneness." This was described in fuller detail later on in the Fo shuo si wen qing jing [sic?] [There seems to be a typographical error in the Chinese text at this point. We have not been able to identify this particular sutra as it is here presented, or even a term in Buddhism corresponding to the phrase si wen qing. Perhaps the term zi was mistaken for the character qing here. In Buddhism, the term si zi qing refers to the so-called Four Self-Injuries,i.e., four ways in which people bring damage to their own bodies and minds. It is possible that there may have been a sutra on the subject--Tr.] translated by Fa Hu [Zhu Fahu]. This idea also bore resemblance to the notion of "simultaneously accomplishing the Deed of the Way" [yu dao ju cheng], which was described and proposed by Ruan Ji in his Da Ren Xiansheng Zhuan [Biographies of Great Men and Forebears]. The sentence "There is no form; therefore it is described as the Void" is very similar to Laozi (Lao Tzu)'s dictum, "The Constant Way has no form." Therefore, it was understood that the mind and the spirit also have no traceable form.

According to people such as Zhi Qian, the human mind-spirit originated from the Way, and only various post-natural influences [such as temptations of desires and appetites] made it impossible for the mind-spirit to return to the state of being one with the Way. In order to be free of these limitations and trammels, therefore, the mind-spirit must empathize with the Way and must understand it. If the mind-spirit was capable of understanding its own original source, it would be able to once again become one with the Way, and thus become Buddha. In fact, this uses the ideas of Laozi (Lao Tzu) and Zhuangzi to explain the tenets of Buddhism.

During the time of the Wei and Jin dynasties, the metaphysical ontology of the Xuanxue [Daoist metaphysics] school, which accepted Laozi (Lao Tzu)'s and Zhuangzi's ideas as its framework, was very popular. Its main focus was the questions of ben-mo [the relationship between the fundamental and the incidental] and you-wu [existence and non-existence]. The ideas of prajna in Buddhist thought came very close to this sort of metaphysical thought. Therefore, at the time, it was convenient and expedient for Buddhist monks to use this sort of Chinese [Daoist] metaphysics to explain Buddhism. The methodology and approach that they adopted was a metaphysical method of the Xuanxue school which moved gradually from the principle of geyi [study of meanings] to the principle of de yi wang yan [discarding the word when the meaning has been attained] or ji yan chu yi [extrapolating the meaning which originates from, and transcends, the word which was its temporary abode].

One very notable phenomenon of the period was that there were many similarities between the ways in which the great monks of Buddhism perceived things and the way in which the great scholars [of the Daoist metaphysical school] looked at the things of the universe. Moreover, they seemed to take pride equally in being free of worldly matters, in being unconventional, unconfined by normal ethical constraints, and "above it all." While the famous scholars employed the so-called san xuan [Three Metaphysical Observations] to develop and promote their xuanxue [Daoist metaphysics], the great monks of the period similarly used the doctrine of san xuan to explain the principles of Buddhism. In the Western Jin dynasty a renowned monk, Zhi Xiaolong, befriended such great scholars of the day as Ruan Zan and Yi Kai and became known to the people of the time as Ba da [He Who Reached Far in All Eight Directions]. In the Eastern Jin, Sun Zuo wrote the book Dao xian lun [On the Good People in the Dao] in which he compared seven famous monks to the legendary "Seven Scholars of the Bamboo Grove."

At the time, many Buddhist monks became extremely well-versed in the teachings of Laozi (Lao Tzu) and Zhuangzi. It was said in the historical record that the Monk Fahu [Zhu Fahu] "was well-read in all the Six Classics, and has been widely exposed to the teachings of all the Hundred Schools [of the pre-Qin period]." Furthermore, the Monk Zhi Dun praised the Monk Yu Falan for "having a comprehensive understanding of the meanings of the Xuanxue." Zhi Xiaolong claimed that he himself "became a free spirit capable of roaming without restriction [xiaoyou] when he achieved the goal of paoyi [the Daoist principle of maintaining singularity, or becoming one with and undifferentiated from the Dao] and arrived at mie [nirvana, or extinction] by way of the cultivation of tranquillity."

The Monk Dao Qian [Zhu Daoqian] "roamed freely for thirty-some years teaching and preaching; in some cases he transmitted the teachings of the Vaipulya sutras; in others he explained the doctrines of Laozi (Lao Tzu) and Zhuangzi." The Monk Zhi Dun was "fond of the teachings of Laozi (Lao Tzu) and Zhuangzi" and annotated the chapter "Xiao yao you" [The Roaming of a Free Spirit] in the book Zhuangzi. The Monk Dao An made a comparison between the [Daoist] doctrines of ke dao [the Way of Possibilities] and chang dao [the Constant Way] and the Buddhist doctrine of the two satya [er ti]. [The two satya, or two forms of noble statements of the truth sees dogma as existing in two forms--or the universal truth as able to be expressed in two dichotomized ways--one, the samvritisatya or vulgar and common statement in which truths are expressed as if phenomena are real, and, secondly, the paramartha-satya, or true statement by the enlightened who has already understood the true unreality and non-existence of phenomena--Tr.] When the Monk Hui Guan annotated the Fa hua jing [Saddharmapundarika sutra, or Sutra of the Lotus of the Wonderful Law] he studied the teachings of Laozi (Lao Tzu) and Zhuangzi. The Monk Hui Yuan was known also for having "broadly studied the Six Classics, and [he] was particularly adept at interpreting the teaching of Laozi (Lao Tzu) and Zhuangzi."

At the time, the majority of the famous monks preached the doctrine of prajna, and, as we have seen already, they were also prone to discuss, if not advocate, the teachings of Lao and Zhuang. Indeed, objectively for the most part the Buddhist teachings introduced into China from India and other "Western countries" at the time belonged to the prajna school, but there were other factors which rendered the popularity of the prajna school in China at that time far from accidental.

In the article Bei nai ye xu [Preface to the Vinaya, or Discipline, Pitaka], the Monk Dao An wrote:

> *Of the twelve volumes herein collected, the most voluminous is the collection of Vaipulya sutras. This occurs because in this country the teachings of Lao and Zhuang have already gained much headway among the people. [These teachings] are quite similar to the teachings of the fangdeng [vaipulya] sutras; there is much that they share in common. That is why the people have already adapted their behavior and ways of life to the teachings [of our sutras].*

The "vaipulya" teachings belonged to the category of the fangdeng [or fangguang, both being the general categorical title give to the Mahayana sutras]. The prajna [wisdom] teachings also belonged to the category of fangdeng. From Dao An's explanation we can see that the popularity of the prajna teachings in China during the Western and Eastern Jin Dynasties had a great deal to do with the influence of Daoist metaphysics, or xuanxue. However, even so, the major pin [segments] among the prajna sutras, namely, the Fangguang banruo boluomi jing [The Prajnaparamita Sutra Emitting Light] and the Guang-han banruo boluomi jing [The Prajnaparamita Sutra Praising Light] did not become truly popular until the early years of the Eastern Jin. That is why the Jian bei jing xu [The Account of the Gradual Fulfillment of the Sutras] said:

Although the great pin has appeared for some decades, at the time of its appearance the learned people for the most part did not study it or practice it. One wonders why the various masters should have done so? . . . However, this situation has gradually changed, and since [through translation] the major pin has arrived in toto [in China], there is not a single pandit today, of either East or West, who does not make it his career and goal to teach it.

The Guangzhan Banruo Boluomi Jing was produced in translation by Zhu Fahụ in the seventh year of the Taikang reign [286], and the Fangguang banruo boluomi jing was translated by Zhu Falan in the third year of the reign of Yuankang [291]. Both became popular only in the early years of the Eastern Jin dynasty [i.e., circa 320]. This popularity was intimately related to the socio-historical conditions of the period. Since the Wei dynasty and the beginning of the Jin dynasty there had been a continuous enlargement of the power and influence of the ruling cliques made up of the menfa shizu [grand noble families and gentry clans]. One can say that this influence reached its peak in the reign of Yuankang [291-299 A.D.] The subsequent "rebellion of the Eight Princes," the invasion of the northwestern minority nationalities and their domination of the Central Chinese Plains, and the southward move of the royal house and central government of the Jin dynasty of the Sima family accelerated the degeneration of the ruling cliques. By this time, this ruling power structure had become extremely helpless and pessimistic about its own fate and the destiny of society. It was natural, therefore, that they then turned their attention to the problems of life, death, and liberation of the individual. This was also one of the reasons for the increasing popularity of the two religions--Buddhism and Daoism (Taoism)--toward the end of the Eastern Jin dynasty.

A society wherein people are seeking a world which transcends the mundane and real provides a very important context and purpose for the emergence of religions. For religions they are able to propose to people that solutions can be found in their own particular worlds of fantasy for the many sufferings which exist in such common measure in the real society where they cannot be resolved, including such problems as living and dying. Buddhism is no exception to this generalization. After the in

troduction of prajna Buddhist teachings into China, it remained in a stage of translation until the Eastern Jin dynasty. That is, the Chinese Buddhist monks had not yet formed their own understanding or interpretation of the prajna teachings. In the Eastern Jin, however, sects and subgroups which represented different understandings of the teachings of prajna Buddhism began to emerge. Later, it was as discussions and responses to the schools of prajna teachings which has emerged since the Eastern Jin dynasty. The Monk Zhao [Seng Zhao] wrote the Bu zhen kong lun [Treatise on the Fallacy of the Doctrine of True Nothingness or Non-existence] to criticize the refute the three schools, namely, the ben wu [Original Nonexistence or Nothingness] school, the zhi se [Identity of Appearances] school, and the xin wu [Non-existence of the Mind] school; during the Song dynasty Tan Ji wrote the treatise Liu Jia Qi Zong Lun [On the Six Schools and Seven Sects]; and the Monk Jing [Zeng Jing] wrote Shi Xiang Liu Jia Lun [The Six Schools of the Sect of the Reality of Appearances].

We do not propose to spend much time in this essay in discussing in any detail the various prajna teachings popular at that time, but two notable issues were the very questions which had occupied the center of attention in the Daoist metaphysical teachings [xuanxue] of the Wei and Jin periods, namely, the questions of ben-mo [relationship between the fundamental and the incidental] and you-wu [substance and unreality, or existence and non-existence]. These were the very same questions posed by the various schools of prajna Buddhism popular at the time. In the following paragraphs I shall attempt to illustrate this problem by taking, in turn, the three schools contradicted and criticized by the Monk Shao in Bu Zhen kong lun.

The meaning of the doctrine of the non-existence of the mind [xin wu yi]. In Bu Zen Kong Lun the Master Monk Shao wrote:

> *By saying that the mind does not really exist they [the adherent of this doctrine] are actually saying that the mind does not have existence in any thing, but they do not actually say that all things do not really have existence. This doctrine is good in that it leads people toward tranquillity of the spirit, but it is faulty in that it is really things, rather than the mind, that are empty and non-existent.*

According to Ji Kang (Chi Kang), in the Er ti yi [The Meaning of the Two Statements]:

Those who espouse the dogma of the non-existence of the Mind have for too long taken the truth of this doctrine for granted. Even before the time of the Great Pandita Kumarajiva, and going as far back as to the time of the Masters Dao An and Zhu Fahu, this dogma has existed. Those who speak of the non-existence of the mind cite the sutras, saying: "Those who say that the nature of appearance is empty and non-existent are in fact clear that appearances cannot by themselves be empty and nonexistent`but are empty or non-existent in the mind. It is because one can achieve this emptiness of vision [of the mind] that one can say that appearances are non-existent. In the final analysis, however, the appearance cannot be non-existent." Master Shao dispelled this dogma; he understood its goodness to lay in its exhortation to the tranquillity of the spirit, but he also faulted it for its ignorance of the fact that it is matter, or things, which are non-existent. To achieve tranquillity of the spirit one must indeed understand the emptiness, or non-existence, of the mind; in this respect the word of that dogma is good, but, in claiming that appearances may not themselves be non-existent, this dogma has exposed its own weakness.

The idea here is to claim that "the significance of the dogma of the nonexistence of the mind" is that "the mind, not the appearances [of matter], is empty and non-existent." To say that it is not the appearances which are nonexistent is to say that "all things are not [necessarily] non-existent."

In the Tang dynasty, in his annotations to Shao Lun So [Commentary on the Arguments of the Grand Monk Shao], Yuan Kang wrote, "It [the dogma of the non-existence of the mind] affirms that matter has substance and is not non-existent"; "it did not understand that the nature of matter is non-existence; [the Monk Shao] called this its fallacy." To "not understand that the nature of matter is non-existence" is to understand the nature of matter as substance, or existence--this is an idea that bears much resemblance to the thought of Guo Xiang. [Although a Daoist metaphysician], Guo Xiang opposed the notion of "taking wu [non-existence, or non-being] as the point of origin." He believed that wan you [all that is, or all existence] does not originate from wu [non-existence] or have wu for its original ontological reality. To Guo Xing, you [existence] is the only real being, and it exists on the basis of the fact that each matter has its own zi xiang [particularity of nature of self-nature]. Therefore, he said, "Each matter, or thing, has its nature." To speak of the non-existence of the mind would therefore be to project the emptiness, or non-existence, of the mind into all things. Yuan Kang annotated this notion, saying, "[To say that the mind is non-existent] is to say that one must also not generate a definite, appropriating mind on the basis of matter; this is what is meant by emptiness or non-existence." This, too, was rather similar to the ideas espoused by Guo Xiang.

In annotating and commenting on the seven "inner" chapters of the book Zhuangzi, Guo Xiang wrote a set of essays which explained, from his viewpoint, the meaning of the title of each of those chapters. In three of these essays, Guo espoused the idea of "the non-existence of the mind [wu xin]." The essay on the chapter Ren jian shi [The Inter-human World], for example, said, "Only those who have no existence of the mind and are not self-serving can go wherever the changes lead and yet not feel the burdens [of change]."

The essay on Da zong shi [The Great Ancestor and Teacher] said, "Out of the great expanse of the universe and the richness of all things, there is only one thing which is worth learning from, and of which it is worth one's while to become master, and that is the emptiness, or non-existence, of the mind." In the essay on the chapter Ying di wang [Response of Emperors and Princes], Guo said, "Those who have no existence of the mind and have learned to allow changes and transformation to come whither they will and lead whither they will are worthy of becoming emperors and princes of men."

According to these sayings, it is evident that Guo Xiang believed that the sage has no existence of the mind and simply follows the [natural] course of matter and is therefore capable of "going wherever changes may lead, and feels no burden."

Nonetheless, although we may say that the [Buddhist] doctrine on the non-existence of the mind resembles Guo Xiang's thinking on the subject in many ways, we have no evidence that the doctrine was directly derived from Guo Xiang's system of thought. We can say only that at that time, under the prevailing influence of xuanxue [Daoist metaphysics], Buddhism often focused on the same problems on which this school of xuanxue concentrated.

The meaning of the doctrine of the Identity of Appearances [ji se yi]. It was Zhi Dun [Zhi Daolin] who advocated the doctrine of the Identity of Appearances. It was said that he wrote about twenty essays [on the subject], including the Shi zhi se ben wu yi [The Buddha's Notion of the Identity of Appearances Originating in Nothing], the Ji se you xuan lun [Treatise on the Free Roaming in the Realm of Metaphysics of the Doctrine of the Identity of Appearances], the Miao guan zhang [The Chapter on the Wondrous Vision or Meditation], and the Xiao yao lun [Treatise on Free Roaming]. Most of these have been lost and only fragments remain. In the segment Wenxue [Literature] in the book Shi shuo xin yu [New Specimens of the Talk of the Times] Zhi Dun's essay Miao guan zhang [Chapter on the Wondrous Vision or Meditation] was cited in one of the notes, and in this citation [the article to which it was attached was itself lost] a certain fragmentary passage read as follows:

The nature of appearances is that appearances do not exist naturally or in and of themselves. Since appearances do not exist naturally or in and of themselves, there are appearances that are kong [empty, or insubstantial]. That is why we say: Appearance [se] is empty, and yet appearance is also separate, or different, from emptiness.

Furthermore, in the Shao Lun Shu [Commentary on the arguments of the Grand Monk Shao] the Monk Hui Da was quoted as saying:

> *The Master of the Laws [fashi] Zhi Daolin said, in the Ji se lun [Treatise on the Identity of Appearances]: I believe that the saying: "The identity of appearances is emptiness, not that the appearances perish, but that*

they are empty, or nonexistent" is a most correct statement. (This saying is derived from the text of the Wei mo jing [Vimalakirti nirdesa Sutra].) Why? Because the nature of appearances lies in that appearances are not by themselves naturally appearances. Although they are appearances, they are empty.

The saying that "appearances are not by themselves appearances" meant that physical phenomena do not have their own nature or character [zixing, or self-nature]. The saying, "appearances do not exist by themselves or naturally" meant that there are no supporting materials or substances behind things in the natural state. By "self-nature" [zi xing] we are actually referring to "substance in itself" [zi ti] or ontological substance [ben ti]. If things did not have their own substances, although there are myriad separate and diverse phenomena, they are all not real. This is the reasoning behind stating that "although they are appearances, they are empty"; i.e., although there are myriad diverse phenomena, there is in reality not a single true substance. In the time of the Wei and Jin dynasties, the term kong [emptiness] was often conceived to be interchangeable with the term wu [non-existence, nonbeing] and xuanxue scholars [metaphysicians] [or adherents of the Buddhist religion who were influenced by the ideas of xuan xue] of the day often also argued that kong [emptiness or insubstantiality or unreality], or, interchangeably wu [non-existence] was the ontological substance of all things. (This, for instance, was the contention of the ben wu yi [Doctrine of the Non-existence of Origin], with which we shall be soon dealing.) Therefore, on the point that it made regarding the absence of ontological substance behind matter, or things, Zhi Dun's idea also came very close to the ideas of Guo Xiang.

The notion of "the non-existence of substance" [wu-ti] proposed that behind se [phenomena or appearances] there is no ontological substance in the kong or wu [i.e., the kong (emptiness) or wu (non-existence) is not actually ontological substance for the se (appearances)]. Although there is phenomenon, there is no ontological substance, and thus "appearances are also separate from emptiness." Since there is no ontological substance to appearances, one cannot say that it is only when appearances have perished that they become "empty" [or, revert to emptiness]--hence the saying: "Not that appearances perish, but that they are empty." From this angle, Zhi Dun's Ji se lun [Treatise on the Identity of Appearances] could have been more appropriately called the Je se ben wu yi [Doctrine of the Identity of Appearances Originating in Nothing].

From one angle, Zhi Dun's idea appeared to be quite similar to Guo Xiang's thought, as when they seemed to hold in common a belief that there is no ontological substance behind things. From another facet, however, their ideas were different. Zhi Dun's belief, as we have seen, was that, if things did not have ontological substance behind them, it meant that things were "empty" to begin with.

From the angle of their separate interpretations of the essay, Xiao yao you [Free Roaming] in the book Zhuangzi, it becomes even more obvious that there were differences between Zhi Dun's ideas and Guo Xiang's thought. According to the "Zhi Dun zhuan" [The Biography of Zhi Dun] in Gao Zeng Zhuan [The Biographies of the Great Monks].

Liu Xizhi et al., when discussing the chapter Xiao yao bian of the book Zhuangzi, said: "Each must accommodate its own nature and only then can it roam totally freely." Dun [Zhi Dun] disagreed, saying: "That is wrong. Jie [a tyrant, and last ruler of the Xia dynasty] and Qi [a notorious bandit and rebel of the late Spring and Autumn period] are by nature cruel and ruinous. If it were indeed all right, and necessary, for each to accommodate its own nature, would not Jie and Qi also be free roaming now?" On that [Zhi Dun] retired to write his own annotation of the Xiao yao bian.

The idea of "each accommodating its own nature and thereby becoming a free roaming spirit" was, of course, precisely the dominant thought in Guo Xiang's own annotation and interpretation of the Xiao yao bian. In the prefatorial note of his commentary to this chapter of Zhuangzi in which he laid down his arguments by way of explaining the chapter's title, he said:

> *Although things may differ in size, if they were each placed in its own appropriate place, where it fits the circumstances, each matter would be able to let loose its own nature and each thing will be suited to its ability; each will be in its proper portion, and all things will be equally free to roam. How then can differences be driven between things?*

Moreover, the first annotation in Guo Xiang's annotative commentary on Xiao yao you read, in part,

> *Zhuangzi's general idea was that one must be essentially free to roam and travel totally free of confinements. One must therefore obtain oneself--be independent--by putting oneself in non-action. Therefore the smallest is also the greatest. One must hence understand the principle of fitting one's nature to one's portion.*

From the above, we can see that it was precisely to this idea of Guo Xiang's that Zhi Dun objected. What then were Zhi Dun's own views on "the freely roaming spirit"? The full text of his commentary on the Xiao yao bian is no longer extant. However, a fragment of it was cited by an annotation in the Wenxue [Literature] portion of Shi shuo xin yu.

Xiaoyao [free roaming] means the fulfillment of the enlightenment of the mind of the Ultimate Man. The Young Master Zhuang established through the Word the Great Way, by putting his ideas into the words of the roc [peng] and the wren [yan]. The roc's pathway of life is a broad one; to accommodate it he has to lose himself outside of his own body; the wren, on the other hand, is but close to the ground, yet it jeered at that which was far away and high up in the heavens. He had a sense of arrogance and conflict in his own mind. The Ultimate Man rides on the wings of the Propriety of Heaven and is glad; he roams in the realm of Infinity and is entirely footloose. To objectify objects and not be objectified by objects is to roam freely and not return to one's condition; to contain a sense of xuan [the metaphysical principle] and not to engage in action, to move swiftly and yet without any haste, is to roam freely and be able to go wherever one wishes. That is what is meant by xiaoyao. If one had a desire in one's mind which has to be met, and if one is content with meeting the desires whose fulfillment meant contentment, then, though one's happiness may appear similar to natural naivete, it would, in fact, be nothing but like the desire of the thirsty for the contentment of a single drink. How can one lose the sense of luxurious food simply because one has been filled up by one good dinner? Or can we put an end to the reality of the grandeur of the ceremonial wine after we have imbibed some rich quaff? The Ultimate Man does not speak of xiaoyao [free roaming] until he is truly satisfied.

It was Guo Xiang's belief that, although things differed in magnitude, they were equal in terms of the ability to "roam freely" under the principle of "each according to its own nature." From this opinion Zhi Dun differed. In his point of view, whether or not one was capable of roaming freely depended on one's perspective. If one could "objectify all objects and not be objectified by objects" [i.e., be in control of all things and not be oneself trammeled by things], and "contain a sense of xuan [the metaphysical principle] and not engage in action, be swift without being in any haste" [i.e., respond objectively to all things and yet not ask, or need, anything of things; respond to change but not change oneself, then one would be capable of "free roaming" that is indeed worthy of that description.

On the other hand, Zhi Dun believed that, if one were to "roam" only to satisfy the requirements of one's own nature and portion, then it would be nothing more than a hungry man seeking a meal or a thirsty man asking for the gratification of a drink. To him, such low levels of demand and satisfaction cannot be considered "free roaming." Therefore, only that which satisfies the Ultimate can be called "roaming freely." Zhi Dun thought of "satisfying the Ultimate" as "riding the wings of the Propriety of Heaven" (according to Zhuangzi's text, the proper citation should have been "the Propriety of Heaven and Earth") and "being glad, traveling in the realm of Infinity and being completely unconfined." This meant living in the universe and yet not being limited by the limited world, and absolutely transcending of the world of matter and being unconfined, unfettered in thought. That is what he meant when he said,

"To roam freely is to attain the full enlightenment of the mind of the Ultimate Man." In Zhi Dun's view "roaming freely" depended solely on the ability of the mind of the Ultimate Man to transcend the limitations of time and space.

Another essay that Zhi Dun wrote, known by the title Ji se you xuan lun [Treatise on Free Roaming in the Realm of the Metaphysical by the Doctrine of the Identity of Appearances] is also no longer extant. It is possible to deduce, however, that it contained a theory which was derived from a combination of his "doctrine of the identity of appearances" [ji se yi] and his doctrine of "free roaming" [xiao yao yi]. If the Ultimate Man was able to realize the principle that "appearances are not by themselves appearances" [se bu zi se], then he would be able to "objectify all things and not be objectified by them", to "contain a sense of the principle of the metaphysical and not engage in action, to be swift and yet not in haste"; such a person would "roam freely everywhere and be able to go wherever he wishes." In other words, such a person's mind would be fully capable of transcending all the limitations of time and space. Therefore, in Zhi Dun's view, to become Buddha meant, in fact, to roam freely and to become completely unconfined by convention--this was precisely the same goals which the xuanxue [Daoist metaphysics] scholars strove to achieve. From this viewpoint, there is, between his "doctrine on free roaming in the realm of the metaphysical by the principle of the identity of appearances" [ji se you xuan lun] and his "doctrine of the identity of appearances originating in nothingness" [ji se ben wu lun], no inconsistency of theoretical contradiction.

From the above analysis, we can see that the questions discussed in Zhi Dun's doctrine of the identity of appearances were the same as those which were raised in the circle of xuanxue. Furthermore, from his own views on the question of xiao yao [free roaming], we can see that he was himself a xuanxue scholar [Daoist metaphysician]. Although his views differed from those of Guo Xiang, they were in fact quite close to the original ideas of Zhuang Zhou [Zhuangzi].

The Meaning of the Doctrine of Original Nothingness [ben wu yi]. From the Liu jia qi zong lun [Treatise of the Six Schools and Seven Sects] written by the Monk Tan Ji, and the Zhong lun shu [Commentary on the Prannyaya mula sastrtika, or Treatise of the Meditation of the Mean] written by the Monk Ji Kang (Chi Kang), the ben wu yi [doctrine of original nothingness] bifurcated into two major channels. One was the ben wu zong [School of Original Nothingness] and the other was known as the ben wu yi zong [the Variant Sect of Original Nothingness]. The former school espoused the form cf the doctrine as championed by the Monk Dao An; the latter was espoused by the Pandita Shen [or Fa Shen, a.k.a. Zhu Daoqian]. In reality they resembled each other in major ways and differed only in minor areas. Here, therefore, we shall not dwell on the differences but analyze only Dao An's "doctrine or original nothingness" [ben wu] in order to illustrate the relationship of this doctrine to the teachings of xuanxue.

In the Zhong lun suo, Ji Kang (Chi Kang) wrote:

> *Before the arrival of Kumarajiva the Pandita, there were three schools of Buddhist teachings in Changan [the Tang dynasty capital of China]. One was the school of the Monk [Shi] Dao An, which was represented by his teachings on Original Nothingness, in which he argued that wu [nothingness, or non-being] existed prior to all creation and that kong [emptiness or non-existence] was the beginning of all forms. He also argued that what was holding people back [from their enlightenment] was the sense of you [existence, or being] when you is in fact a product rather than a point of origin. If people could only rest their minds in contentment with Original Nothingness, they would be able to quell all devious thought. . . . To understand this significance is to maintain tranquillity in the universal enlightenment of Original Nothingness. All the myriad dharma [fa, or things] have, as their original nature, emptiness and extinction; that is what we mean when we say Original Nothingness.*

This quotation suggests that Dao An first of all posited that the prior existence of all dharma, together with all their forms and phenomena, was wu [nothingness, or non-being] and kong [emptiness or non-existence]. However, kong wu [non-existence and emptiness, or non-being] was not the same as xu kong [void]. Dao An, therefore, said "Wu [non-existence] existed before the original transformation [or creation]; kong [emptiness] was the beginning of all forms [formed substance]; that is what we mean when we speak of original nothingness. This does not mean that it was from a [specific] void that all things were given birth." (See the citation of Tan Ji's Liu jia qi zong lun in the Ming Zeng Zhuan chao [Handcopy of the Biographies of the Renowned Monks].) Therefore, when [Dao An] argued that "the wan you [all things] were generated from kong wu" [emptiness and non-existence], the term kong wu did not mean xu kong [void]; the meaning, rather, was that kong [emptiness] or wu [non-existence] was the original ontological substance of wan you [all things]. Only in this way could it exist "prior to all existences" [wan you].

It should be noted that Dao An's understanding of the Kong zong [Emptiness Sect, or Sect of Non-being] in Buddhist prajna teaching was not quite in conformity to that sect's understanding of its own teachings, in which "original nothingness" seemed to have been taken to mean that "all dharma did not originally have a nature unto themselves [zi xing]," or, in other words, nothing has a real ontological substance in itself. (We shall have more to say on this issue later.) Instead, Dao An's doctrine of original nothingness can be said to have borne certain resemblances to Wang Bi's idea of "accepting wu [non-existence] as the origin" [yi wu wei ben]. In fact, it may be closer even to the ideas of Zhang Zhan. Like Wang Bi, Zhang Zhan posited "non-existence as the origin" [yi wu wei ben], but when he spoke of wu [non-existence] he seemed to have been referring to something outside of [and over and above] you [existence]. For example, he said: "Because there is such a thing as Ultimate Non-existence [zhi wu], it can therefore be the origination and source of all changes and transformations [from which came creation]." He also said: "That which is not born can therefore be the origin of all that is born." In these illustrations, Zhang Zhan affirmed in his mind that there was, above and beyond wan you [all existence], a transcendental Absolute which served as the Origin from which and by which all existence is born. This viewpoint differed substantially from that of Wang Bi. Wang believed that, although "non-existence" [wu] was the ontological substance of "existence" [you], it did not exist outside of you. He said: "Non-existence cannot be without name; it must have cause in existence." Also, Wang believed that substance [ti] cannot be divorced from usage [yong]. He said: "We shall take non-existence for usage; we cannot abandon non-existence as substance alone." On the other hand, Dao An, when he talked of Original Nothingness, saw wu [non-existence] as existing prior to wan you [all existences, or all being]. He was, therefore, closer to Zhang Zhan's ideas. Furthermore, Dao An, in a way similar to Zhang Zhan, even used the "theory of the Original Breath, or Spirit" [yuan qi lun] to explain the construction of the Universe and the formation of all things. It was thus recorded in Tan Ji's Liu Jia Qi Zong Lun:

In the first place, thus spoke the Founder of the Sect of Original Nothingness: Ru lai [He That Was as He Came, i.e., Buddha] came to prosper the world. He taught the doctrine of Original Nothingness to extend his teachings. That is why the profound vaipulya sutras all contain enlightenment on the doctrine of the original nothingness of the wu yin [the five negative elements, or agencies]. For the longest time, the doctrine of original nothingness has been accepted and broadened. . . . How so? Prior to primal and Covert Creation, there was nothing but the frame. It was when the Original Spirit or Breath began to mold and transform that the myriad phenomena began to be endowed with forms. ... This is not to say that it is out of Emptiness that the many things were born. What holds people back is that they remain stagnated [in their understanding] in the realm of the you [being] which is merely the product, or result [and not the origin]. If a person is capable of investing his mind in the Original Nothingness, he would be able to shed this very burden. This is what we mean when we say that, if only one would pursue and exalt the origin, the inconsequential ends would be put to rest.

By wu [non-existence] Dao An meant the Original Spirit or Breath [yuan qi] which he conceived to be a frame without form or phenomenon. This viewpoint was consistent with the interpretation which the Buddhist monks, from the Han-Wei period up to this time, held with regard to the notion of the formation of the universe, and followed from those interpretations. The Monk Kang Hui, when he translated the Liu Du Ji Jing [Collected Sutra of the Six Paramitas] wrote, in its volume 8, under the Cha Wei Wang Jing [Sutra of the Observations of the Covert Meanings of the Words of the King]:

> *What we have observed has rendered us profoundly aware that, when Man was in a primitive original state, he was born of the Original Nothingness. Then the Original Breath became differentiated: that part which was solid and strong became earth, that which was soft became water, that which was warm became fire, and that which was mobile became wind. . . . These four things met in harmony and the Knowing Spirit was born. Arising, it became enlightened as to its capacities and senses, and it ceased to desire, becoming thus empty of mind, and the spirit was reverted to Original Nothingness. This Breath, or Spirit, of the Knowing and the Origin was delicate, subtle, and imperceptible.*

Again, in the Yin Chi Ru Jing Zhu [Annotations to the Sutra of the Entrance to Truth by Way of Covert Maintenance], the wu yin zhong [Five Negative Elements species] were described as being "akin to the yuan qi [original breath or spirit]." Therefore, the idea was not that "all existences" were born of "emptiness," but that "all existences" came about as the result of the transformation of the Original Breath or Spirit which had neither form nor phenomenon. All things were born of this formless, phenomenon-less Original Breath or Spirit, and man was no exception.

The argument continues that Man was confused because he was holding on to the various forms and appearances which had temporary existence, but if he was able to comprehend that wu [non-existence] existed before the myriad transformations, and that kong [emptiness] was the origin of the many forms, he would be able to revert to his own source, transcend life and death, become delivered, and merge as one with the universe and all things, that is, attain the dao (tao) [way] and revert to the yuan qi [original Spirit].

Therefore, in Dao An's doctrine of Original Nothingness, the key to deliverance was to eliminate the incorrect understanding of things. In nonaction and absence of desire and purity of the mind one would be able to achieve that state of being "commensurate with the Ultimate Emptiness and roam with the Creator Force in tranquil and serene happiness." (See Ren Ben Yu Sheng Jing Zhu [Annotations on the Sutra on the Origin of the Life of Man in Desires].)

The way to deliverance described by Dao An was almost identical to that proposed by Zhang Zhan. Zhang believed that if man were able to relinquish all tenets and understand the origins and the ultimate destinations of life and death--i.e., that Man came from the Ultimate Emptiness and shall return unto that Ultimate Emptiness, Man would be able to attain deliverance and become the Ultimate Being, which has attained the dao (tao) [way]. Furthermore, the Ultimate Being is one "whose mind has been re-joined, re-connected with the Original Spirit or Breath, and whose body, covertly, was in harmony with the Yin and Yang." (See the book Lie Zi Zhu [Annotations on Lie Zi].)

In the Bu zhen kong lun [Treatise on the Fallacy of the Doctrine of True Non-existence] the Monk Shao criticized the doctrine of Original Nothingness, saying:

> *The advocates of Original Nothingness align their sentiments on the side of wu [nothingness] and then write their words of teaching to support that argument. They refute, to begin with, the notion of existence and say that you [existence or being] was in fact wu [non-existence]. Even if one refuted the notion of non-existence will nonetheless still be nonexistence. The original meaning of the Buddhist canons is that fei you [not being] is not really being and that fei wu [not non-being] is not really non-being. Why must one insist on refuting the notion of being and say that "this being is not," or refute the notion of non-being and say that "non-being is not"?*

What this passage says is: The school of Original Nothingness maintains a biased affinity for wu [non-being]. They accept the idea that nonbeing is the ontological substance of reality, and all its arguments are based on this philosophy of non-being. Therefore the adherents of this school do not recognize you [being]; rather, they believe that being cannot be divorced from non-being; i.e., they accept "non-being as the origin." They believe, moreover, that non-being itself could not be separated from non-being; i.e., they maintain the notion of the fundamentality of non-being, insist upon it, and see non-being as true non-being. However, according to the original intent of the Buddhist sutras, what is important, and to be maintained, was that "not being" is not truly being [fei you bu shi zhen di you], and not non-being is also not truly non-being [fei wu ye bu shi zhen di wu]. Why, therefore, should anyone insist that "not being" meant the non-being of any particular thing or that "not non-being" meant the absence of any particular non-being?

[From the above] it appears that the Monk Shao took the original intent of the Kong zong [Emptiness school] of prajna Buddhism as his point of departure in criticizing the doctrine of Original Nothingness and its adherents for their insistence on wu [non-existence] and their failure to comprehend that "non-being" was itself a jiaming [false name, or illusion] and not a real being. His argument, ultimately, was that only "the refutation of both being and non-being" was the true principle taught by Buddhism. In doing so, in the Bu zhen kong lun [Treatise on the Fallacy of the Doctrine of True Nothingness] the Monk Shao criticized not only the doctrine of Original Nothingness itself, but also Wang Bi's idea of "valuing nothingness" and Guo Xiang's idea of "exalting being" as well, and thereby developed [not just Buddhist teachings but also] the teachings of xuanxue [Daoist metaphysics] of the Wei and Jin periods.

The Meaning of the Doctrine of Non-Real, Non-Existence or Emptiness [bu shen kong yi]. It can be argued that the criticism contained in the Monk Shao's Bu zhen kong lun of the three schools of prajna Buddhism which were popular in China at that time was based on the original intent of the Indian teachings of Buddhist prajna. By positing that "emptiness is not real" [bu zhen kong] he suggested that all things do not truly exist, or that all things not truly are, but rather, the existence of all things is unreal, and that that is why we can call [existence] kong [emptiness or unreality]. In other words, "emptiness" equals "unreality." This was the Chinese expression of the fundamental premise of the Kong zong [Emptiness school] of Indian Buddhist prajna teaching, namely, the premise that "all fa [dharma, or things] do not have ontological self-substance" [zhu fa ben wu zi xing].

The Monk Shao said that the Zhong lun [Treatise on the Mean] posited the paradox that while, from one angle, "all fa [dharma] were not existent," from another angle, "all fa were also, and at the same time, not non-existent." He argued that to understand this principle of "not being and yet not non-being" would be to understand the ultimate truth. This is because, he argued, although there were very many things of various forms and appearances, under analysis they can all be found to be formed only by causes and effects and their combinations and have no zi xing [self-nature, or ontological substance, or reality in and of themselves]. This would therefore be "non-existence." On the other hand, although all dharma had no real ontological substance, there were nonetheless phenomena in many diverse forms and appearances, and dharma was therefore also "not non-existence." Hence, he argued, one cannot say that there are no things, but only that there are no real things.

In what way, then, can there be such "unreal existence" [jia you]?

According the Monk Shao's interpretation of Zhong lun, all things are formed of the combinations and permutations of causes and effects and therefore have no ontological substance. However, once made up by the combination of causes and effects, things also then become "not non-existent" and cannot be said to be fundamentally non-existent. By further applying logical reasoning to this issue, the Monk Shao concluded that this principle was the very basic truth. If "being" was "real being," he argued, "being" would have existed at the beginning and should exist to the very end, and there would have been no need to wait for the combination of causes and effects to bring "being" into existence. If, on the other hand, "non-being" was real non-being, "non-being" itself should also have existed at the very beginning and to the very end, and there would also have been no need to wait for the combination of causes and effects to bring about "non-being."

If one were to accept that "being" cannot be "being in itself," but had to wait for the combination of causes and effects to bring it into being, then one would be able to realize that "being" was not "real being." [He said], "Being is not real being; therefore, though there is being, we do not say that there is real being." At the same time, one must also say that there is "not non-being." If there was real "non-being" it would be monolithic and totally immobile [zhan ran bu dong] [i.e., totally incapable of transformation] and no phenomenon could then be generated. Only such a totally immobile "non-existence" could be called "real non-existence." Therefore, if we were to say that "all fa" [dharma] were "truly nonexistent" there would not be the generation of all fa, and nothing would come of causes and effects. Since "all fa" do come as a result of causes and effects, then one cannot say that there is real "non-existence."

Both in terms of contents and methodology, one can say that the Monk Shao's Bu zhen kong lun was closer in meaning to the original intents of Indian Buddhist prajna teaching. It was not by accident that his doctrine of the Bu zhen kong lun came about; it was, rather, because by that time two conditions had already come into existence. The first was the fact that Kumarajiva was already in possession of the various sutras that provided full explanation [to the Chinese] of the prajna teachings, such as Da zhi du lun [Treatise on the Paramita, or ferrying across by way of the Great Wisdom], Zhong lun [Treatise on the Mean]. Bai lun [The Hundred Treatises], and Shi er men lun [Treatise on the Twelve Sects]. This made it possible by that time to have a clearer understanding of the teachings of the Indian prajna school of Buddhism. The second was that contemporary developments in the teachings of xuanxue [Daoist metaphysics] made it possible for such theories as "non-being and yet not nonbeing" [fei you fei wu] to appear in the Chinese mind and exert an impact on Chinese thinkers (more on this later).

CULTURE–BUDDHISM

The question of the importation of an alien ideological culture and its interaction with an existing native ideological culture is a very complicated one, and there is great significance in studying this problem. Our country's philosophical thinking [and, in fact, its entire culture and society] underwent a major transformation in the time of the Wei and Jin dynasties and the North and South dynasties; it can easily be said that the introduction of Buddhism was one of the most significant causes of this transformation. As for China Buddhism was an alien ideological culture, it is very helpful to study the interaction between the two and the process by which this alien ideological culture integrated with China's own pre-existing traditional ideological culture. This would include its development from being formalistically attached to the body of China's traditional ideological culture, to emerging with its own characteristics which clearly conflicted with and were contradictory to China's ideological culture, and finally to becoming an integral part of the Chinese ideological culture.

The formation of an ideological culture is certain to have its roots in social history; thus in the history of the world various ideological cultures have emerged which are separate and different in both type and form. To understand the characteristics of an ideological culture and the level of its development, one must compare it with other ideological cultures. If we were to compare the Buddhism introduced into China during the period of the Wei, Jin, and North and South dynasties with what existed at that time as China's native traditional ideological culture, we would be able to understand more profoundly not only the characteristics and level of development of that traditional Chinese ideological culture, but also the reasons for which an alien ideological culture was able to be assimilated by the Chinese. The method of analytically studying the comparisons between the ideological culture of one nation [or country or region] and that of another is known as comparative philosophy, which is guided by Marxist thought.

Another significant phenomenon which emerged in the period of the Wei, Jin, and North and South dynasties was the Daoist religion. This was formed in the late years of the Eastern Han dynasty and acquired its own theoretical system. Although it can be said that the formation of the Daoist religion was influenced or stimulated by the introduction of Buddhism, it was nonetheless a religion peculiar to the Chinese, particularly to the Han people, and was bound, therefore, to have characteristics which set it apart from Buddhism. Prior to the Wei and the Jin, Buddhism had just been introduced and in the early stages of its introduction had been grafted to the already existing body of the daoshu [Daoist techniques and crafts].

Hence, the contradictions between the two religions, although already real, were not obvious or outstanding. Since the Wei and Jin, however, because the Daoist religion's own system of thought and theory had gradually formed and because Buddhism, as an imported alien ideological culture, needed to shed gradually its own earlier attachment to the pre-existing native ideological culture, the contradictions and conflict between the two religions became daily more acute and intensified. If we were to analyze and draw comparisons [between these two religions] on the issues upon which they debated, it would be easy for us to see more clearly the characteristics of the Daoist religion as well as the mutual influence which their two religions had upon one another in the midst of their contradictions and polemical struggles. This is the task of those who undertake the study of comparative religion. At this time, we ought also to develop and promote this field of investigation, so that we may form a comparative study of religions, guided, also, by Marxist thought.

What were the most notable characteristics in Buddhism after it was introduced into China and as it became popularized and developed in China? What are the ones we should study and what general laws [of development] can we extract from [such a study]? What conclusions can be drawn? In the following discussion we shall suggest three major problem areas for analysis.

Adaptation to Tradition

When Buddhism was introduced into China at first it was grafted upon the body of pre-existing Chinese ideological culture; then it gradually developed on its own and began to exert its own influence on that culture and Chinese society. It should be understood that Buddhism did not have a great deal of influence immediately after its introduction.

After being introduced into China in the Han dynasty, Buddhism at first attached itself to the daoshu. In the Wei and Jin period, because of the popularity and influence of xuanxue [Daoist metaphysics] Buddhism switched and was attached to the latter. During the time of the Han dynasty, the central tenets of [Chinese] Buddhism were "the imperishability of the soul, or spirit," and "causes and effects." These were ideas that were already originally carried within traditional Chinese thought, or, in some cases, were at least similar in ways to certain ideas which already existed in Chinese philosophical traditions.

Furthermore, the Hinayana methods of chan meditation [dhyana] which were preached at that time also generally were quite similar to the breathing exercises taught by the Huang-Lao School of Daoism (Taoism) and the Immortality [shen xian jia] school. By the time of the Wei and Jin Daoist metaphysical teachings had become popular, and, since Kong zong [the Emptiness sect] of Buddhist prajna teachings was somewhat similar to these Daoist metaphysical teachings, this branch of Buddhism was therefore able to gain popularity by attaching itself to the body of xuanxue. However, it was not until Kumarajiva translated the sutras and commentaries [sastras] such as the Zhong lun that the Chinese understanding of the teachings of the Kong zong of Indian Buddhist prajna philosophy came close to capturing the original intents of those teachings. From the above brief description, we can see that, when Buddhism was first introduced into China, it had first to exist as an attachment, or graft, on the body of some previously existing ideology, and only thus was it able to achieve popularity of its own.

There is one question here which needs to be raised and calls for some discussion. When Zhi-lou-jian translated the Dao Xing Jing [Sutra on the Practice, or Way, of the Truth] in the year 179 A.D., there was in it a pin [segment, or folio] known as the ben wu pin [segment of Original Nothingness]. This appeared long before the [xuanxue] ideas of gui wu [exalting nothingness] and yi wu wei ben [taking nothingness as the origin] which are identified with He Yan [190-249] and Wang Bi [226-249]. Does this then mean that Wang and He's idea of "taking nothingness as the origin" was a product, a result of the influence of Buddhism? We do not believe that this is the answer; it would accord with the facts of the historical record to think that Daoist metaphysical thinking [or, xuanxue] was generated only under the influence of Buddhism.

First of all, the formation of Daoist metaphysical thinking responded to the social needs at the time. Moreover, the emergence of xuanxue should be considered in the light and context of other intellectual developments, either of the period or slightly earlier. These include the development of the teachings of ming li zhi xue [on names and principles] and the distinction between cai [ability] and xing [nature, or character] which appeared during the interim period between the fall of the Han and the rise of Wei, as well as the revival of various schools of Confucianism, Daoism (Taoism), the School of Names [Ming jia] and Legalism, and their mutual intersection and influence. This makes it possible to see that, from the angle of certain inevitable trends in ideological and intellectual development, this emergence of xuanxue was a product of the natural processes of China's indigenous intellectual evolution.

We have not found any convincing evidence that Wang Bi and He Yan were influenced by Buddhism. Even if one or two pieces of evidence were to be discovered indicating that Wang, He, and company may have been in contact with the Buddhism of the day, either directly or indirectly, nonetheless we must still maintain that the ideas of xuanxue were products of the development of preexisting indigenous Chinese ideas themselves. Furthermore, there is a great deal of evidence showing that by and large, during the Han-Wei period, the Chinese officer-scholar gentry did not in the least think highly of Buddhism. For instance, Mouzi in Li huo lun [Treatise on the Disposition of Error] said for the record that "the people of the age, and scholars, mostly sneer at it [i.e., Buddhism] and defame it," and, "we have not heard that, among the rules and teachings accepted by the five talents or among the discussions taken up in the Forest of Confucianist Scholars, the practicing of the ways of Buddha is valued or self-disfigurement is esteemed."

One thing serves to illustrate this point even more clearly and conclusively, namely that, while in the prajna Buddhist teachings of the time the term ben wu [original nothingness] was used, it did not mean the same thing as Wang Bi's idea of yi wu wei ben [taking nothingness to be the origin]. In the various prajna sutras, the idea of ben wu was taken to mean that "all fa [dharma] do not have ontological self-substance" [zhu fa ben wu zi xing]--that is, that all things did not, in and of themselves, have real substance. This, if fact, negated the notion that there was original substance to things. When Wang Bi spoke of ben wu [original nothingness], on the other hand, he meant that "nothingness was the original substance"--that is, ontological reality--of existence [wu shi you di ben ti].

The Buddhist teachings that were imported into China in the Wei-Jin period were for the most part teachings of the Mahayana prajna Kong zong [Emptiness school]. Its fundamental premise was that "all things did not originally have ontological substance, or self-substance" [zi xing]. In this, the term fa [dharma] referred to all things, material but also spiritual. These were known as adharma in the Buddhist sutras. In the Da bo you jing [Great Collection of Prajna Sutras], volume 556, we find the following passage:

> *Take ourselves, for instance; we are, ultimately, not life. We are jia ming [false names or unreal names] [i.e., we are illusions, or falsehoods.] We have no zi xing [self-nature, or nature in and of ourselves]. Likewise, all*

dharma--they too are nothing but false names, and no nature in and of themselves. What is se [appearance]? It cannot be assumed and cannot be born. What is shou [acceptance, or destiny] or xiang [thought] or xing [action] or shi [perception, or understanding]? They, too, are incapable of being assumed or being born.

The Kong zong [Emptiness school] of prajna teaching believed that while people have always held to the notion that there was something which could be called you wuo [having oneself, or self-existence], i.e., zi ti [self-substance], they have done so without realizing that "self" was nothing but the combination produced by the five elements [wu yin] of se [appearance], shou [acceptance or destiny], xiang [thought], xing [action], and shi [perception or understanding]. They were indeed wrong to have believed that there was such a thing as "self." How could "self" exist apart from or independent of these five elements? Therefore, it argued, the term "self" was really nothing but a hypothesis, an unreal name [jia ming], and did not contain any self-nature. Not only was this true of people but of all dharma [things] as well. Therefore, the Guan si ti pin [Segment of the Meditation on the Catvariarya satyani, or Four Noble True Statements] in the Zhong lun argued:

The various causes and effects generate the dharma. The idea of self is but an idea of emptiness, and also a false name. This is the meaning of the Central Way, or the Mean.

The argument here, apparently, was that, since all things were generated by causes and effects, there is in reality no such thing as zi xing [self-nature, or real self-substance] but only kong [non-existence]. The idea of self, therefore, is itself a "non-existence."

However, although things did not contain "self-substance," there are, nonetheless, all sorts of separate phenomena in the world after all. What then are such things? To say that they do not have real existence; still possible, however, are all sorts of unreal existences or phenomena. For purposes of convenience, the argument went, these are given hypothetical, or false, names. The Fangguang banruo jing [Prajnaparamita Sutra Emitting Light] said:

> *Buddha spoke thus to Subhuti [One of the Ten Major Disciples of Buddha, said to have been the best exponent of the Sunya, or Doctrine of the Void--Tr.]: Names are not real; an unreal designation is given and is known as a name, or as the five yin [elements] or as a human being, man or woman.*

The Monk Shao, in Bu zhen kong lun, provided the following explanation:

> *The Fangguang [sutra] said: All dharma have false designations which are not real. For example, Man is the product of the transformation of illusions; this is not to say that there is no man who is the product of the transformation of illusions, but simply that Man who is the product of the transformation of illusions is not really Man [i.e., there is no reality to Man who is produced by the transformation of illusions].*

This raises a secondary question which must be discussed here. Does the idea of kong [emptiness or non-existence] in the saying "self, as it is expressed, is kong, or empty or non-existent" [wuo shuo ji shi kong] signify the position that while things, phenomenologically speaking, did not really exist, there was, nonetheless, an ontologically real "non-existence" [similar to Wang Bi's ontologically real wu, or non-being] which itself was true? This, we shall see, was not the viewpoint of the Kong zong [Emptiness school] of prajna Buddhist teaching. To the adherents of the Kong zong, kong simply referred to the absence "of ontological self-substance in all dharma." This arose because the dictum "dharma is produced or generated by causes and effects; the statement of self is itself non-existent" was proposed for the very purpose of dispelling people's insistence on holding to the idea of real ontological substance in all things. But if people were simply to switch to insist on [the idea of the reality of] non-existence, alluded to in the sentence "the statement of self is itself a non-existence," then the purpose would be defeated, because people would still be insisting on the reality of something-i.e., of "non-existence." That is why, the Kong zong believed, it was necessary to add: "Even this [non-existence itself] is but a false name." Hence the formulation, completed, would be: Not only are the names of things, i.e., phenomena, jia ming [false names] and merely hypothetical; kong [emptiness, or non-existence] itself is a false name also.

Volume 556 of the Da Bo You Jing contained this parable:

> *At one time, the various sons of heaven asked He Who Appeared in Goodness [a name for Buddha]: Is it possible to be in Nirvana and still revert to the realm of illusion? He Who Appeared in Goodness replied: If there was a thing [dharma] that overcame Nirvana and yet, then, reverted to the state of illusion, what would Nirvana then be?*

One must, therefore, not only understand that all dharma do not have real ontological substance; one must at the same time not insist on [the reality of] non-existence. The Da zhi du lun [Treatise on the Ferrying Across by Means of the Great Wisdom] said:

> *The situation is like the taking of medicine. Medicine can dispel the sickness. When the illness has been dispelled, the medicine should also be expelled. If not, then an illness will be acquired. Kong [non-existence] is something that was used to dispel all our troubles, but we should be wary lest kong itself remain to plague us. Therefore, what we suggest is that we must use kong to shed kong--that is, we must understand the non-existence of non-existence itself.*

This means that the assertion of "non-existence" was for the purpose of dispelling the insistence on existence. When and if the notion of existence has been dispelled, the time would come for one to know that "non-existence" is itself an illusion, an unreality, or false name. Yet one cannot say that all is "non-existence" (because there is still, for example, Man who is the product of the transformation of illusions). To understand both of these aspects would be to achieve the Zhong dao guan [True Meditation of the Middle Way, or Mean]. It was, however, not until the late years of the Eastern Jin dynasty, after Kumarajiva had already translated such treatises as the Zhong lun, that this idea of "not existence and yet not non-existence" [fei you fei wu] was truly accepted and understood among Chinese Buddhists and epitomized in the Bu zhen kong lun of the Monk Shao.

Prior to the time of the Monk Shao, the general understanding which the Chinese monks had regarding prajna teaching was on the whole derived from the perspectives of the Daoist metaphysical [xuanxue] thought which was popular at the time. This is something we have already discussed. To further substantiate this argument, let us now analyze again some of the problems raised in connection with Dao An's theory of Original Nothingness. We have, earlier, cited the following passage from Ji Kang (Chi Kang)'s Zhong Lun Shu[Commentary on the Treatise of the Mean]:

When Master An expressed [the doctrine of] Original Nothingness, he meant that all dharma's original nature was emptiness and extinction. That is why he said "Original Nothingness."

Is this not the same idea as that contained in the saying: "All dharma do not originally have any ontological self-substance"? In fact it is not. The sentence here, "all dharma's original nature is emptiness and extinction," meant that emptiness and extinction made up the original nature of all dharma, or, in other words, all things have emptiness and extinction for their original nature or ontological substance. This was an interpretation that could be traced as far back as the Monk Hui Da's Shao lun Shu[Commentary on the Arguments of the Monk Shao]. There he criticized Dao An's theory of Original Nothingness by saying: "[He, Dao An,] was simply unable to realize that originally all dharma was nothing; and therefore he called original non-existence real, but resulting existence vulgar."

The same idea was contained in An Cheng's Zhong Lun Shu[Commentary on the Treatise of the Mean], which said: "The Bie ji [Alternative Record] says" 'The true statement [zhen ti] is the origin of the vulgar statement [shu ti].' That is why we say that Non-existence existed prior to the Original, or Primeval, Transformation." From all the above illustrations, we can see that, in Dao An's understanding of kong [non-existence] or wu [non-being], he still took them to be the ontological substance for you [existence].

Why did such a set of circumstances come about? Because, as Engels pointed out, tradition is an immense force of conservatism. It appears that every ideological cultural tradition is bound to have its conservative aspect which resists imported alien ideological cultural influences. For that reason, an imported ideological culture must first adapt itself to the requirements and demands of the originally existing native ideological culture and be grafted onto its body. Those elements within the imported ideological culture which are relatively close to the original native ideological culture or which resemble it will be easier to be propagated; only then, after the grafting and the initial propagation, will it be possible for the various parts of the imported culture gradually to infiltrate the original culture and exert some of their own influence, until eventually [the imported culture] modifies, or effects transformations in, the original ideological culture.

THE ENRICHMENT AND INTENSIFICATION OF TRADITION

When an imported ideological culture is capable of having a relatively great impact on the country [or nation or region] to which it was imported, in addition to the real and practical societal needs, this would often also occur because the imported culture in general approximated a potential or possible product of the evolution--or certain aspects of the evolution--of the original indigenous ideological culture itself.

It is possible to trace a line of development in the ideas of xuanxue [Daoist metaphysics] from Wang Bi and He Yan's ideas of gui wu [valuing nothingness or non-being] which were based on the notion of "taking non-being as the origin" to Guo Xiang's idea of cong you [exalting being] which was based on the notion of "all things generating themselves" [wan wu zi sheng]. Subsequently, the ideas of Zhang Zhan emerged during the time of the Eastern Jin, which were exemplified in the saying, "Things are generated by themselves spontaneously and instantly, and yet they share one common origin in non-being" [fu er er zi sheng, ze ben tong yu wu]. What then followed in this line of development was the notion of "not being and yet not non-being" [fei you fei wu]. This was similar to the doctrine of "not real non-existence" [bu zhen kong] in the Kong zong [Emptiness school] of prajna Buddhist teaching. Why was it possible for Wei-Jin Daoist metaphysics to develop into the idea of "not being and yet not non-being?" One may say that this was a "potential" product of the evolution of Wei-Jin Daoist metaphysics, or, in other words, it can be said that such an evolution was not only not antithetical or contradictory to the essence of Wei-Jin Daoist metaphysics; it was in fact an enrichment of Wei-Jin Daoist metaphysics.

Beginning with Wang Bi and He Yan, and particularly in the case of Wang Bi, Wei-Jin Daoist metaphysical thought carried out rather penetrating examinations and logical reasoning on the question of the relationship between you [being] and wu [non-being]. Wang Bi used the idea of ti [substance] and yong [effect, function, usage, or phenomenon] to illustrate the relationship between being and non-being. He posited that "non-being cannot be without expression, and therefore must have cause in being." Therefore he believed that, while "non-being" was the ontological substance, it was contained in "being" and had expression in "being." Therefore he viewed substance [ti] and use [yong] as essentially one and the same thing. However, since there was an emphasis in Wang Bi's system of thought on the absoluteness of "non-being," the idea of "exalting the origin and ending the result" [cong ben shi mo] emerged. This brought about an inconsistency in Wang Bi's system of thought. From the perspective of this cong ben shi mo idea, it can be said that there was a notion of negating the being, or, an idea of "not being." Through Xiang Xiu and Pei Wei, Wang Bi's idea of gui wu [valuing the non-being] later made the transition to Guo Xiang's idea of cong you [exalting being].

In Guo's view, being was the only existence, and there was nothing that existed over and beyond wan wu [all things] and that could have served as the ontological substance for wan you [i.e., a Creator substance]. He believed that the existence of all things was based on their respective "self-nature" [zi xing] and that this self-nature was generated spontaneously and instantaneously. For this reason he argued: "Non-being is non-being; that is it. It cannot generate being." In this way he directly challenged and refuted the idea of an ontologically substantial non-being. This idea in itself contained the notion of "not non-being."

In the Eastern Jin dynasty, Zhang Zhan wrote a commentary and annotations to the book Lie Zi, and in it he attempted to bring together in his own way the ideas of Wang Bi and Guo Xiang. On the one hand he argued that "all beings [qun you] have the Ultimate Void [zhi xu] as their ancestor [zong]"--i.e., wu [non-being] or zhi xu [the Ultimate Void] was the basis for the existence of you [being]. This was his idea of wu as ontological substance. To him, Non-being was neither created nor perishable; it does not come together and does not dissipate, whereas all being is created and is perishable, and clusters and dissipates. Moreover, he believed that all species [wan pin] have their ultimate test in their ultimate perishability and, therefore, are "not being." Yet, at the same time, Zhang argued that all things were instantaneously and spontaneously created--their existence was neither purposeful nor conditional. This had the potential or possibility of leading toward the idea of "not non-being."

Nevertheless, in the case of Zhang Zhan, these two ideas were put together mechanistically and were mutually incompatible and contradictory. His system of thought was not one which was tightly woven. And yet, incidentally, it was at this juncture that prajna Buddhist teachings, in particular those of the Kong zong, posited the idea of fei you fei wu [not being and yet not non-being], which itself was far more solid and tightly argued in theory and reasoning methods. For that reason, one can say that the doctrine of the Bu zhen kong lun [Treatise on the Fallacy of Real Nothingness] proposed by the Monk Shao was a development of the ideas of xuanxue [Daoist metaphysics] after Wang Bi and Guo Xiang. Although the ideas of the Monk Shao came directly from Indian prajna Buddhist teaching, they in fact became an important component of Chinese philosophy itself and helped to make up the following circle in the development of Wei-Jin xuanxue-Wang Bi-Guo Xiang-the Monk Shao.

Why was such a development possible? One may ascribe it to the demands or requirements of the heritage or continuity of ideological cultures [as they came into contact with one another]. As long as the development of an ideological culture is not drastically interrupted, what follows must be the product of a continuous evolution from what preceded it. The development of preceding ideas often would contain several possibilities, and the idea(s) which would continue to be developed, representing the subsequent parts of the development, would be bound to take the shape of one or another of these possibilities. If an imported alien ideological culture can, on the whole, adapt or conform to a certain aspect of a potential or possible development of the original indigenous culture and ideology [or fit into a trend or tendency of one of the possible developments], not only will it be itself developed and thus exert relatively great influence in itself, but it may even become directly a component part of the original indigenous ideological culture and perhaps even to some extent alter the course of the development of that original ideological culture.

RELATIVE EXCELLENCE AND REAL CONTRIBUTION

If an imported alien ideological culture affects the original indigenous ideological culture, and if this is not a temporary influence but a long lasting one, in some aspects or even in all aspects in general it would have to achieve a higher level of development than that of the indigenous culture. Only in this way can the imported ideological culture serve as a stimulus to the native culture and affect the development of the native culture itself.

Whether or not the level of development and sophistication in reasoning achieved by the Kong zong [Emptiness school] of Indian prajna Buddhist teaching was generally higher than that of China's own native and traditional ideological culture which existed at that time is a question which may not be realistically and honestly resolved until very careful and meticulous analysis has been made. This is not a problem which we may attempt to discuss here. However, in one specific aspect of its ways of reasoning and philosophizing, namely, its analysis of the questions of being and non-being [you wu], the Kong zong of prajna Buddhism, in postulating the dialectical thesis of "not being and yet not non-being" [fei you fei wu], clearly demonstrated a superior level of theory and reasoning in comparison with the ideas of Wang Bi and Guo Xiang, although its own ideas, like those of Wang and Guo, were drawn from the general source of idealism. In terms of development, although it appeared to have been derived out of Wang Bi and Guo Xiang's xuanxue thought, the Monk Shao's doctrine of bu zhen kong [not real emptiness] was closer to the original intents of the Kong zong's teachings and should be acknowledged as having made certain advances beyond Wang and Guo's ideas.

As I see it, it was after the baptism of the introduction and assimilation of prajna philosophy introduced from India that the idealist philosophies of the Chinese tradition became themselves a truly influential and meaningful system of thought. In them, the doctrine of the Creator [a spiritual ontological substance which created Heaven and Earth and all things] no longer occupied a central position.

In its stead, abstract concepts such as li [principle] or dao [Way], which determined, rather than personally created, the existence of Heaven, Earth, and all things, were put into the position of first or primal importance. In another case, it was the mind that was put into that position, as in ideas which posited that "mind equals principle" [xin ji li] or "the principle is possessed in the mind" [li ju yu xin]; i.e., the notions that the principles of Heaven, Earth, and all things were all present in the mind. It was only after such idealistic concepts were developed that the fundamental forms of China's traditional idealist philosophy were set. This itself set the stage for the emergence of the li xue [neo-Confucianist philosophy of Principle] in the Song and Ming dynasties, whether it be the Cheng and Zhu [Cheng Hao, Cheng Yi, and Zhu Xi] school or the Lu-Wang [Lu Xiangshan, Wang Yangming] school.

However, for an imported alien ideological culture, even one with a relatively higher level of development in reasoning, to have a great and long-lasting impact on the country [nation or region] to which it is introduced, it not only would have to subject itself, nonetheless, to the limitations of the political and socioeconomic conditions of the host country, nation, or region, but it must also be in possession of the first and second sets of conditions described in the afore-discussed sections. This is particularly true of ideological cultures, especially if the original, indigenous ideological culture did not experience an abrupt and radical interruption, or if such an interruption was not to be caused by the introduction of the alien culture. Only in such a way could the new culture affect the original culture in a profound and long-lasting way. Without these conditions, no matter how advanced or superior the imported ideological culture may be, it would be difficult for it to strike roots into the soil of the host country and over the long run exert any deep influence.

For example, the Wei shi [Vidjnana, or Consciousness Only school] teachings of Buddhism introduced [later] by the [Tang dynasty] Monk Xuan Zang, and the related teachings of vidjna [yin ming, or hetuvidya, or nyaya teachings] which were introduced at about the same time and in conjunction with the Consciousness Only school, were also superior in the levels of their reasoning and development, and yet, though they gained much ground in establishing a reputation for themselves for a time, they did not eventually have a very long-lasting impact on the development of Chinese thought as a whole. Even though specific categories of thought in the Consciousness Only [Wei shi] school, such as the dual categories of neng [ability or possibility] and suo [identity or proper placement], were individually absorbed into Chinese thought, on the whole the Wei shi school did not become an integrated component of the Chinese traditional ideological culture, and to this day we still have the tendency to think of the Wei shi [vidjnana, or Consciousness Only] teachings as an Indian ideology.

Out of the three points of argumentation outlined above, we may draw out one proposition: that it is meaningful, at least in one aspect, to focus the comparative study of philosophies on the general and historical laws which govern the extent to which an imported alien ideological culture may influence [the ideological culture(s) of] the country, or nation or region to which it was introduced, and on the conditions without which such an influence may not take place. In comparing and analyzing, for example, two ideological cultures which stemmed from different traditions we must understand, first, the characteristics and level of development and reasoning which have been achieved by the original indigenous ideological culture [i.e., that which, of the two, is the host culture] and, second, the differences and similarities between these two cultures, their mutual influences, their assimilation and conflict, the amelioration of their conflict, and so on.

As we study the introduction of Buddhism from India to China in the first century A.D., and its subsequent development we must ask its meaning for the practical way of life today. The tendencies in the development of current world ideological cultures are manifested as patterns conflict and harmony between many different ideological cultures stemming from many different traditions. The instability, contradictions and conflicts in the world today may also be ascribed, in addition to certain other [political and economic] factors, in part to differences in ideological and cultural [i.e., philosophical and religious] traditions. The contradictions between the Arab and Islamic world, on the one hand, and the West, on the other, for example, are themselves fraught with philosophical and religious factors. At the same time, because of the increasing frequency and intimacy in terms of intercultural contacts in today's world, the propensity for mutual interaction and influence and for harmonization and assimilation between various ideological cultures is also very obvious.

In particular, the broad spread of Marxism throughout the world today has provided many new lessons to be learned and emulated in the relations between ideological cultures which stem from different traditions and backgrounds. Marxism itself was generated in Western Europe under historical conditions peculiar to Western Europe and therefore as an ideological culture it was alien to many other parts of the world. Out of this, problems have surfaced in the relationship between Marxism and the various indigenous ideological cultures of the places to which it has been introduced. Even though Marxism is a proletarian philosophy and the cause of the proletariat is not confined by national boundaries--[Marxism] is the ideological weapon with which the proletariat and the revolutionary peoples of all countries carry out their revolutionary struggles--in order for Marxism to take root in any country [or nation or region] in a certain sense it will still have to become integrated with the native ideological culture of that country [nation or region]. Or, shall we say, it must undertake critically to carry on the legacy of that original indigenous ideological cultural tradition. Unless this is achieved, Marxism will not be able to exert any real influence.

Is it possible then for Marxism to be enriched and furthered in its development by, say, the study of the relations between Marxism and China's traditional indigenous ideological culture? We believe so. In the essay "The Task of the Youth League," Lenin said: "It is only when we have indeed understood fully the culture which is created through the entire developmental process of humanity at large, and are capable of transforming this culture of the past, that we can proceed to construct a truly proletarian culture." Undoubtedly Marxism is a methodology which will guide us in dealing accurately with our various ideological cultural traditions. It is "not a doctrine, but a methodology. It provides, not ready-made dogma, but points of departure for further investigation and a methodology which may be employed in such an investigation" (see The Complete Works of Marx and Engels [Chinese edition], vol. 39, p. 406]).

It should be acknowledged that in the history of human civilization each nation or people had, and has, its own special contribution to make. If we were to study, with the correct method, these contributions, we would be able to render accurate assessments regarding them and turn these assessments into parts of the legacy of the spiritual civilization of humanity, which we are to inherit. It is not the intent of Marxism to reject the spiritual cultures which have made contributions to the human society; rather, it hopes to absorb them, and transform them, and in the process continue to enrich and develop itself.

THE COMPARATIVE STUDY OF PHILOSOPHIES AND RELIGIONS

The present age is vastly different from past ages. As the world marches into the 1980s, developments in science and technology and social progress have made the interaction between the various countries and nations of the world immensely different from that of the past when the world was still in a stage of feudalism.

These objective circumstances compel us to absorb imported alien ideological cultures more quickly. What methods can we use to turn those parts of alien ideas which are of use and value to us more speedily into integrated parts of our own ideological culture?

One important method would be to engage in the comparative study of philosophies. In the past, the absorption of alien ideological cultures as a natural and spontaneous process was often slow and sluggish, and incidental and accidental factors tended to have a great deal of influence on the process. If we were to carry out such work today in a conscious and deliberate fashion, we are bound to be able to absorb the valuable and refined portions of an alien ideological culture more speedily. This problem applies to Marxism as well.

If we are able to deal correctly with the relationship between Marxism and our own ideological cultural tradition, so that Marxism may become even more compatible with the circumstances and sentiments of the people in our country, if we may create a Sinicized Marxism, then it not only would take deeper and stronger roots in China, but would also more effectively absorb and retain the good and valuable parts of Chinese ideological cultural tradition and expel those which are valueless or corrupted so that our country's fine spiritual culture may be further developed. Therefore, the establishment of comparative philosophical studies under the guidance of Marxism is a most important task for us. The question is, how we should undertake the study of comparative philosophy?

THE SEARCH FOR COMMON LAWS

In comparatively studying two ideological cultures from different traditions we should attend to the discovery of certain common laws which govern the evolution of human ideological culture.

The study of comparative philosophy, like the comparative study of religions and literature, has a specific meaning of its own. The study of comparative philosophy does not mean simply the comparison between two, any two, philosophers (taking, for instance, Zhu Xi and Wang Shouren [Wang Yangming]), any more than the study of comparative religion means the simple comparison of any two Buddhist monks [say, Zhi Dun and Dao An].

Comparative philosophy or comparative religion refers to comparing two systems of philosophical thought which stem from different traditions, or two religious systems that come from different sources and origins. Therefore, such comparative studies must be comparative analyses of two different countries [such as China and India] or regions [such as East and West] or nations [such as the Chinese people and some other nationality].

Philosophy is the most general science in the study of Nature, society, and human reasoning, and the laws which govern the development of human thought are, fundamentally speaking, similar or for the most part identical. Thus, when we have understood the laws which governed and sustained the evolution of the philosophical thought of a certain ideological cultural tradition, analyze the philosophical thoughts of another ideological cultural tradition promises to be of great help. In "On the Problems of the Dialectical Method," Lenin said:

> [These are] the circles which describe the history of philosophy: The Ancient World: Dialectics from Democritus through Plato to Heraclitus; The Modern Age: Feuerbach to Hegel [through Berkeley, Hume, and Kant]; Hegel to Feuerbach to Marx.

In his "Outline to Hegel's 'Notes on the History of Philosophy'" Lenin also said:

It is possible to see the history of philosophy in terms of circles . . . Each type of philosophical thinking equals a smaller circle on the big circle (spiral) of the evolution of human thought.

Hegel's idea of "the history of Philosophy as a circle," which Lenin cited in the above-mentioned essays, is not only a law which summarizes the development of Western thought, but also a profound reflection of the general law of the history of the development of philosophy and of thought in the universal sense. If we took this idea to be a compass to guide us in studying the laws which governed the development of traditional Chinese philosophy, we could see that, in general, traditional Chinese philosophy was also made up of three major spirals? The first would be the philosophy of the pre-Qin period: From Confucius to Mencius to Xunzi [through the philosophies of other schools of the time]: the second would be Wei-Jin xuanxue [Daoist metaphysics]: Wang Bi to Guo Xiang to the Monk Shao; the third would be Song-Ming neo-Confucianism: Zhang Zai to Zhu Xi to Wang Fuzhi.

Between these three circles, which are to be seen as being put together as spirals, there would be the connecting tissues of development--the Han Classical scholarship [jingxue] which made up the transition from the first circle to the second one, and the development of Sui-Tang Buddhism, which made up the transition from the second circle to the third. Together these three ascending circles would make up a vast circle which would express the whole of Chinese philosophical tradition: from the pre-Qin and Han philosophy, whose primary substance was Confucianism; to the Wei-Jin and Sui-Tang philosophy, whose primary substance was xuanxue [metaphysics] built on the foundation and framework of the ideas of Laozi (Lao Tzu) and Zhuangzi as well as a gradually Sinicized Buddhism; to the neo-Confucianism [Song-Ming Confucianism], which absorbed the thought of both Daoism (Taoism) and Buddhism, and on that basis developed [Confucianism] to a higher stage of evolution.

In the book Comparative Religion F. B. Jevons cited one example which quite clearly demonstrated the general significance of the study of comparative religion. He said that it was difficult to understand, or explain, the demotion of the Thunder God in the religion of ancient Babylon from his original status to the rank of a demon. The answer seemed to lie, he also said, in the study of comparative religion and its methodology, because in the history of the development of various religions we often encounter in the history of the development of various religions, the phenomenon of deities of an earlier religion being demoted to another rank in a new religion when the older, earlier religion is overcome and replaced. In this case, the method of the study of comparative religion provides us with a rational explanation for such a phenomenon as the demotion of the Thunder God of Babylon to the rank of a demon.

At the present time, the methods of comparative studies generally fall into two categories: namely, "parallel studies" and "influence studies." The former refers to conducting comparative studies between two different ideological cultures which do not have direct or indirect influences upon one another, and yet between whom there obviously are comparable points. In this case, the task would be to discover the similar as well as the dissimilar phenomena between the two and to demonstrate common laws and dissimilar, individual qualities. The latter is to conduct comparative studies where there are direct or indirect mutual influences, or, in some cases, unilateral influence, in order to discover the shared phenomena as well as points of dissimilarity so as to demonstrate the contradictions, conflicts, assimilations and compromises that exist between them.

No matter to which category it may belong, when a comparison is made it should not simply draw one or two elements from the ideological culture of a country, nation, or region and study them in comparison with a few sayings or one or two isolated phenomena from the ideological culture of another country, nation, or region. This would be what is known as piecemeal comparison which, strictly speaking, has hardly anything to do with the study of comparative philosophy or comparative religion. The comparative study of two different ideological cultural traditions ought to be conducted on the basis of a rather comprehensive and exhaustive comparison of a problem or problems found in both traditions. Only in this way can we discover the phenomena [within each] which reflect the presence of laws, and only then can we be led from knowledge or its absence to knowledge regarding this particular law of the development of human ideological culture, and from the understanding of the individual to an understanding of the general.

ATTENTION TO THE SPECIFIC CHARACTERISTICS OF A CULTURE

In undertaking to study comparatively the ideological cultures of two different traditions, we should base conclusions on the special characteristics and features of both of these cultures. Only when a certain ideological culture is compared and analyzed in the light of a different ideological cultural tradition that its own special characteristics and features can become clarified. It is impossible to express the special characteristics of an ideological culture when it is studied only by itself or internally.

In the first and second part of this essay we discussed the fact that, although there were apparent similarities between metaphysics [xuanxue] in China during the Wei-Jin period and the prajna teachings of Indian Buddhism, they ultimately were separate and not the same, each having its own special characteristics. We were able to draw such a conclusion because we had made a comparative study of these two ideological cultures which stemmed from separate traditions. For example, we came to know that the analysis which Wei-Jin xuanxue made of "being" and "non-being" was made from the angle or perspective of "existence," that is, from the perspective of the relationship between "ontological substance" and "phenomenon," with the latter being seen as the various expressions of ontological substance. Indian prajna Buddhist teaching, on the other hand, often analyzed wu [or kong, or non-existence] and you [being] as a pair of abstract concepts. Therefore, although both may have appeared to be speaking of ben wu [nothingness or origin], when Wang Bi employed the term he was referring to the idea of yi wu wei ben [taking nothingness to be the origin]--i.e., non-being [wu] being the substance behind being [you]--whereas when prajna teaching used the same term it referred to the idea that "all dharma did not have original self-nature" [zhu fa ben wu zi xing]. In this latter formulation, wu [or kong, or non-existence] did not refer to substance, but rather [to the idea] that all things did not have real self-substance [zi ti] and therefore that the existence of all things was merely illusory. Furthermore, the method of reasoning behind Wei-Jin metaphysics and that behind Indian Buddhist prajna teaching were also different. The tendency for the Indian Buddhist prajna teachers was to employ an analytical method to reason out their viewpoints whereas the Wei-Jin xuanxue metaphysicists would reason by way of the philosophical methods represented by such sayings as: de yi wang yan [Once the meaning, or intent, is attained, the words may be forgotten] and ji yu chu yan [The meaning resides outside of the words, which are only its temporary abode].

For example, in the Kong zong [Emptiness school] of prajna Buddhism, the postulate "all dharma did not originally have self-nature" [zhu fa ben wu zi xing] would often be analyzed in the following logical manner:

(1) When things are analyzed at the utmost level of minutiae, further analysis would, presumably, bring the object of analysis to the realm of lin xu [the neighborhood of Void or Nothingness]. That is, further analysis would bring about the logical conclusion that the object of analysis does not really have substance or a self--thus the saying: "Observe and contemplate the minutiae of things; when the final minutiae is reached, there would be found no substance."

(2) When one analyzes things from the angle of the relationship between time and object, one will understand that neither wu xiang [material or physical phenomenon or appearance] nor xin xiang [mental or psychological phenomenon] is real. First, all things are generated instantaneously and also perish equally

instantaneously, that is, all things are no sooner generated than they perish. Second, nothing lasts at all, that is, not things are first generated and then perish, but that they are generated and perish all at once: generation and perishing happen at one and the same time. For these two reasons therefore things cannot be said to have any real self-substance.

(3) The analysis of the object itself leads inevitably to the conclusion that it is made up of the combination of causes and effects and therefore it does not have any real ontological substance of its own. Since all dharma does not have real self-substance, all things or phenomena are therefore without original existence--thus the saying: "not that appearances (phenomena) perish, but that they are non-existent."

The method which the Wei-Jin xuanxue [Daoist metaphysics] scholars, such as Wang Bi, used to argue for their idea of "having origin in non-being" [yi wu wei ben] was very different from that of the prajna Buddhists. In the Laozi (Lao Tzu) Zhi Lue [An Outline of the Intentions of Laozi (Lao Tzu)], Wang Bi said:

The cause for the generation of a thing and the fulfilling of its achievement is this: It must be born of the Form-less [wu xing] and have origin in the Name-less [wu ming]. The Form-less and the Name-less is the origin of all things. It is neither warm nor cold, neither gong nor shang [Gong and shang are sounds of special characters--Tr.]; its sound cannot be heard; one cannot see its expression if one were to look at it, nor know it by feeling, nor taste it. This is made of a primal combination of forces; as a phenomenon it does not have a form, as a noise it has but a little sound, and in terms of taste it does not have any presentation. It is for this reason that it can be the origin of all species and objects. It exists as an embryo, in which all Heaven and Earth is contained and all parts of Heaven and Earth are connected. There is nowhere it cannot go, and yet it will not be directed.

If something is warm, it cannot be cool; if something is gong, it cannot be shang. Once things take form, they are inevitably divided; sounds, too, naturally belong to separate divisions. Therefore, if something that is a phenomenon has form, it cannot be the Great Phenomenon; the sound that has noise cannot be the Great Sound. Nevertheless, if the Four Phenomena did not have form, the Great Phenomenon cannot be free. If the Five Sounds did not have noise, the Great Sound cannot arrive. If the Four Phenomena do take form, and yet objects are not made to submit to a master, the Great Phenomenon will be free; if the Five Sounds have noise but the mind does not follow them, the Great Sound will arrive.

In Wang Bi's view, Heaven and Earth and all things have many forms and appearances. What is one thing therefore cannot be any other thing at the same time; if something has a specific form, it cannot take another form. Thus, it is only the Form-less that can accomplish any form, only the Sound-less that can become any sound, only the Non-being [that which is not any specific being] that can accomplish being [can become anything]. It is because Non-being can become, or accomplish all being that it can be the foundation of the existence of all existence. Therefore:

All things under heaven are born of "being." The beginning of being is in having non-being as its origin. If one desired to accomplish "being" one must first revert to "non-being" (see Laozi (Lao Tzu) Zhu [Annotations on Laozi (Lao Tzu)]).

All things under heaven are specific and concrete existences with forms and phenomena. That these things with forms and phenomena can come into being, or be generated, is because they have "non-being" as their ontological substance; only then can this substance be expressed as many specific things with many forms and appearances. For example, it was argued, the water of the sea is manifested in waves and billows of many different colors and shapes. That it can be manifested in these many phenomena is precisely because it has its origins in water. Therefore, in order to preserve all things of various forms and phenomena, one must grasp the "non-being" which is their ontological substance.

However, the "non-being" which is the ontological substance is not a "thing" which exists outside of "all things." Although one can say that "a phenomenon which has form is not the Great Phenomenon," unless "the Four Phenomena have form the Great Phenomenon cannot be free." Therefore, it is only when one can understand things through specific forms and phenomena, and yet not be confined by the specific forms and phenomena, that one can grasp "the phenomenon which is without phenomenon" [wu xiang zhi xiang], or, "the scenery outside of the picture" [hua wai zhi jing]. It is only when one can understand through specific sounds and yet not be insistent on, or confined by, specific sounds that one can grasp "the sound that has no noise" [wu sheng zhi yin] or, "the sounds outside the chords" [xuan wai zhi yin], and it is only through the understanding of language [words] and yet not insisting on language that one can attain the "meaning without words" [wu yan zhi yi] or, the "meaning outside the words" [yan wai zhi yi].

From the above we can see quite clearly that the method with which the argument "taking non-being as the origin" [yi wu wei ben] was made by Wang Bi was very different from the analytical approach adopted by the Kong zong of prajna Buddhist teaching. The approach taken by Wang Bi was the method of de yi wang yan [attain the meaning and lose, or forget, the words] which is a peculiarly metaphysical method of the xuanxue scholars.

When we have compared and studied the various aspects of the gui wu [valuing non-being] school of Wei-Jin xuanxue, as exemplified by Wang Bi, and the Kong zong [Emptiness school] of Indian prajna teaching, we shall be able to see more clearly each school's characteristics and its level of development. Only on such a basis can we clarify the relationship between Buddhism and Wei-Jin Daoist metaphysics during the period immediately or shortly after the introduction of Buddhism into China.

In issue no. 1, 1980 of Zhexue Yanjiu [Philosophical Studies], an article was published on "A Brief Discussion on the Theories of Early Daoist Religion on the Questions of Life and Death and Form and Spirit." In that essay, comparisons were made of the Daoist religion and Buddhism during the period of the Wei, Jin, and North and South dynasties, focusing on their respective views regarding life and death, and the question of jietuo [emancipation, or, in the Buddhist case, more commonly known as deliverance; in Sanskrit, mukti, or moksa]. The article pointed out that on these questions between these two religions, both of which were popular at the time, there were three major differences:

(1) On the question of life and death, the Daoist religion advocated adopting the notion of "everlasting life" [i.e., non-perishing] as the goal, whereas Buddhism advocated taking "eternal extinction" [i.e., non-life] as the goal. Daoism (Taoism)'s idea of emancipation advocated the transformation of mortal flesh into immortality by way of an integration of the body and the spirit such that this integrated substance may live on in non-perishable eternal life and in so doing be separated from the trouble-laden world of the present and enter the spiritual world of fantasy and illusion. Buddhism, on the other hand, believed that the source of the pains of human life was the "life of being," which was the state in which the spirit was connected to the body. Within this state of "life of being," until the spirit achieves Nirvana it must always return in the cycles of incarnation. Only by transcending these cycles of incarnation becoming separated from the body and returning to everlasting extinction, can the spirit be delivered from the sea of bitterness that is human life.

(2) On the question of form and spirit, Daoism (Taoism) advocated the achievement of immortality by having the spirit and form become one. Buddhism advocated having the form and spirit separated from one another and thereby achieving Buddhahood. Buddhism believed that, unless the spirit became separated from the form, it would not be able to escape the cycles of incarnation and could not be delivered: to be delivered the spirit must be separated from the form, and, in response to its own completed destiny, enter extinction and perish. Daoism (Taoism) believed that the path of transcending

life and death and becoming liberated did not lie in this sort of completed destiny or extinction but in the immortalization of the flesh and for the flesh to become immortal it cannot, and must not, be separated from the spirit.

(3) As to the methods of achieving liberation or deliverance Daoism (Taoism) advocated the tempering of the form, whereas Buddhism advocated the nurturing of the spirit. As Buddhism believed that the achievement of Buddhahood depended on enlightenment and realization, the chief means of achieving Nirvana was to cultivate the inner mind and enhance one's own realization or awareness. As Daoism (Taoism) believed that the achievement of immortality depended on the accumulation of successes and attainments, its chief means of achieving liberation was to temper body and mind, nurture life, and be assisted by external matter [foreign substances].

From these three points of comparison, we generally can know the characteristics of the Daoist and the Buddhist religions in China during the period of the Wei, Jin, and North and South dynasties. Daoism (Taoism)'s goal was the achievement of immortality. Though this was an impossibility, because of this people's attention was directed toward the tempering and nurturing of the functions of their own bodies and spirits [e.g., the qi gong, or breathing exercises] and to the study of external matter such as the manufacturing of pills and elixirs (foreign substances) whose assistance they counted upon for the achievement of the goal of immortality. The goal of Buddhism was to achieve Buddhahood. Though this, too, was obviously an unattainable goal, nevertheless it directed people's attentions toward the analysis of psychological activities and to the study of the cognitive processes.

Therefore, we have been able to discover that in Daoism (Taoism) there was, and is, much material related to understanding of "the way of materials" and to knowledge concerning the human body that is worthy of our own efforts of analysis and investigation. For example, the book Dao Zang

[The Treasury of the Way] comprised of 5,000 to 6,000 volumes all of which, unfortunately, have yet to be systematically organized and studied, contains a wealth of information on such things as breathing exercises, medicines and herbacology (pharmacology), chemistry, hygiene, and physical education.

On the other hand, there are also over 10,000 volumes of Buddhist sutras [including sastras, annotations, and other exegetical treatises] in Chinese. In many areas, such as the analysis of psychological and psychic activity, of the processes of knowledge and cognition, the analysis of the relationship between subject and object, the analysis of concepts, perception and conceptualization, and the logical process known as vidjnana, or sometimes hetu-vidya-these Buddhist canons have much to add to our enlightenment. If we could but purge from these Daoist and Buddhist materials those parts which are unscientific, fabulous, fantastic or superstitious and analyze the remaining parts which are of positive value, it would be a most meaningful endeavor.

One of the purposes of studying comparative philosophy or comparative religion is to discover, through comparison and analysis, the characteristics of individual ideological cultures of various traditions, to identify and establish their peculiarities so that people may correctly understand and assess the status and role of these particular ideological cultures in the development of world history, and to ascertain the contributions they have made.

The great treasure trove of human ideological and intellectual culture inevitably is made up of the good and superior parts of many individual ideological cultures, each with its own tradition and characteristics. If an ideological culture did not contain any special characteristic of its own, it would be difficult for it to make any contribution to human intellectual civilization.

On the other hand, a culture which becomes the ideological culture of a nation, or a part thereof, is bound to have its own special characteristics and therefore is bound to make some contribution to the ideological culture of the human race as a whole.

THE ISOLATION OF OLD TOPICS AND NEW ISSUES

Finally, in the comparative study of two ideological cultures of different traditions we should attend to the discovery and re-discovery of problems to be mulled over and solved, and to proposing new topics or lessons for investigation and study.

Jin Kemu, in his article "Shi lun fan yu zhong di 'you yi chuanzai'" [A Tentative Discussion of the Terms, or Expressions, for 'Being, Unity and Existence' in Sanskrit] pointed out that there are several roots, or radicals, for the expressions in Sanskrit that stand for the notions of being, unity, or existence. The more common ones, he tells us--and there are two of them--are as and bhu. These are both translated in the Chinese language as you [being]. For example, in the translation of the Zhong bian fen bie lun [The Treatise on the Differences between the Mean and the Extremes] [written by Vasubandhu] made by Chen Zhenti, and in the translation of the Bian zhong bian lun [The Treatise on the Debate Between the Doctrines of the Mean and the Extremes] made by Xuan Zang, the term "sattvau." was consistently translated as you [being]. However, bhava [having, or possession], one of the dvadasanga pratityasamutpada, or Twelve yinyuan [nidanas, or combinations of causes], was also translated as you [being]. As refers to existence or being in the simple, abstract sense, or, if you will, the static, absolute sense, whereas bhu refers to existence in the transforming or specific sense, or in the moving, relative sense.

We also know that in ancient Greek philosophy, particularly in the Aristotelian system of thought, "substance" was also divided into two categories: primary substance and secondary substance. The two possessed different meanings. The former does not refer to simple and pure matter, nor to the general form common to the various matters, but to the individual units of matter and their forms. The second meaning of substance [or, secondary substance] referred, on the other hand, to the general form, or concept or category of matter, which becomes individualized in each separate matter.

Does this fact--that, while in Sanskrit, corresponding to various linguistic radicals, the terms for "being, unity, and existence" have different meanings, and that the term "substance" in the Aristotelian system of thought also has various meanings--enlighten us in any way? In the Chinese translations of the Buddhist canons the term for existence and being, which had different meanings in the original, all were translated as you. In Chinese traditional philosophy, then, did the concept conveyed by the term you also have various meanings? When Pei Wei, in his Cong you lun [Treatise on the Exaltation of Being] spoke of "self-generating and inevitably existent in substance" [zi sheng er bie ti you] did the term you there refer to specifically existent matters or to the general existence of matter? Again, in the usage of Guo Xiang's Zhuangzi Zhu [Annotations on Zhuangzi] did the term you sometimes refer to the specifically existent matters and sometimes to the general existence of matter? These are all questions which call for further investigation and require deeper analyses of the meaning(s) contained in the term you in traditional Chinese philosophy.

In his book Ti yong lun [On Substance and Use], Xiong Shili proposed that the essential and fundamental difference between traditional Chinese philosophy and Indian Buddhism was that where traditional Chinese philosophy talked about the "one-ness of substance and use" [ti yong ru yi] Indian Buddhism separated substance from use, rending the two asunder. Whether or not Xiong's conclusion was correct is not something we wish to make a point of in our discussion here, but certainly it can be said that the problem which he raised in his study of these two ideological cultures stemming from different traditions is most likely to have considerable significance for the study of the characteristics of the Chinese philosophical tradition itself.

From the perspective of the general trends in the development of traditional Chinese philosophy, it can be seen that the notions of tian dao [Heaven's Way] and ren dao [the way of humanity] generally are considered to be consistent and integrated one with the other--in other words, it was assumed that the ideal should and could be realized in present reality. Even in the xuanxue metaphysics of the Wei-Jin period, although this system of thought took the ideas of Lao Zi and Zhuangzi to be its framework, the ultimate pursuit of the metaphysicians was still to achieve the "way of the inner sage and the outward monarch combined" [nei sheng wai wang zhi dao] which was contained in the "paradise which is naturally possessed by the Great Teaching" [ming jiao zhong zi you le di], i.e., in Confucianism. When the Song-Ming neo-Confucianists opposed Buddhism and Daoism (Taoism), they did so chiefly on the grounds that Buddhists and Daoists, according to the neo-Confucianists, "pursued the illusory transcendental periphery of the universe of that which was real."

The neo-Confucianists claimed to believe fundamentally that "the ethics of the norm" [gang chang] and the great teaching [ming jiao] equaled "the principle of heaven" [tian li]. On the other hand, in Chinese Buddhism, too, and particularly in the Chan School, the teaching was that "achieving Buddhahood" did not require leaping out of, or being separated from a life of reality. The Chan Buddhists said, "Carrying water, cutting firewood, all these contained the most wonderful way and truth"--that is, it was possible for one to become enlightened to the wonderful way of achieving Buddhahood even in the mundane routines of everyday life.

When we compare China's traditional philosophy with the transcendentalist "going outside of the world" notion in Indian Buddhism, can we say that Chinese philosophy, after all, remained indeed faithful to the idea of "one-ness of substance and use" and that it was for this reason that the notions of complete transcendentalism were never able to become part of the mainstream of traditional Chinese thought? As I see it, this, too, is a question which merits further and more penetrating investigation. If we were to apply the comparative method to the study of the philosophical ideas and religious doctrines of various ideological cultures which stemmed from different traditions, such as the ideological culture of China and that of India, or that of the Western world, we will, I believe, discover even more lessons to be learned and topics to be discussed.

Over a hundred years ago that Marx and Engels pointed out: "Because the bourgeoisie opened up a world market, the production and consumption of the various countries have become universalized. . . . This is true not only of material production, but of the products of the mind and spirit as well. The spiritual products of the nations have become their common property, and the partialism and parochialism of the individual nations have become daily increasingly impossible. Therefore, out of the literature of the many nations and places of the world a world literature has been formed."

According to the editor-annotator, the term "literature" here referred to writing in many areas, including science, art and philosophy. We have now reached the 1980s; our age is much more advanced than that of 1848 when Marx and Engels wrote the Communist Manifesto. The interflow of ideas and culture and the interaction between peoples and civilizations have become even more widespread and profound. The comparative study of philosophy and religion is bound to promote the study of the history of Chinese philosophy. In the comparative study of ideological cultures of different traditions we can discover the common laws which govern the development of things; we can expose and demonstrate the characteristics and levels of development of various ideological cultures and expand the contents and scope of our study. Will this also play a part in the enrichment and enhancement of the development of Marxism? I am sure that it will.

3

The Importation of Buddhism

Historically, there were three major occasions when China imported foreign culture and ideology. The first was the importation of Buddhism--the focus of this paper.

The second cultural incursion was that of Western culture, an event which, for a time, gave rise to debate over the respective merits of things past and present, Chinese and foreign. From a philosophical standpoint, this event raised questions concerning the relationships between Western and Chinese philosophy. Many modern philosophers, whether or not they were aware of it, were in actuality striving to reconcile these two vastly different cultures. Before Liberation, Feng Youlan (Feng Youlan) was perhaps most successful in reconciling the two. His "New Rationalism" may be seen as an attempt to use Western pragmatism to resolve several traditional Chinese philosophical questions. That he did not succeed in determining the true course of Chinese philosophical development can be seen in the fact that, in practice, he failed to solve China's social problems.

The third event was the importation of Marxism, a European ideology developed in response to European historical conditions. In order for Marxism to take root in China, it must also, in a certain sense, merge with traditional Chinese culture and thought. That is to say, it must pass through a stage of critical acceptance of traditional culture.

Jia Yi in his "Guo Chin Lun" (Treatise on the Failings of Ch'in) quoted an old adage: "The unforgotten events of the past are teachers of the future." Can we today learn anything from the contacts between imported Buddhism and traditional Chinese culture? I think we can.

I would like to discuss three important elements which characterized Buddhism's spread in China.

First, is the fact that when Buddhism first entered China, it tended to attach itself to native ideologies. Only later did it gradually develop and begin to influence those ideologies.

When, during the Han dynasty, Buddhism entered China, it identified itself with native religious practitioners. During the Wei-Jin period, Buddhism identified itself with the "Mysterious Learning" then popular.

During the Han Dynasty, Buddhism was often seen as on par with the Huang-Lao School. Thus, King Ying of Chu is reported as having "recited the subtle words of Huang-Laoe and respectfully performed human sacrifices to the Buddha," while Emperor Huan "set up shrines to Huang-Lao and the Buddha in his palace."

Buddhist disciples of the period even identified themselves as "practitioners of the techniques of the Way." The "Lihuo lun" (Treatise on Rectifying Error) of the Mozi (Mo Tzu) states: "There are ninety-six distinct ways, but, among those worthy of veneration, none is so great as the teachings of the Buddha." The Sutra in Forty-two Sectionsi also styles itself "the Way of the Buddha."

At that time the principal tenets preached by Buddhist missionaries were the immortality of the soul and karmic retribution; such Indian concepts as the "non-existence of the self" were simply not understood. The immortality of the soul was already present in traditional Chinese thought, but only in the concept of spirits. The Wen Wang Ode of the Shi Jing (Shih Ching)j says of the former Zhou Kings, "The Three Directors are in Heaven," that is, their souls have ascended. The "Jingshen Xun" of the Huai Nan Zik asserts that "the form may be ground away, but the spirit is not transformed." As a result of these beliefs, Huan Tanl held that "when the form comes to an end, the spirit is easily destroyed," while Wang Chong argued that "when men die, they do not become ghosts (spirits)." That the immortality of the soul or spirit depended on "refining and nurturing" was also a native Chinese concept.

As for karmic retribution, while the Buddhist conception did not exactly accord with that of China, it was promulgated during the Han and was compatible with the Chinese notion that "good fortune comes to those who are good and evil to the dissolute." Witness the Wen-yen gloss to the Qian hexagram of the Yi Jing (I Ching): "Those who accumulate good deeds will certainly have an excess of blessings, while those who accumulate bad deeds will have an excess of calamity."

During the end of the Han and the beginning of the Three Kingdoms period, as Buddhist translations increased, Buddhism divided into two main schools. The first was the An Shi Gaoo lineage of Hinayana Buddhism, emphasizing meditation. The second was the Lokak sema lineage of Mahayana Buddhism, which emphasized prajna.

An Shi Gao translated a number of sutras among which the most influential were the Anapansmrti-sutra (T602) and the Yin chi Ru Jing (T1694). The former emphasis breath control, a practice comparable to the "inhalation and exhalation" (tu-na) methods of Chinese seekers of transcendence. The latter explicates Buddhist numerical categories and may be compared to Han exegetical studies.

With regard to man's place in the cosmos, the theories of these sutras are based on the concept of "primal breath" and state that primal breath encompasses the Five Phases which they equate with the five skandas. It can be seen that the Hinayana practices expounded by the An Shi Gao lineage were assimilated to the popular religious practices and thought of the day which then used them to explicate Buddhism.

The prajna concept taught by the Lokaksema lineage held as its most important truth the "return of the spirit to its original perfection and union with the Way." In this we see already the influence of the philosophy of the Laozi (Lao Tzu) and the Zhuangzi.

Zhi Qian (Chih Ch'ien), the disciple of Lokaksema's disciple Zhi Lian, re-translated the Prajnaparamita sutra as the Ta

Ming Du Wu Ji Jing This title itself betrays the influence of the Laozi (Lao Tzu) and Zhuangzi. His translation of "Grand luminescence" for prajna probably draws on the phrase, "He who knows the eternal nature of things appears luminous," from the Laozi (Lao Tzu). The translation "cross to the illimitable" for paramita also means to reach a state of union with the Way, that is the illimitable Dao.

Zhi Qian (Chih Ch'ien)'s gloss for the first chapter states: "My Master (that is Chih Liàng) said: "The heart of the Bodhisativa treads the Great Way. Wishing to embody the Way, his heart and the way merge. For this reason, the formless is called the `empty void'." This is the same point reached in Ruan Ji's': Biography of the Prior-born Great Man," wherein the great man merges with the way. The latter phrase recalls as well the Laozi (Lao Tzu) statement, "The constant nature of the Way is formless."

Zhi Qian (Chih Ch'ien) and the others believed that man's heart and spirit originated in the Dao, but, because of such flaws of the latter heavens as desire, man can no longer join with the Dao. For the heart and spirit to escape these limitations, one must embody one's origin, the Dao, and become a Buddha. This is undoubtedly a Buddhism assimilated to the thought of the Laozi (Lao Tzu) and Zhuangzi.

During the Wei-Jin period the ontology of Mysterious Learning, based on the Laozi (Lao Tzu) and the Zhuangzi, was very popular. The central issues discussed in the Mysterious Learning were questions of fundamental cause and secondary effects as well as existence and non-existence. Buddhist prajna studies were fairly similar to the concerns of Mysterious Learning, so many monks used it to explain Buddhist principles. Dao An, for example, wrote in his Pi-nai-yehx (Preface to the Vinaya):

Among the twelve sections of the Tripitaka, the vaipulya section is the largest due to the fact that Laozi (Lao Tzu) and Zhuangzi have spread teachings in this country similar to the Fang-teng Jing and Prajnaparamita sutra and thus it has been easy to travel with the wind. Even the clerics of that time recognized that the popularity of Buddhism was due to the thought of the Laozi (Lao Tzu) and Zhuangzi. What is the reason for this situation? As Engels has said: "Tradition is a great conservative force." It seems that any cultural ideology has its conservative aspects and will resist foreign culture. Because of this, foreign ideologies must first adapt themselves to the requirements of the native ideology, attaching themselves to a native thought system. Elements of the foreign ideology which are similar or identical to the native ideology are easily transmitted, while dissimilar elements seep in only gradually to eventually change the native ideology.

The second element involves the reason why Buddhism, as a foreign importation, was able to have such a strong impact on Chinese culture. In addition to the fact that it met certain social needs, it often accorded with the natural development of Chinese thought.

The Mysterious Learning of the Wei-Chin period developed from Wang Bix and He Yan'sy emphasis on Non-being as the source of all existence through Guo Xiangg'sz emphasis on Being ("The ten-thousand things are born of themselves,") to Chang Chanaa of the Eastern Chin, who contended that "in being suddenly born of themselves, the Source of all things resides in Non-being." Finally there was Seng Zhao,ab who held that "the Emptiness of the Unreal" consisted of a negation of both Being and Non-being. Why was the Mysterious Learning of the Wei Chin period summed up in Seng Zhao's prajna inspired doctrine? Precisely because this was one possible outcome to which this philosophical system tended.

Beginning with He Yan and particularly Wang Bi, Mysterious Learning was much engrossed with the relationship between Being and Non-being, which was explained in terms of substance and function. It was held that "Non-being may not be understood in terms of Non-being, (so) it draws its name from Being." Thus Non-being was held to be the Original substance, which expressed itself as Being so that its substance and function were as one. However, since Wang Bi emphasized the unconditional nature of Non-being, there was also the tendency to glorify the Original substance while neglecting its expression as Being. This was an internal contradiction in the thought of Wang Bi. From just this element of Wang Bi's thought, we can extrapolate the negation of Being (which was fully realized in Seng Zhao's system).

Wang Bi's emphasis on Non-being was further refined by Xiang Xiuac and Pei Guad and eventually developed into Guo Xiangg's emphasis on Being. According to Guo Xiang, all existence was comprised of individual concrete objects. Beyond these material objects there was no Original substance (i.e., no creator). The existence of the ten-thousand things was based solely on their "self-nature." This self-nature was self-generated. He wrote "Non-being has no reality and thus cannot give birth to Being." This direct contradiction of non-existence contains within it the seeds of (Seng Zhao's) negation of existence.

These two developments fit exactly the Prajna School's negation of Being and Non-being. So Seng Zhao's doctrine of the Emptiness of the Unreal continues the philosophical development begun by Wang Bi and Guo Xiangg. We may, then, trace the historical development of Mysterious Learning from Wang Bi through Guo Xiangg to Seng Zhao. Later, the San-lun Schoolae (Madhyamika) would develop Seng Zhao's doctrine and Hui Nengaf of the Chan Schoolag would further refine it and eventually influence the Neo-Confucianism of the Song and Ming dynasties.

The reason for this development is that ideologies have certain set principles of development. Unless interrupted, later developments always grow out of earlier tendencies. Also, an ideology often has several possible ways in which it might develop, so that, if an important ideology accords in important respects with one possible line of development, it can have a very great impact. The important ideology may then become a constituent element of the native ideology and, to a greater or lesser extent, influence the development of the native culture.

Thirdly, the reason that Buddhism was able to work such a lasting influence on Chinese thought and culture, was that, in certain respects, it was superior to native Chinese systems of thought. In this way it was able to act as a stimulus in the development of Chinese culture. The question of the Indian Buddhist prajna doctrine's superiority to native Chinese modes of thought is one that must be examined closely from every angle before a conclusion can be reached. This we are not able to do here, so we will only examine the prajna system's resolution of the contradiction inherent in the doctrine of the negation of Being and Non-being. Despite the fact that, like the thought of Wang Bi and Guo Xiangg, this doctrine is an instance of idealism, it is undoubtedly superior to theirs in that it can be used to analyze problems from two opposite directions. Even though Seng Zhao's doctrine of the "Emptiness of the Unreal" can be seen as an extension of Wang Bi and Guo Xiangg, it goes beyond their systems in that it accords fairly well with the Indian prajna system.

In my opinion, after its absorption into Indian Buddhism, the idea of a creator or a spiritual entity which fashioned heaven and earth never again occupied an important position in China's idealism. This was replaced by such abstract concepts as the Confucian liah (the "natural pattern") and Daoai ("the Way"), which, as first principles, determined human existence in the universe. Sometimes "Heart mind"aj was made a first principle; it was held that "the heart is the natural pattern" or that "the natural pattern merges in the heart." This is a feature of Sung and Ming dynasty philosophy. As this sort of idealism developed, it became the most important form of Chinese traditional philosophy.

However, even for a relatively superior foreign ideology to influence another culture it must, in addition to satisfying certain economic and political conditions, also meet the first two requirements we have discussed. If it does not, then even a superior ideology will fail to take root in the host country. For example, the "Treatise on the Completion of Ideation Only" (Wei-shih hun)ak brought in by Xuan Zangal and Hetuvidya (Yin-ming xüeam) are both fairly lofty constructions, but, despite Xuan Zang's reputation, they were not influential in China and failed to become a constituent of Chinese philosophy.

I think that the above three points are significant phenomena attending Buddhism's importation into China. With these in mind, I would like to bring up a question of current concern: can Marxism merge with traditional Chinese thought and culture. This is a large and difficult question. Predictions are hard to make, but it can be explained. In the abstract, most people respond that they wish for a merger of the two, but the question is whether this is possible and how it could be achieved.

Here I wish only to discuss a few thoughts drawn from the second of the points above: If Marxism is to take root in China, continuing lines of development begun in traditional Chinese thought and culture, the chief issue is to find points of convergence between the two so both Chinese philosophy and Marxism will progress.

Marxism is undoubtedly a superior ideology. Moreover, it developed in the West so that there are great differences between it and traditional Chinese thought. It is also a vast system of thought, so that it is difficult to know just where to search for points of convergence. Naturally, I cannot here discuss the problem in its entirety. I merely wish to raise a few examples.

The dialectical methodology of Marxism centers on the law of the unity of opposites, and takes actual practice as the only standard of determining truth. This I believe to be correct. If related principles can be found among those fundamental to traditional Chinese philosophy, then cannot Marxism be sinified and become a further development of Chinese philosophy?

The central problem of traditional Chinese philosophy as defined by ancient philosophers and historians is the question of the relationship between man and heaven. The traditional answer to this question, in most cases, has been that heaven (that is the natural world, or the way of heaven) and man (society, or the way of man) are one. From this unity derives the unity of thought and action and, in art, the unity of subjective feeling and objective expression. (This is what Wang Fu calls the interface of emotion and scene.)

These three unities of man and heaven, of thought and action, and the unity of subjectivity and objectivity are questions of "truth," "goodness" and "beauty." Chinese philosophy, then, emphasizes unity, a fact which may have something to do with Chinese thought processes or social conditions. Confucian thought has always emphasized the Grand Unity and the Way of the Mean, and opposed excess. If we correctly understand this unity and do not regard it as inflexible, then it is easy to see it as an active unification as in the Yi Zhuan (I Chuan) phrases "giving birth without cessation" and "Heavens movements enduring while the Xunzi (Hsün Tzu)an never ceases in expanding himself."

Would it be wrong, then, to see struggle, (or "movement") as the traditional technique of Chinese philosophy by which union was achieved, with the unities of heaven and man, knowledge and action, subjective and objective as the goals of this striving? If so, then this is a point of convergence between traditional Chinese philosophy and Marxism. From one standpoint, the Marxist law of the reconciliation of opposites is a superior summation and more scientific continuation of traditional Chinese philosophy. From another, absorbing Chinese ideas of unity would enrich Marxism.

Another special characteristic of Chinese philosophy is that it has never separated its theories of knowledge from questions of moral cultivation. Thus questions of knowledge and action are at once epistemological and moral. To know one must be able to put something into practice. The unity of thought and action, then, is an important concept.

From the point of view of the development of thought, it is proper and even necessary to separate epistemological and moral questions. The failure to do so may have been a shortcoming. Looked at from another angle, however, the traditional Chinese concept of putting moral theories into action has a great significance.

"Practice" in Marxism primarily denotes production struggle, class struggle and scientific experimentation. Of course, such things as the "struggle against Japan," an example of social practice, also included moral practice. "Is it not meaningful, then, to emphasize moral practice"?

I think that such an emphasis would have two important results: first, it would raise our self-evaluation and cause us to view ourselves as moral human beings; second, it would cause us to pay attention to the results of our actions.

I think that if we can overcome the confusion of traditional Chinese philosophy with respect to practice and, moreover, refine it through reference to Marxist views, we can make it more scientific and more correct.

This would serve both to advance traditional Chinese philosophy and to sinify Marxism. The moral emphasis on the unity of thought and action in practice would also enrich Marxism. If this is so, then here is yet another point of convergence between traditional Chinese philosophy and Marxism.

Undoubtedly Marxism must develop, thus it must be an open system, and not a closed one. If it is to develop in China, then it must resolve the question of its merger with traditional Chinese culture. Naturally, the convergence of two such extremely different entities is difficult, but the need to advance Chinese philosophy requires that we strive to do so.

The advancement of Chinese philosophy depends on Marxism's union with the better elements of that philosophy. The modern generation of philosophers is faced with this responsibility. I myself am without special abilities. I can only express my feelings through an old adage: "Though I cannot achieve it, I aspire to do so."

THE ATTEMPT OF MATTEO RICCI TO LINK CHINESE AND WESTERN CULTURES

When introduced into another country or nation a foreign culture is confronted by the problem of how to treat that cultural tradition. If it wishes to spread easily and exert influence in the country in which it is introduced it must identify with that country's native culture. Hence, as the attitude of Matteo Ricci towards traditional Chinese culture is related to his missionary goals in contacting Chinese and especially Confucianist culture, he developed an intensive knowledge of that culture and recognized its very positive value. Therefore, his missionary work is related to an important issue in the history of culture: how effectively to blend not only into one but to communicate between two cultural traditions with different backgrounds. This is the heart of the problem of cultural transplantation.

Most probably, he appreciated well the significance of solving the problem and on the hole took a positive attitude towards Confucianist culture. We may observe this problem in two aspects: one is his own description of the problem; the other is how the literati of the period or a little later looked upon Matteo Ricci.

Matteo Ricci not only had a good command of Chinese, but also knew a great deal about Chinese customs and etiquette. He not only dressed in Confucianist style and called himself a "Western Confucianist" (xiru) with a square piece of cloth on his head, but also followed the etiquette of a Chinese scholar when meeting visitors. He made a careful study of ancient Chinese classics and records and regarded Confucius as a great man of wide knowledge. Of The Four Books (sishu) which he translated he wrote that it "was written by the four great philosophers and is full of reasonable ethical thought."1 To his mind, "it is no use at all just to know our learning without the knowledge of theirs."

But how did he treat Chinese culture? In a letter of February 15, 1609, to another missionary he wrote:

As I have gradually illustrated, they (the Chinese) also appreciate very much the principle of filial piety, although one might hold different views. To date from its very beginning, they faithfully followed natural law in ancient times, just like the case in our country. In 1500, this nation did not simply worship any idols. Even though they did worship some, these idols were not so detestable as those worshipped by our Egyptians, Greeks and Romans. Some of the gods were even very moral and well-known for their good conduct. As a matter of fact, in the most ancient and authoritative works of the literati, they only worshipped Heaven and Nature and their common master. When making a careful study of all these works, we may find few things contrary to reason, but instead, most of them are corresponding to reason. And their natural philosophers are no worse than anyone else.

The above quotations make clear the following: (1) Ricci knew very well traditional--especially Confucian--Chinese culture. As in ancient society, China was dominated by the patriarchal clan system and moral importance was attached to filial piety based on the principle of blood relation and "natural law." In China worship of Heaven and Nature also is moral and hence naturally "reasonable." Being quite knowledgeable regarding Chinese culture, Ricci regarded Confucianism not as a kind of religion, but rather as based on "natural law." Ricci highly appreciated China's Confucianist culture.

He saw that the idolatry in ancient Chinese culture was not like that of the Egyptians, Greeks and Romans and hence that ancient Chinese philosophy, in speaking of human nature and heavenly principles, transcended Western philosophy. This appears in his answer to Xu Guangqi's question, "China now, when virtue and rite and cultural relics are all prevailing, really flourishes culturally as though it has dispelled clouds and seen the sun again."

This may be due to the fact that as Catholic he attached great importance to opposing idolatry and advocating morality. Matteo Ricci was strongly against the idolatry of Buddhism and Daoism (Taoism), but he did not regard Confucian worship as a kind of idolatry. Thus we can say, that, on the whole, Matteo Ricci agreed with and appreciated the orthodox Confucianist thought of Chinese culture.

As Xu Guangqi believed in Catholicism through his contact with Ricci, he respected Ricci both for his learning and for his morality. He noted that in Ricci's speech, "you cannot find even a single word which runs counter to the principle of loyalty and piety, nor can you find one harmful to the will of the people and the world." That Xu Guangqi should attach special importance to "loyalty and piety" was influenced strongly by traditional Chinese ideas and it is on this basis that Matteo Ricci preached the Catholic doctrines and received Chinese culture. One passage in Ten Discourses by a Paradoxical Man describes the statement of Gong Dacan made on Matteo Ricci:

On hearing his wise talk, I feel that the Confucian classics of China and those of his country corroborate each other. Thus those who believe in the real sages, either from the East or from the West, from the North or from the South, are actually all the same.

All the Chinese scholars mentioned above think that what Ricci preached corresponded to traditional Chinese thought, especially to that of Confucianism, the most fundamental linking point of which lies in "the principle of loyalty and piety." As far as we know, although the Chinese intellectuals at the time set store in Ricci's knowledge of astronomy, almanac, science and technology, they valued even more highly his attempt to combine Western with Chinese culture. This probably is one of the earliest manifestations of "regarding Chinese learning as the body and Western learning for use." I shall discuss this problem later on.

MODES OF RELATING ORIENTAL AND OCCIDENTAL CULTURES

Judging from the above two aspects we see that, while doing missionary work in China, Matteo Ricci actually was trying to link Oriental and Occidental cultures. On this premise, we would conclude that his attempt adopted the methods of "linking Catholicism with Confucianism" (heru), "using the Catholic doctrines as a complement to Confucianism" (buru), "making in some respects the Catholic doctrines transcend the Confucian ones" (chaoru) "and making some revisions of the Catholic doctrines so that they would concord with the Confucianist ones" (furu). In short, on the above bases Ricci attempted to discover the point at which Oriental and Occidental cultures could be linked.

Linking Catholicism with Confucianism (heru)

Matteo Ricci wrote three important books on Catholic doctrines: The True Meaning of the Lord of Heaven, Ten Discoursed by a Paradoxical Man and Twenty-five Sayings from Epictetus. The original title of the first one is "The True Meaning of the Learning of Heaven." Obviously, he first thought of avoiding the name "the Lord of Heaven" because there is no such thing in China, to facilitate its reception by the Chinese. Fang Yingjing explains in the Preface as follows:

> *This book is about the questions and answers between Matteo Ricci and his fellow friends and five Chinese. What is the Lord of Heaven? It is God. It does exist.*

The edition of The True Meaning of the Lord of Heaven in the Ming Dynasty often used the titles "God" and "Heaven" for "the Lord of Heaven" or "the Lord of Supremacy," while the present edition often uses instead "the Lord of Heaven" and "the Lord of Supremacy" simply because Ricci used those titles in order to be easily received by the Chinese. Thus in ancient times the Chinese people worshipped Heaven, their state and their forefathers, but not "the Lord of Heaven." He tries to conform to this by quoting the classics to show that in ancient China "the Lord of Heaven" is God himself. The Chinese classics which he quotes include The Book of Songs (shi), The Book of History (shu), The Book of Rites (li), The Book of Changes (yi) and The Doctrine of the Mean (zhongyong).

These quotes appear more frequently in The True Meaning of the Lord of Heaven. For instance, in Discourse 6 of Vol. II, where he answers the question about "rewarding the good and punishing the evil," he more than once quotes Chinese classics to confirm that the doctrines of Catholicism should be combined with those of Confucianism.

(1) Matteo Ricci is quite aware of the existence of a supreme personal "God" in ancient China, regarding which he argues that the "Lord of Heaven" in Western Catholicism and "God" in China are one thing with different names.

(2) Criticizing Zhu Xi's explanation, he argues that there is only one "supreme lord," not two (heaven and earth). In his Introduction to The True Meaning of the Lord of Heaven he notes that the ancient sage advised that the subject should be faithful, but that they cannot be faithful to two lords. Of the three Cardinal Guides, ruler guiding subject stands first for since a state has its head, how can heaven and earth not have their lord? As a state should be unified, how can heaven and earth have two lords? All these ideas obviously show his interpretations of the Catholic doctrines in relation to Confucianism.

(3) Quoting the ancient classics he also states that God wills to impose fortune and misfortune on humanity.

(4) So God has his own "sphere" (ting) which is different from the "heaven" (tian) in nature. From all these we

can see that what Matteo Ricci attempts to prove that Catholicism coincides with Confucianism and the ancient Chinese classics.

COMPLEMENTING CONFUCIANISM (BURU)

Lettere dalla China is a note written by Matteo Ricci in Italian in China. Later a British missionary translated it from Italian into Latin and added something concerning the history of missionary work as well as of Matteo Ricci, the missionary. It also has an appendix relating the missionary's posthumous glory and pathos. One passage in the book reads as follows:

In answering what the main content of Christianity is, Dr. Xu Guangqi sums it up very exactly in four Chinese characters: "expelling Buddhism and complementing Confucianism" (qufuburu). That is to say, he wants to expel the idol of Buddhism and add something to the doctrines of Confucianism.7

As generally any religion is characterized by excluding others, Ricci criticized Buddhism and Daoism (Taoism), especially the former, since he wanted to bring Catholicism to China; this shows signs in nearly all his works. St. Augustine once pointed out that the main content of a heathen religion should resolutely be given up, but that the ideas put forward by some heathen philosophers should be taken into account, accepted or approved if they were really reasonable. Matteo Ricci took this approach to the doctrines of Confucianism. He declared that Confucianism had nothing to do with religion, but was rather a kind of philosophy. He particularly esteemed Confucius, noting that as Confucius lived five centuries before the birth of Jesus Christ he could not know what was to happen 500 years later. "Ricci just quotes the classics of Confucianism in their own terms, saying nothing of how they should be evaluated after the death of Confucius."

In Ten Discourses by a Paradoxical Man there is a passage about Gong Dacan's discussion with Ricci on the issue: "whether good or evil will be rewarded posthumously." Gong first notes that the Chinese classics, because Emperor Qin Shihuang burned books and persecuted scholars after the death of Confucius, lost the records of the paradise, hell and retribution, which are still in a good state of preservation in the West: "Thus the stories about the paradise and hell are well preserved."

In China, the story of retribution in later ages "is both vague and strange to scholars, who half believe and half doubt its existence." Gong also tries to prove the probable existence of the paradise by quoting ancient classics, but he still doubts the idea that "bestowing charity is bound to be rewarded a place and stand long." Ricci explains this according to the doctrines of Catholicism in which retribution to those who bestow favor does not consist in "place" or "life span." A man living in the world should work hard for the Lord of Heaven instead of intending to be rewarded in his lifetime; he should be confident that he will finally go to the paradise. Therefore, answering Xu Guangqi he says: "Those who suffer simply for benefit and emolument or fame and official rank or lasciviousness rather than the sacred cause are actually tragic. But those who suffer for the Lord of Heaven are obviously happy and seem to live in the paradise." It is apparent that he wants to complement the thought of Confucianism with Catholic doctrines, but the approach he adopts is not to negate the Confucian classics but to extend and develop them so as to show that the Confucian ideas do not run counter to those of Western religions but may be complemented by them.

In The True Meaning of the Lord of Heaven many passages deal with the "retribution of good and evil." In Discourse VI "On Man's Being Rewarded with Heaven or Punished with Hell after Death," he more or less complements and revises the Confucianist concept that "the family always doing good is bound to be fortunate, whereas the family always doing evil is doomed to misfortune." To him, there is not only retribution in one's lifetime or to one's descendants (he seems not to be favor of that to one's descendants). What is more important is posthumous retribution: those who do good will go to Heaven instead of going to Hell after death. But as their purpose is not just this, Ricci adds:

All those who do good usually have three intentions: (1) to go to Heaven instead of going to Hell; (2) to reward the kindness bestowed by the Lord of Heaven; and (3) just to follow the imperial edict given by the Lord of Heaven. The first intention serves as a bridge in order for one to reach the third; that is, doing good is after all following the imperial edict. However, the Confucianists did not know this, and even criticized the concepts of Heaven and Hell simply because they could not understand their deep significance: "The Confucianists criticize the concepts of the Heaven and Hell because they do not know truth." We can see roughly the difference between Catholicism and China's Confucianist tradition. Since the Confucianists talk about "the retribution of good or evil" just from personal moral cultivation, so everyone should "have self-cultivation" or "stick to morality" only for the purpose of reaching one's inner moral accomplishment. In this sense, it is pursuing a kind of "inner transcendence." But the Catholic doing good is after all for "the Lord of Heaven," which is a kind of power of "outer transcendence." So it pursues or follows a kind of "outer transcendence." I shall discuss this problem later on.

Transcending Confucianism (chaoru)

The aim of China's Confucianist theory is to pursue "inner transcendence," whereas that of Catholicism is to pursue "outer transcendence." In The True Meaning of the Lord of Heaven Matteo Ricci points out this shortcoming of Confucianism and criticizes it.

As far as we know, traditional Chinese philosophy, and Confucianist philosophy in particular, is strikingly different from Western philosophy and religion. The Greek philosophy of Plato and Aristotle already had divided the world into two parts: a transcendental noumenon and a real world. Thereafter Christianity was concerned especially with an outer transcendent God, whereas traditional Chinese philosophy was characterized by "inner transcendence." What Confucius means by "nature and the doctrine of Heaven" is a matter of inner transcendence, and what Mencius meant by "thinking hard, knowing nature and Heaven" is also a matter of "inner transcendence." There is a sentence in Xici saying: "A feminine (yin) and a masculine (yang) equals a word, and it is followed by virtue (shan) and will have a nature," which is a matter of "inner transcendence." According to this, one may reach a realm leading to a transcendental "way of Heaven" through one's own inner moral cultivation, without the help of an outer transcendent power. But for Ricci, one can hardly reach the culminating realm just through one's inner moral cultivation; one must be pushed by an outer transcendent power or God; thus it is necessary to believe in God. That is to say, Ricci considers the doctrines of Catholicism to be more perfect than those of Confucianism.

Concordance with Confucianism (furu)

This concept means that it is necessary to make some revisions of the Catholic doctrines or to yield to some of the Confucianist ideas in order to concord or chime in with China's traditional Confucianist thought.

The editor's Preface to the French 1978 edition of Lettere dalla China says:

> Immediately before Ricci's death, the methods adapted by the Chinese missionary group led by him had already become an issue argued both at home and abroad. It was disputed with two objections. In practice, he was accused of paying too much attention to developing his relation to the Confucianist elite instead of pushing forward the missionary cause. In theory, he was also opposed for his positive evaluation of Confucianism. Some people even pointed out that, if so, it would run a risk of sullying the purity of Christianity. Only by means of a heightened religious emphasis can the missionary preach the Gospel to the broad masses of people and make evident the characteristics of Christianity.

I have already pointed out that Matteo Ricci had some opinions of China's Confucianist tradition and attempted to link Western and Eastern cultures. Naturally, he knew clearly that there were many differences and conflicts between Confucianism and Catholicism and probably would have dealt with these by the methods of "complementing Confucianism" and "transcending Confucianism." If his missionary work were completely according to Catholic doctrines, however, he would have been confronted with more difficulties. Therefore, he had to make some revisions of the Catholic doctrines so as to cater to the Chinese tradition and it is not strange that he was criticized. As to how he adapted Catholicism to Confucianism, the following should be noted.

a. In order to fit Catholicism to Chinese society, he explained its differences from Chinese society. In the Italian edition of his Lettere dalla China, there is a passage describing how the Confucianist offers sacrifices to gods.

   However, according to an old law, there is a grand Confucian temple in every big city where the literati gather, with a figure of Confucius enshrined and his name; every year, the literati offer sacrifices to him four times, with a candle burning and a beast is killed. However, as they do not think of him as godly or want anything of him, such a rite cannot be called a real offering.

   In Matteo Ricci's books, there are many signs of the Catholic stance against idolatry; the criticism of Buddhist idolatry is particularly strong. However, he never criticizes Confucian offerings to the Sage, nor does he criticize the Chinese offerings to their ancestors. The issue concerning offerings is an important reason why China later forbad the preaching of Catholicism. In 1704, the Vatican gave orders that Chinese Catholics should not follow traditional Chinese rites that did not conform to Catholicism. Obviously, offering sacrifices to Confucius as well as to ancestors is especially counter to Catholicism; this led the Chinese government to limit and even forbid the preaching of Catholicism. Since Matteo Ricci well understood Chinese conditions, he adopted the method of compromising with the Chinese tradition for the sake of adapting to Chinese society as well as his missionary work, although the attempts did not conform to the doctrines of Catholicism.

b. He makes some Catholic ideas conform to traditional Chinese Confucianist thought so as to enable the Chinese to accept Catholicism. As mentioned previously, the "Lord of Heaven" in Catholicism is, of course, the supreme personified God, but Ricci's The True Meaning of the Lord of Heaven does not mean this according to its original title. In that book he often uses such words as "God" and "Heaven" of Chinese origin, instead of the "Lord of Heaven." According to Fang Hao's Collected Essays on The History of Chinese Catholicism, in contrast to the edition of the Ming Dynasty, it is found that the later edition has changed the words "God" or "Heaven" in the Ming to "Lord of Heaven" or "Supreme Lord" in 79 places.15 In the Chinese language there are already such words as "God" (shangdi) and "Heaven" (tian), but in traditional Chinese thought tian has several meanings. Among these Ricci takes the meanings "God," "Heaven" and the supreme personified God, but for the Chinese people there may be some other meanings. In 1715, after Ricci's death, the Pope gave an edict that the name "Lord of Heaven" was a legal one and such names as "God" and "Heaven" should no longer be used because they could be interpreted in different ways.

Also, according to Professor Luo Guang, Ricci says in his Twenty-five Sayings from Epictetus, "This book is actually composed of 25 chapters. Every chapter is short and concise. It advises people to live simply and to restrain desire and feeling. Happiness lies in one's secure state of mind without having stirred either by good fortune or misfortune. The purpose of human life lies in one's obedience to the Lord of Heaven." It is apparent then that the book is intended to conform to Chinese conditions.

c. Ricci made some revisions in the "idea of sin" in order that it should approach more closely the "idea of virtue" in China's Confucianist tradition. As the "idea of sin" in Catholicism implies, human nature cannot be considered "virtuous," which is entirely different from the "idea of human nature being virtuous" in China's traditional Confucianist thought. In accordance with St. Augustine's interpretation, man is born to be "sinful" because of his rational choice. In the final analysis, what causes man to choose evil with reason is his vanity, or an ego-centric desire that puts himself over God. Such a desire usually drives him into following his own intention and holding in contempt God's decree, which is particularly apparent in human desire. Augustine then adds that, since man intentionally chooses evil and commits sins violating God, he can never recover his original state with his own effort. For such a "sin" causes him to degenerate inevitably, being characteristically ego-centric in willing and desiring and able only to choose "committing sin" or tending to "evil."

In this regard in the 7th discourse of The True Meaning of the Lord of Heaven, Ricci thinks that the "human nature" refers to what differentiates man from metal and stone, grass and wood, bird, beast and even spirit, and this is why man "can reason things out." So he says: "What can reason things out is alone called human nature, which is different from other creatures." "Virtue and morality come after reason, which itself is something dependent, and not human nature itself." Thus, "reasoning things out" refers simply to this virtuous "ability," and "human nature is born to be virtuous." This obviously caters to Confucianist ideas. But since Matteo Ricci could not completely violate the doctrines of the Lord of Heaven, he thinks that man is "able to reason things out." How can he get such an ability? Just as farmers plough, weed, remove the stones and irrigate before they sow seeds in order to get good harvests, so "learners should first of all get rid of evil before they could be virtuous. Only by standing aloof from worldly success can they be successful." As this idea is associated with that of "sin" in Catholicism, it could not but conflict with the so-called idea of "good ability." Thus it is quite difficult to reconcile one cultural tradition with another.

From the above four points we can see that Matteo Ricci preached the doctrines of Catholicism for the purpose of linking Oriental and Occidental culture together. Whether his attempt was successful or not will not be evaluated here, but that he was the very first Westerner to make such an attempt is certainly of historical importance.

"BODY AND USE" AND THE CORRELATION OF CHINESE AND WESTERN HARMONY

In trying to link Western and Chinese culture, often we encounter the problem of the "body and use" (tiyong), of Chinese learning and Western learning. In preaching Catholicism in China, Matteo Ricci could not but consider his relation to traditional Chinese thought and culture. Similarly, in receiving Catholicism, the Chinese had to consider such a relation. Above I have discussed how he dealt with this problem. Now let us consider how the Chinese intellectuals at the time received Catholicism. In my opinion, such receivers of Catholicism at the time as Xu Guangqi, Li Zhizao and others in receiving or studying Western learning took the attitude: "Chinese learning as body and Western learning for use, we know that although the Protestants were active at that time even at the court in Beijing, yet "the Chinese court made use of them only by employing their techniques." "For example, Ricci once repaired clocks and other machines in the court, and Tang Ruowang and Nan Huairen and others joined in revising the calendar." "What China's enlightened literati were particularly interested in was to learn from them their science and knowledge." "They did not have great success in shaping China's intellectuals" for few Chinese intellectuals received the doctrines of Catholicism. As these were received chiefly due to his association with traditional Chinese thought, especially the Confucianist morality, his attempt can be regarded as another earlier form of "regarding Chinese learning as body and Western learning for use" formulated in the 1860s.

During subsequent centuries there have been various attempts to correlate "Chinese learning" and "Western learning" with that between "body" (ti) and "use" (yong), such as "Chinese learning as body and Western learning for use," or "Western learning as body and Chinese learning for use" and even "both the two learnings as body and Chinese learning for use" are called "all-Westernizers" (quanpan xihua pai); those who regard

"Chinese learning as body and Western learning for use: are called "Chinese culture supremacists" (guocui pai). Such confusions are caused by the attempt to describe the relationship between "Chinese learning" and "Western learning" with that between "body and use." As a matter of fact, none of the above ideas are tenable.

As a pair of important categories in the history of Chinese philosophy, "body" and "use" are not substantial categories, but rather fundamental relations. "Body" (ti) generally refers to the "inner transcendental spirit" or "transcendental noumenon." It corresponds to what Mencius means by "conscience" (liangzhi or liangneng) and Wang Yangming by "mind" (xin), etc.; the latter corresponds to "God's will" (tianming), "taiji," "God's word" (tianli) and "logos" (dao), etc. "use" (yong) refers to the various functions demonstrated by such an "inner transcendental spirit" or "transcendental noumenon." According to traditional Chinese philosophy, ti and yong are unified, with the former presenting the latter for, as Wang Bi in the Wei-Jin Dynasty pointed out, there would be no corresponding yong without ti. The so-called concept of "Chinese learning as body and Western learning for use" is nothing but an effort to preserve the inner transcendental noumenon in Chinese tradition, so as to reject the Western spirit. For how could we make "Western learning for use" if we should do like that? Similarly, it is impossible to regard "Western learning as body and Chinese learning for use." The former will inevitably result in "Chinese learning both as body and for use" and, the latter, "Western learning both as body and for use."

As for "both the learnings as body and for use interchangeably," it can be interpreted as: if something in Chinese learning is good we should regard "Chinese learning as body and Western learning for use"; also, if something in Western learning is good we should in turn regard "Western learning as body and Chinese learning for use." Such an idea is obviously untenable. It will do nothing but include both attitudes in the so-called concept of regarding "both learnings as body and for use interchangeably," which is just eclectic. Professor Fang Keli involves himself in a confused eclectic situation although he criticizes the above two attitudes in his "`Chinese Learning as Body and Western Learning for Use' and `Western Learning as Body and Chinese Learning for Use'".

It would give rise to "stealthily substituting one culture for another" if we use the relation of tiyong to explain the relationship between Chinese culture and Western culture. If we do not improve the cultural soil and other conditions, but just stealthily substitute one culture for another, the cultural foundation will not be solid. Thus to my mind, our modern society should have its modern spirit and various systems embodying such a spirit. If we use the relation of tiyong to explain this problem, we might probably regard "the modern spirit as body and the systems and their functions embodying such a spirit for use." If so, one might ask: what is the "modern spirit"? and what are the "systems and their functions embodying the spirit"?

Here I would refer to the point of view put forward by Mr. Yan Fu, who once criticized the idea of regarding "Chinese learning as body and Western learning for use." He also points out that body and use should be unified rather than dual. Particularly, he lays emphasis on the significance of science and puts forward a very meaningful proposition: "liberty as body and democracy for use." I do think that such an idea of his is probably of certain modern significance. So in my opinion, "liberty" is the concentrative embodiment of the modern spirit, or an inner spirit in the modern era and a universal ideal that the people in modern society are pursuing; whereas "democracy" consists of various systems of modern society ensuring one "liberty," rather than certain people only. We now live Chinese society. It is most important to give everyone "liberty" and have a set of democratic systems ensuring its realization if we want to enable our society to become modernized. Only in this way, can people give full play to their enthusiasm and creativity, and our country set foot on the road not only of the "four modernization" but also of all-around modernization.

4

Buddhism and Traditional Chinese Philosophy

At present Chinese philosophy in its development is combined with two important issues:

(1) how to meet the challenge of Western philosophy and

(2) how to approach Marxist philosophy.

To understand both the characteristics and values of traditional Chinese philosophy will be beneficial in resolving the above two issues.

The viewpoint concerning the true, the good and the beautiful in traditional Chinese philosophy is fully embodied in three propositions which have long been discussed by ancient Chinese philosophers, namely: (1) "the integration of heaven and man"; (2) "the integration of knowledge and practice"; and (3) "the integration of feelings and scenery." The integration of heaven and man refers to the relationship between man and the universe, a concept in which man is considered the center of the whole universe. The conduct of the sages should not only conform to the "way of heaven." Living between heaven and earth man should not adopt a pessimistic attitude but should make unremitting efforts to improve himself, thereby giving expression to the prevalence of changes in the universe. By so doing, man should set a standard for himself, have a principle of conduct, and possess a lofty spiritual state.

The most important of these qualities is to do everything in the light of integrating knowledge and practice, to cultivate morally the integration of knowledge and practice. In addition, man should take pleasure in realizing the ideal state of "integrating heaven and man" and the principle of "integrating knowledge and practice." Man has to conduct himself properly and, at the same time, enjoy the pleasure of conducting himself properly.

Man has to comprehend the wonder of the creation of heaven and earth. To do this man must display his powers of creation in reproducing the wonders of creation by producing essays as "perfect essays," paintings as "godly works" and music as "heavenly music." Therefore, the demand for art should be in the spirit of "integrating feelings and scenery." When man has entered into such a state of creation, he has attained a state in which the true, the good, and the beautiful are unified. The meaning of man's life and the most lofty ideal of mankind consist precisely in this. In the eyes of China's ancient sages, to conduct oneself properly is difficult, and to bring nature, society, and the inner and outer aspects of one's body and soul--as well as those of others--into full harmony is even more difficult.

Traditional Chinese philosophy has had a profound influence on the psychology of the entire Chinese nation and has been expressed in the unique psychological characteristics of the Chinese people. These characteristics have long influenced the nation in all respects and express both the strengths and weaknesses of the Chinese tradition of thought and culture. Traditional Chinese philosophy has exercised great influence on the whole nation by means of the following concepts:

Utopian Idealism. Most of the principal philosophers in traditional Chinese philosophy had an intense of responsibility and mission towards their country and people. They adopted an active and warm-hearted attitude toward social reality which they tried to transform with their doctrines and ideas. However, these doctrines and ideas failed to transform political reality in China and turned out to be tools used for its embellishment. Therefore, many influential thinkers in Chinese history turned out to be tragic figures. The actual role which utopian idealism played in China was quite contrary to their wonderful but subjective hopes.

Practical Moral Concepts. In traditional humanistic Chinese philosophy there has been a tendency which differs from Western humanism. Chinese humanism emphasizes the place of man in the universe and society. In any given social relationship it dwells on how man should behave himself, on how he should take responsibility, and how he should fulfill his duty to society and to others. But traditional Chinese philosophy is seldom concerned with human rights, thus hindering the development of personal character and restricting creativity.

Unitary Way of Thinking. Most major figures in traditional Chinese philosophy considered it their duty to establish a harmonious and unified society. Therefore, traditional Chinese philosophy has been rich in dialectical thinking, which emphasizes unity and harmony and opposes both the "overdone" and the "underdone." In these respects, this unitary way of thinking has positive meaning. Unfortunately, being a worldview often lacking in analysis, it is not easy for Chinese unitary thinking itself to develop into a modern science, since it is unable to set up a systematic theory of logic and knowledge.

Intuitive Rationalism. Most traditional Chinese philosophers have paid great attention to the functions of the "mind." Confucian scholars pursued the full play of mental intuition from a positive viewpoint. According to Mencius, "the function of the eyes and ears is not thinking, for they are only blocked by objects." "The function of the mind is thinking. Think and then you gain, otherwise you gain nothing." The school of idealist philosophy of the Song and Ming dynasties even centered on the study of the "nature of the mind." As for Daoist scholars, they tended to treat man's subjective intuition from a pessimistic position. Laozi (Lao Tzu) advocated "sweeping away the dust from the mirror" and told people to get rid of the dark spots and make the "mind" as clear as a mirror able to reflect the outside world correctly.

Wang Bi, metaphysician of the Wei and Jin dynasties, held that sages were different from the common people because their "godly wisdom" (wisdom of the mind) is higher than that of others: "The better part in sages is their godly wisdom."

Overemphasizing the intuitions of the "mind," this kind of nationalism could not be based on the analysis of things since it focused on "experience" while ignoring "verification." Intuitive rationalism tended to be tinged with mystery.

Traditional Chinese philosophy has already made its contribution once to human civilization. To let it make an even greater contribution, we must undertake its thorough study and analysis to understand clearly both its strengths and weaknesses, so that it can develop further and play an even greater role in the present world.

THEORIES OF LIFE AND DEATH IN CONFUCIANISM, BUDDHISM, AND DAOISM

Theories of life and death in Confucianism, Buddhism, and Daoism (Taoism) can be discussed by comparing the following: (1) Confucianism and Daoism (Taoism) and (2) Buddhism and Daoism (Taoism).

Confucianism and Daoism

Confucianism regards both life and death as a responsibility to society, while Daoism (Taoism) holds that both life and death should be in conformity to nature.

The fundamental concept of the Confucian view of life and death is: "Life and death are determined by fate, and wealth and nobleness are determined by heaven," thereby emphasizing life rather than death. Confucius once said, "How can one know about death before he knows clearly about life?" In one's lifetime, one should fulfill one's responsibility in realizing the ideal of a harmonious society. "It is man who can find and develop ways and ideas, and not vice versa." Man should consider it his duty to testify to the workings of the "way of heaven." Heaven pursues its eternal movement, and a gentleman should make unremitting efforts to improve himself." Since Confucianism lays more emphasis on responsibility in one's lifetime, it neglects the world after death. According to Confucianism, man can be "immortal." Zuo Zhuan proposes that man can be "immortal in three ways": to set a fine example in virtue; to achieve a great career; and to leave behind great writings.

This "immortality," in spirit only, has social and ethical significance, but has not direct connection with life. When Zhang Zai, a famous Confucianist in the Song Dynasty, wrote Xi Ming, his final sentences were: "When living, I work with the social trend; and, when I am gone, the world will be in peace." When living, man should try his best to fulfill his social responsibility and strive to realize an ideal society. One should ask oneself "to set a goal for the world, to live for the people, to study sages of the past, and to work for a peaceful world in the future." This idea of Zhang Zai is actually what Confucius sought after as "the way of heaven prevailing all over the world" and also the "three programs and eight items" in Da Xue and the idea of Great Harmony in Li Ji--Li Yun (Book of Rites). If a man does what he can to fulfill his responsibility before his death, he will feel composed and have no qualms when he leaves this world.

Therefore, Confucianism does not lay too much emphasis on death. To realize one's idea, one can "end one's life for benevolence" and "give one's life for righteousness." This thought once exerted profound influence on China's literati and officialdom in feudal society. Before his execution, Wen Tianxiang, a national hero in China's history, wrote the following on his clothing belt: "Confucius teaches benevolence and Mencius teaches righteousness. For the sake of righteousness, perfect benevolence could be attained. What else can a man learn from the sages? After my death, I will feel no qualms at all." In the last analysis, life in Confucianism is to fulfill one's responsibility to society and death is the same. If one fulfilled his social responsibility before death, he will die "immortal."

The founder of Daoism (Taoism), Laozi (Lao Tzu), did not much discuss the issue of life and death. At one place in his work, he touched upon the issue as "enjoying longevity," a notion which has something to do with his idea that, if one does not play too much emphasis on his life, it may be easier for him to preserve his thought. However, Zhuang Zhou (Zhuangzi) discussed this issue and considered both life and death as natural phenomena. When living, one should do everything in conformity to the law of nature and not seek anything beyond one's ability. In Ying Di Wang (Fit for Emperors and Kings), there is a story in which Hundun (Chaos) was killed when he helped to bore seven openings for seeing, hearing, eating and breathing. According to Zhuangzi, "death" is nothing but a "rest." "When death befalls me, I begin my rest." So when his wife died, he sang to the beating of bronze bowls. But there were "Perfect Men" or "Godly Men" who were beyond life and death. They could attain a state in which "both heaven and earth exist with them and all things are one with them." However, this "living beyond life and death" is somewhat different from "living in eternity" and it is only meant for a "spiritual state."

By the Wei and Jin dynasties, the Metaphysical School became popular and was often referred to as "New Daoism (Taoism)." It developed the thought of Laozi (Lao Tzu) and particularly that of Zhuangzi. In Zuang Zi as interpreted by Guo Xiang, both life and death were but different states in which all things existed. To life, life is life, but to death, life is death; to life, death is death, but to death, death is life. So whenever life or death is mentioned, people just give out different views from different viewpoints. Since life and death are both states in which all things exist, when living, one should live in composure and, when dying, one should die in composure. This idea of Guo Xiang was evidently derived from that of Zhuangzi.

Another philosopher named Zhang Zhan interpreted the work of Lie Zi (Great Thinkers in Ancient China). He thought that everything had its beginning and end, sometimes gathered together and sometimes dispersed. The life of anything was supposed to be its beginning: "gathering takes a certain shape." The death of anything was supposed to be its end: "when dispersing, things go to nothingness." "By life is meant an air that gathers temporarily the ether of anything. Temporary gathering will eventually disperse and temporary ether will finally go to nothingness." Therefore, man should know his source and his final destination, namely deliverance. Both Guo Xiang and Zhang Zhan were influenced by the Daoist thought that both life and death were but natural phenomena.

BUDDHISM AND DAOISM

Almost all religions seek to solve the problem of what will happen to man after his death, but Daoism (Taoism) in China alone chooses to tackle the problem of "how can man avoid death." The basic belief of Daoism (Taoism) is "living in eternity" and for "the body of flesh to become immortal." Tai Ping Jing states, "Daoism (Taoism) has all along taught conservation. Man can live in eternity and get away from death." Laozi (Lao Tzu) Xiang Er Zhu also says, "The reason people are converted to Daoism (Taoism) is the wish to live in eternity." Therefore, finding a solution to the question of life and death, seeking deliverance and immortality, and finally reaching the state of "living in eternity" are the characteristics of Daoism (Taoism).

Xiao Dao Lun, published in the North Zhou Dynasty, quoted The Preface to Laozi (Lao Tzu) written by Ge Xun, "Daoism (Taoism) preaches life, while Buddhism preaches death." San Tian Nei Jie Jing also said, "Lao Jun (Daoist Buddha) advocates achieving life and Sakyamuni advocates achieving death." According to Buddhism, the sufferings and pains of man lie in "being in life." Being in life means the spirit is associated with flesh and cannot be freed, that is, the spirit is still in the circle of samsara (wheel of life) before it reaches nirvana. Only when the spirit leaves the flesh can it arrive at the state of nothingness and he delivered from the sea of bitterness.

Daoism (Taoism) advocates realizing immortality in the flesh, that is, a body combined with spirit achieves immortality. In this way, man can leave bitter reality and enter the world of immortality. When commenting on the difference between Daoism (Taoism) and Buddhism on the issue of life and death, the Daoist monk Qi said, "The wonder of Daoist teachings lies in the seeking of oneness through intense meditation, in achieving immortality without dying. The essence of Buddhist teachings leads to meditation by ridding oneself of miscellaneous disturbing thoughts, by seeking no life and naming death clay eternity. I never heard of not dying by seeking death." Tang Falin also said in Bian Zheng Lun (Book of Dialectics), "Wai Er Yi said that Lao Jun elaborates the preaching of living in eternity with no life or death. Sakyamuni establishes the religion of eternal nothingness with no life or death. Nei Er Yu said that Li Ran explains the essence of both life and death: "Fearing life that troubles life will bring about grey hairs. Sakyamuni reveals the sign that explains both life and death. Going to the final nothingness that silences nothingness will honor the body in gold." Buddhism advocates "no life," for whenever there is life there is death. Daoism (Taoism) advocates "no death," for "no death" means living in eternity. Though their views are totally different, both Buddhism and Daoism (Taoism) seek deliverance by dealing with the issue of life and death.

THE ENTRY OF INDIAN BUDDHISM INTO CHINA: THE MERGER OF TWO CULTURES

In China's history there have been three occasions when foreign cultures were introduced into China. The first was a little after the first century A.D. when Indian Buddhism spread into China. The second was in the middle of the 17th century when missionaries brought along with them the civilization of the West. The third was at the time of China's Fourth of May Movement in 1919 when various trends of thought of the West, especially Marxism, were brought into China. By analyzing some social phenomena that appeared after Indian Buddhism entered China, we shall discuss the question of how the two cultures merged. The entry of Indian Buddhism into China went through the following process.

Indian Buddhism, after its entry into China, was first attached to China's existing culture and, from this base, began to develop and exert its influence.

When Buddhism spread into China during the Han Dynasty, it was first attached to Daoshu or Fangshu (Daoist practices or techniques). When metaphysics became popular in the Wei and Jin dynasties, Buddhism was also attached to metaphysics. In the Han Dynasty, both Futu and Huang-Lao were treated equally, even the Buddhism was Daoshu. At that time the content Buddhism preached was similar to such ideas as "souls are immortal" and "preordained fate" which already existed in China, but the concept of Wu Wo (without myself) was unknown to people at that time. Two branches of Buddhism were popular in the last Han and early Wei dynasties. One was the An Shiguo Theravedic school (known in Chinese as Xiaocheng) which emphasized Zen practices. An Ban Shou Yi Jing (Sutra on the Maintenance of Thought by the Practice of Anapana) was a book on a breathing method to "keep one's thought in place"; this was similar to the breathing and respiration exercises and techniques espoused by the Daoists, and especially by the School of Immortals. Yin Shi Ru Jing, based on the concept of Yuanqi (Original Breath), explained the theory of Wu Yin (Five Negatives), which was later translated into Buddhist terminology as Wu Yun (Five Inward Contents, namely, color, feeling, thinking, practice and knowledge.

Another branch was Zhi Lou Jia Gan School, which belonged to the Mahayana (known in Chinese as Dacheng). This school emphasized that the fundamental principle of life was to make spirit revert to its virginal truth or reality and that life would then conform to the dao (tao) (the way of nature). From this we can see the apparent influence of the ideas of Laozi (Lao Tzu) and Zhuangzi. In the early East Jin Dynasty, the Ban Ru School was prosperous and encompassed the so-called Six Schools and Seven Sects. The issues they discussed were fundamentally those of "Source and Outcome" and "Existence and Non-Existence" which had been discussed by the Metaphysical schools in the Wei and Jin Dynasties.

The wide spread of Buddhism after the East Jin Dynasty brought about a clash and conflict between traditional Chinese culture and thought and those of India, a foreign culture,which gave an impetus to the further development of Chinese culture and thought.

In the period of the South and North Dynasties, the conflict between Buddhism and China's pre-existing culture occurred in all areas. There were questions concerning both political and economic interests, as well as questions concerning interests, as well as questions concerning philosophical thought and religious ethics. In the area of thought, there were controversies on "whether or not immortals were perishable," "whether or not there was preordained fate," "whether or not the Buddhist monks should worship royalty," and the relationship between human beings and other living creatures, between the Chinese nationality and other minority nationalities. The laws to abolish Buddhism, which came into effect during the period of Prince Tai Wu Di in the North Wei Dynasty, had political causes.

Meanwhile, the clash between Buddhism and Daoism (Taoism), the pre-existing national religion of China, became sharper and sharper. All these controversies were but an expression of the clashes and conflicts between two different cultures. Some of these conflicts lasted until the Sui and Tang dynasties.

After the Sui and Tang dynasties, Indian Buddhism was assimilated by Chinese culture and a Buddhist sect with a typically Chinese spirit came into being. By the Song Dynasty, Buddhism had completely merged with traditional Chinese culture and had become a part of Chinese culture. It was the time when the Lixue School in the Song and Ming dynasties was formed. This was called also the New Confucian School.

During the Sui and Teng dynasties, there appeared in China a number of Buddhist sects. Among them were Tian Tai, Hua Yan and Chan Zong--actually Buddhist sects with a typically Chinese spirit. The most important issues these three sects discussed concerned theory and practice and the nature of the mind. The issue of the nature of the mind was originally an important one in traditional Chinese philosophy. It could be traced back to Confucius and, especially, to Mencius. As for the relation between theory and practice, Hua Yan Zong said "theory and practice are mutually independent" and "practices are individually independent"--notions which were related to the idea of "theory and practice are one" elaborated by the Metaphysical School in the Wei and Jin dynasties. Later in China Hua Yan Zong and Chan Zong exerted the greatest influence, just because they were forms of Buddhism in the Chinese spirit. In contrast, Wei Shi Xue, though advocated by the famous monk Xuan Zang, was popular for only thirty years or so and then declined, since it was pure Indian Buddhism.

Lixue School or the New Confucian School in the Song and Ming dynasties criticized Buddhism and at the same time, assimilated and merged with it, thus bringing to Chinese philosophy an even more comprehensive system encompassing the original system, the theory of values and the philosophy of life. From the West and East Han to the Song and Ming dynasties, Chinese philosophy, in the midst of clashes and conflicts with foreign cultures, went through a process of "positive-negative-convergence" that advanced Chinese philosophy.

Any individual culture has its own unique characteristics which set it apart from other cultures. For the culture to remain unique, its distinctive characteristics must remain intact. Otherwise, this culture would only exist in history and have no function as a real culture in present reality. In comparison with Indian culture, the unique feature of traditional Chinese culture is to teach people how to "conduct oneself" so as to realize the ideal of "running the country in a peaceful state" in reality.

This spirit of "living in the real world" runs absolutely counter to the idea of "living beyond the real world" espoused by Indian Buddhism. After Indian Buddhism was introduced into China, though it did exercise some profound influence on the Chinese way of life and changed Chinese social life in many areas, the fundamental spirit of "living in the real world" in Chinese culture was never modified by the alien Indian culture. Chinese culture, as a unique cultural system, remained and continued to develop. The trend of development among China's Buddhist religious sects has never been to adapt China's social life to the needs of Indian culture. On the contrary, Indian Buddhism has been developing in the direction of Chinese culture. This became especially so when Chan Zong (the Zen) appeared and destroyed important features of Buddhism as a religion. Chan Zong advocated that the Buddha and reading Buddhist classics were not necessary and that reproaching Buddhas and cursing ancestors were permitted. Chan Zong holds that "Fetching water and cutting wood are both good ways of life," so that men can realize the ideal of immortality in real life. Therefore, to go one step further, once men are good at serving their fathers and kings, they can eventually be perfect sages. In this way, traditional Chinese culture was able to take the place of Buddhism.

TRENDS IN THE DEVELOPMENT OF CONTEMPORARY CHINESE PHILOSOPHY

Since the conclusion of the Great Cultural Revolution, the study of traditional Chinese philosophy has gone through three periods.* From October 1976 to early 1979, the task was to bring to the study of traditional Chinese philosophy an end to the chaos that resulted from the Cultural Revolution. What was unique during this period was the adoption of an attitude of "seeking truth from the facts" in the evaluation of Confucius. However, negative influence from two sources still existed: (1) that academic work must serve politics and (2) the application of dogmatic research methods that kept the field of study from making any important advances.

Since 1979, however, the study of traditional Chinese philosophy has begun to break through the bounds of dogmatism, and some important issues have been discussed. I made an analysis of progress during this period in an essay, "New Developments in the Study of the History of Chinese Philosophy," published in the Min Bao monthly journal in Hong Kong and also in the Journal of Chinese Philosophy. This essay discussed new developments during that period in the following four areas: (1) the study of the history of Chinese philosophy as the history of the development of knowledge of the Chinese nation; (2) the study of concept categories and systems of Chinese philosophy; (3) the problem of method in establishing a philosophical system for traditional Chinese philosophy; and (4) the comparative study of traditional Chinese philosophy and foreign philosophies.

Since 1983, with the deepening of the study of traditional Chinese philosophy in the People's Republic of China, it is natural that the issue of future prospects in the development of Chinese philosophy be advanced. This issue is not only connected with the development of the study of philosophy in China, but also with the study of Chinese philosophy abroad. In August 1983, I presented a paper at the 17th World

Philosophy Conference in Montreal, Canada, on "An Inquiry into the Possibility of a Third Phase of Development of Confucianism." This paper confirmed the realistic value of traditional Chinese philosophy as a whole and was appreciated by many scholars both at home and abroad. To find a solution to the issue of future prospects for the development of Chinese philosophy, the value of traditional Chinese philosophy must be recognized. For this purpose, some Chinese scholars have made a special study of this problem.

Li Zehou, for example, holds that the history of the development of traditional Chinese philosophy is a history of the cumulative knowledge of the value of man. The core of Confucian teaching is "benevolence," that is, to treat other individuals as "man," an approach which makes people realize that the meaning, position, and value of an individual as man lies in his dealings with other individuals. "To be open and sensible" was advocated by the Metaphysical School in the Wei and Jin dynasties is, in a sense, an expression of the emancipation of "human nature." By the Song Dynasty, Confucianist philosophy expressed consciousness of knowledge of the value of man as man. Therefore, the characteristic feature of traditional Chinese philosophy lies in the fact that people come to know themselves gradually in moral practice, seeking to realize their ideals in present society. Li names this "Practical Rationalism" or "Chinese Wisdom."

Pang Pu holds that the characteristic feature of Chinese philosophy is a kind of "humanism" that emphasizes the meaning and value of "man" in social reality. Even Daoism (Taoism), the original Chinese religion, affirmed this characteristic feature. Daoism (Taoism) preaches "living in eternity" and "immortality of the flesh," the purpose of which is for "man" to attain a state of "immortality" in social reality.

Wang Ruoshui published an essay, "Man in Reality is the Point of Departure in Marxism," in response to Hu Qiaomu's essay criticizing humanism and alienation.

Why are there so many Chinese scholars at present who all take "man" and the value of man as the focus for the development of Chinese philosophy? It is clear that the development of Chinese society has been closely connected with the issue of the value of man.

Since the winter of 1984, a series of conferences have been convened to discuss Chinese culture and the comparative study of Chinese and Western cultures. First, a seminar on the "History of Contemporary Chinese Culture" was held in Loyang, Henan Province, then a seminar on the "Comparative Study of Oriental and Occidental Cultures" was held in Shanghai. In April 1985, a coordinated conference on the "Comparative Study of Oriental and Occidental Cultures" was held in Shenzhen, and, in December, a seminar on "The Philosophical Thought of Xiong Shili" was held in Hubei. In January 1986, the first session of a seminar on Chinese culture was convened in Shanghai. From the above conferences, we can discern three closely-related problems that form the general topic of the development of Chinese philosophy, thought and culture.

A. At present, Chinese philosophy is confronted by a challenge from Western philosophy, including various Marxist philosophies in the West, and the problem is whether or not we can make immediate and active responses. To modernize China must introduce modern science and technology from the West and Western experience in economic management. But at the same time, does China have to usher in Western philosophical thought to enrich her own philosophy? Here three problems are involved: (1) whether China's Marxism can develop an open system to confront new scientific theories and new creative approaches to philosophical issues; (2) how to understand the similarities and differences between "modernization" and "Westernization"; and (3) whether China can preserve her own rich tradition of philosophy.

B. How or in what way can Marxism be combined with China's traditional philosophy? Marxism was introduced into China during the May Fourth Movement in 1919, and politically it met the needs of China at that time. In this sense, a fusion was achieved. Nevertheless, Marxism has not been integrated very well with China's philosophical thought. On the contrary, Marxism adopted a negative attitude towards China's traditional philosophy. But to face the challenge of Western philosophy, this synthesis must be achieved, because only by so doing can Marxism take root in China and become a Marxist philosophy in a Chinese environment. And, again, only by so doing can traditional Chinese philosophy develop into a modern Chinese culture which can assimilate both Western and Marxist philosophy.

C. How can we make a historical re-evaluation of traditional Chinese philosophy as a whole? Whether or not we can solve the first two problems depends basically on whether or not we can make such a reevaluation. This must be conducted in the light of the development of contemporary world philosophy, and in view of the specific conditions of Marxism in China.

It is a pleasure to participate in this United Nations Vesak Day celebration for 2008. One part of the program has been devoted to the issues of Buddhism and technology. In this first panel, we will have an opportunity to hear from three important projects in Europe, Asia, and Australia that have added much to our understanding of Buddhist culture. Subsequent panels bring the opportunity for the delegates to hear descriptions of various approaches and strategies to the use of technology. As part of the activity, we will try to provide support and information for any who are interested in starting work on some aspect of Buddhism that includes technical issues. Our participants are a very special group of experts and scholars who have already achieve much in their own work and are now able to share that expertise with the Buddhist communities.

The problems faced by Buddhism and the new technology are not limited to the religious tradition; they are matters of concern to all research in the fields of cultural heritage. If we consider this issues, it is important to recognize that Buddhism and technology share problems and solutions with a wide range of academic and media groups.

Humanities computing got underway nearly three decades ago. From experience, we already have seen that our first clumsy efforts to build silos of information are no longer adequate. From the time of stand-alone computers with software constructed specifically for one scholar to the present day internet connectivity, it has been a short journey in time but a very long one in terms of technology development. During these decades, we have, at times, been saddened to see how often the ill-constructed silos of the past have become empty of usable information. Some exceptional data prepared in the earliest days of the personal computer have already been lost. Scholars retire, servers are closed, projects come to the end of funding, universities stop support of functional software, and as a result scholarly work that would still have value in the Humanities has disappeared.

Today, our silos of information are lot more sophisticated and numerous. In fact, it is just the numbers of silos that causes concern. We are overwhelmed by having to go into one silo, extract information, go out and find another and repeat the same entrance and exit strategy. How can we work with copyright laws and intellectual property restrictions that impede rather than aid in the distribution of information...information that has after all often been gathered and paid for by society in the salaries and grants we receive? Is it time to review our ethical stand with regard to ownership of digital information and ask funding agencies to state that open access be a requirement for awarding grants?

At a recent meeting of librarians, someone said that we have a "9-5 problem." Our reference desks are open from 9:00 a.m. to 5:00 p.m. but our students are doing their research and writing from the internet from 9:00 p.m. to 5:00 a.m. What should the new reference services attempt to do in a digital world? It is obvious that our great libraries, and we have just heard some encouraging words from one of them, need to be very involved in the construction of a digital reference service. It is not an easy problem.

Our past approach was to train and empower reference librarians who could provide suggestions for codex material held within their building. For the internet world of digital information, we must empower not just the librarian but also, the user. Therefore, the role of the reference librarian must dramatically shift to construct the tools for this empowerment of others. If I use a metaphoric statement, in the past, we looked at users of libraries as those who were confronting a barrier that had to be surmounted. We had to help students and researchers figure out the best way and strategy of answering questions. They had to get over the mountain or barrier that blocked their access to the information that lay beyond the reference desk in the stacks of the library. In the digital world, it is not enough to merely give researchers a list of resources, books, or articles. We want to take them directly to the full text source. That changes the landscape. It is not like going over a mountain pass to information, it is a matter of perspective rather like an aerial view. We need to see the context of our data along with the ability to access it here and there when appropriate and relative to our search.

Recently at a conference in Taiwan, Professor David Germano of the Tibetan and Himalayan Digital Library at the University of Virginia in the U.S. stunned us all. He reported that after constructing a large database, it became clear that they had built a giant pyramid. But the pyramid presented a problem since it became more complex with each new tier and when finally completed had a very small capstone surmounting the whole. Only one or two persons can climb the entire way to the top of this pyramid and make full use of the resource. And as the old adage goes, the capstone of a pyramid is the only part of the structure that has no supporting role. Bravely facing the pyramid problem, Professor Germano and his staff have decided to disassemble the digital library, in his words, "reduce the pyramid to rubble." Out of the rubble they plan to construct a whole series of databases that are centered on specific items of information. The challenge will be to figure out how to link these many new constructions in a way that makes them all interoperate with one another in a matrix.

The Electronic Cultural Atlas Initiative has been focusing on problems of referencing and archiving material. As a result of this intense research supported by the National Endowment for Humanities, the National Science Foundation, the Institute of Museum and Library Services, and the Luce Foundation, we have developed a program of working toward the 4 Ws. Where? When? Who? and What? are well known in the field of journalism and they work well in digital data. In ECAI, we started with Where? and that led us to Geographic Information Systems (GIS). The use of latitude and longitude has proven to be one of the simplest metadata categories for placing and finding information.

When? has been a surprisingly difficult category. We very early saw that calendar dates in the Common Era numerical format are not the only time references we find in the data itself. Instead of 1932, we find named time periods such as "The Mauryan Empire" "The Tang Empire" "Vietnam War." In geology, named time periods are necessary to deal with vast spans that cannot be easily broken into short intervals of months or days. Our research in this arena was aided by the support of the Library of Congress that allowed us to use their digital catalogue for finding all of the named time periods listed in that repository. Through the software developed for this project, we can now identify nearly 3000 named time periods and relate them to other information. At a meeting of Virtual Reality researchers in Rome, I began to note the use of named timed periods and just to explore the problem made a listing of all that appeared in the papers of that three day conference. When you see over two hundred named time periods from one conference, it is brings to our attention the problem of dealing with time.

Who? came next for us. In terms of cultural study, identification of the place and the time must always involve actors. We are constantly constructing Who? When? and Where?. This led to the question of how useful the three elements are in markup and it opened up a new vista for ECAI. At the instant of the combination of Who? When? and Where? we have identified an event and this has become for us the 4th W ... What?

Consider our situation right now. We are in Hanoi in 2008 with scholars and researchers from many nations and this is an Event. If we try to understand this Event, we will have to contextualize all of the information available to us. What is 2008 in terms of its characteristics? What is the role of Hanoi and its institutions in the world of information technology? Who are we delegates? Can we track the biography of each one of us and finally have a full Event markup and structure for this meeting? Event markup is needed as we do context building. At the Semantic Web Conference in Korea last summer, I presented this idea to a group made up of librarians, archivists, and software developers. Some of the European librarians cried out when I suggested that in the future our digital libraries should be catalogued or marked up not only as "objects" but also as "events." They all said that our library catalogues are made to index "objects." Of course, we need object identification and markup but if we see our objects as "Events" we will know much more about them and be able to combine information about Who? When? Where?. Even a book is an "Event" it has a history that includes authoring, editing, publishing, distributing, cataloguing, using, and referencing. I am suggesting that a major step toward interoperability between "objects" found in "silos" is going to be the strategy of seeing the event structures that put those "objects" into a context.

These are a few of the difficulties that people face who want to put Buddhist information into digital format. Much has already been accomplished and some of it is being shown in the panels. Let me just discuss one aspect of Buddhist technological efforts, those concerned with the texts of the tradition.

The initial digital input of Buddhist information centered on the canonic literature. Because of the size and variety of these canons, the computer offered an appealing method of housing and retrieving data. At the same time, the texts of the religion were held in high esteem by the religious communities and from these sources it was possible to raise the sizable sums of money needed for input activity. Scholars were also supportive of the enterprises, although slow to give recognition to the digital sources when annotating articles and books. While a passage might be located by searching the CDs and online versions of the canons, the older form of notation referring to the print copy was more acceptable for footnotes. Standard rules for citation had to be developed and scholars needed to be reminded that using a digital source without giving reference to that fact constituted a new variety of plagiarism. As with all of the technologies, the early use is an imitation of the former methods. When Buddhist texts became available in a digital format, they were seen to be simply another form of print. Later use of the digital canons began to utilize the potential of having an electronic version; a version that can be used for search and retrieval but can also be analyzed for structure and patterns through complex algorithms.

The first major project for digital versions of the Buddhist texts was the input of the Pali canon. Completed on May 30, 1988, Visakha Puja Day, the Digital Tipitaka Development Team under the Mahidol University Computing Center, Thailand, announced the completion of the project. The Siam Edition of the Pali Tipitaka in 45 volumes had been successfully put into a computer format. At the same time, there was the release of an application program, BUDSIR (BUDdhist Scriptures Information Retrieval). The work had been directed by Prof. W. Supachai and the Digital Tipitaka Development team. At first the data was available on a WORM (Write Once Read Many) hard disk. Later it became available on a CD ROM (Compact Disk Read Only Memory) and several hundred copies were distributed by the American Association of Religion and Mahidol University. The availability of the entire Tipitaka meant that researchers need not seek for those few libraries in the world that contained the whole Pali canon in their holdings.

The program developed to archive and retrieve was BUDSIR (BUDdhist Scripture Information Retrieval). For the first time, it was possible to digitally search for and retrieve every example of any word, sentence, or phrase occurring in the Tipitaka. The next step in development was taken in 1991, when King Bhumibol Adulyadej issued a memorial that the 70 volumes of the Attakatha (Commentary) be included along with the Tipitaka texts. This latter task was completed in 1994 and all 115 volumes were released on CD ROM with the improved BUDSIR IV software. This pioneering project reflected all of the necessary responses to new software, international standards, and user needs. The need for upgrade was followed by the release in 1996 of the BUDSIR IV software for Windows. This was enhanced by the use of GUI (Graphic User Interface) for the display of multiple windows for comparison of texts. An added feature was capability for digitally producing sounding of the words of the Pali texts. Continued work on the data came in 1997 when the Thai transcription was added with a new search engine that was able to display multi-script retrieval. In addition, translation tables from Roman and Thai script added the ability to view the texts in either Devanagari, Singhalese, Burmese, or Khmer. At this point in the development of technology, a dictionary of Pali-Thai equivalents was linked to the database allowing quick reference for Thai language readers. Finally in 2002, BUDSIR was upgraded to an internet software, allowing user to access and search the data through online connection. A continual stream of new features were put in place by 2004 when the Devanagari and Singhalese scripts could be used for retrieval.

Within a decade of the release of the Siam digital version of the Pali, a number of other groups began to input other editions. The Vipassana Research Institute (VRI) in India, chose to put the Chattha Sangaya edition into digital form. This version was produced in Myanmar at the time of the Sixth Council of Buddhism in 1956. The Indian government had commissioned the Nalanda Institute to prepare a print version of the Chattha Sangaya edition in devanagari. VRI prepared a new print edition of 135 volumes. By 1997, a CD ROM was available for the devanagari edition along with the software to convert the devanagari script into either Roman or Burmese script. Upgrades of the software included addition of five more script options and the ability to install the data on Chinese Windows. In the subsequent release the number of texts in the data was expanded to 216.

Sri Lanka

In 1991, the input of the Sri Lankan version of the Pali Tipitaka was started by the Vajiragnana Dharmayatana, a Bhikkhu training center in Maharagama. The edition that was used as the basis for the input was from the 58 volume Buddha Jayanti Tipitaka that had been compiled and published during the 1960s and 1970s with government support. The digital input was under the auspices of the Amarapura branch of the Sangha headed by Venerable Madihe Pagnnaeha Mahanayake. The work of creating the machine readable versions was completed in 1994. At that point, the data was not fully proofed and a number of errors remained in the digital version. In order to help with the process, the project was adopted by the Colombo Branch of the Sasana Sevaka Society and further proof reading as well as some annotation was done. The project is known as the Sri Lanka Tripitaka Project (SLTP). In 1999, it was mirror sited with the Journal of Buddhist Ethics.

Dhammakaya and Pali Text Society

The most commonly used version of the Pali canon for scholarship has been the edition prepared by the Pali Text Society of London. Formed by Professor Thomas Williams Rhys Davids and Charoline A.F. Rhys Davids in 1881, the Society had the purpose of translating and publishing Buddhist Literature. Scholars recognized the importance of putting the PTS version into digital form.

In 1988, Professor Jamie Hubbard and Professors Robert Thurman prepared a proposal to the National Endowment for Humanities seeking for the funds. Unfortunately, the NEH did not select the project for support. The next step was to make the Buddhist community aware of the potential for digital versions of Buddhist materials. Professor Hubbard joined Lewis Lancaster at the meeting of the World Buddhist Federation in Hsilai Temple in Los Angeles.

A demonstration was given for the future use of computers for reading and working with text material. Hearing of this presentation, in 1989, the Dhammakaya Foundation indicated an interest in helping produce the digital version of the PTS. By 1990, the input was underway manned by volunteers of the Dhammakaya group who did the input and the proof reading. It was not possible for the team to locate all of the PTS texts in Thailand and the missing ones were used from the library of the University of California, Berkeley. There were difficult issues involving the copyright of the material. It was not until 1996 that a mutually agreeable memorandum of understanding was drawn up between the Society and the Dhammakaya Foundation. Prof. K.R. Norman went to Thailand in April of that year and signed the agreement for a joint venture between the two institutions. After the agreements were in place the CD ROM called EPaliTexti version 1.0 was released in June, 1996 containing the digital version of the Pali language volumes of PTS along with a search engine. The publication came at the time of the celebration of the Golden Jubilee of the Coronation of the King and the first copies of a revised version known as Palitext ver. 1.0 were presented to the monarch on November, 1996. Five hundred copies of the CD ROM were made and distributed world wide. At the same time that the Pali language version was being input, the Dhammakaya group also started work on the English translations of the PTS. To date, this English material has not yet appeared in digital format.

Pali Manuscripts

Palm leaf technology has not disappeared as a format for recording Buddhist texts. However, after printing became an accepted format for the canonic texts, manuscripts were less important. The existing palm-leaf documents often date to the 19th century when the copying of Pali texts was still a major form of merit making. By the latter part of the 20th century, the preservation of the manuscripts was no longer assured. In order to rescue these documents from neglect and destruction, a group was formed under the name of "Fragile Palm Leaves Collection."

One of the leaders of this movement to collect and preserve the older manuscripts was Peter Skilling. By 2000, the Fragile Palm Leaves Foundation housed more than 5,000 manuscripts with 10,000 titles. A catalogue of the manuscripts in Pali and Burmese was made in cooperation with the Pali Text Society. As new computer technology came into use, it was decided to scan the images of the manuscripts into digital form. This was established in cooperation with the Lumbini International Research Institute in Nepal.

Tibetan Canon Editions and Commentaries

The major work on the digitization of Tibetan canonic texts was started through the efforts of Michael Roach. He was influenced by his contact with Geshe Lobsang Tharchin, when the former abbot for Sera Mey Monastery in Tibet moved to New Jersey as the head lama of the Mongolian Monastery at Freewood Acres. The endeavor was given the title Asian Classics Input Project (ACIP). Centered on the Tibetan Buddhist material, the work of input was coordinated from the ACIP office in the U.S. with monastic colleges in India such as the Sera Mey Tibetan Monastic University, Sera Jey, Ganden Jangtse, Drepung Loseling, and Sakya (Rajpur).

Another site for the input has been the refugee camps primarily in south India. The major facility of this group was the Hunsur Tibetan Settlement, and the other important places were the Rabling and Dekey Larsoe Settlements. Working with the refugee council of His Holiness the Dalai Lama, space was made available by the local groups in India while ACIP provided the hardware, training, and salary for the input. The project has been closely tied to the education of Tibetan youth in computer technology.

ACIP, in addition to the input of the Tibetan texts, has undertaken the work of creating a digital catalogue for the Tibetan woodblock prints in Russia. There are two large collections of these prints. The St. Petersburg Branch of the Institute of Oriental Studies of the Russian Academy of Sciences has 25,000 volumes containing nearly 200,000 titles. A smaller set of xylograph copies exists at the Oriental Library at the University of St. Peterburg where 3,300 titles are located. By 2005, the total number of catalogued titles reached 50,000 entries. Even at a preliminary stage, the number of text titles recorded far exceed the largest print catalogue content of about 1,000 entries. This is a good example of how the amount of data that became available online and in distributed digital formats surpasses that contained in print. Following up on the preparation of the digital catalogue of the materials at St. Petersburg, ACIP turned it attention to the collections of Tibetan materials in Mongolia.

It is estimated that 1.4 million titles are found in the archives, many of them duplicate copies. When finally catalogued, ACIP estimated that the Mongolia materials will be far larger than the collections in St. Peterburg. In particular, the Gangdan Tekchen Ling monastic complex has preserved many texts. However, during the troubled times of the 20th century after 1937, the texts were often scattered or ill-housed and the first task was putting the physical objects back in order before preparing digital catalogues and input or scans.

In addition to ACIP, there are a number of projects in Nepal and India that are working to create digital versions of the literary traditions of major schools of Tibetan Buddhism. These projects focus on the writings of important figures in Tibetan history. Many of these efforts are combining printing with digital publications of the rare texts. For example, The Nitartha Document Input Center in Kathmandu used computer generated script to print the collections of the Karma Kagyu masters. The ability to create and use new fonts and produce clear copies for printing have enhanced many of the publications. Ironically, it is the computer that has spurred much of the growth of paper publication.

The Drukpa Kagyu Heritage Project (DKHP) has been closely associated with these attempts to collect and publish the texts of the writings of particular masters. Led by Tsoknyi Rinpoche and Tony Duff, the DKHP has led the way in development of software for dealing with Tibetan materials and shared it with other projects. There are a host of projects in this field. Leigh Brassington and Marvin Moser were software engineers involved in the early development of Tibetan software strategy. Some of the most advanced input projects are:

Sanskrit Editions

The digitization of Sanskrit materials has been delayed because there is no religious community to provide the support for such work. The most significant project to preserve the images of the Sanskrit texts was done through the Nepal-German Manscript Preservation Project founded by Dr. Wolgang Voigt and Professor Dr. Klaus Ludwig Janert. This work of microfilming was started in 1970 in an agreement between the Nepalese government and the German Research council. Prof. Dr. Albrech Wezler served as the Director from 1982 until the work was completed in 2002. The project has provided microfilm for more than 180,000 Sanskrit and Tibetan manuscripts that include nearly five million folios. A number of Buddhist texts have been included in this international project and it is an excellent target for future digitization.

Since there has never been a coordinated effort to input all of the existing Sanskrit found in either manuscript format or published critical editions, the early attempts came from individuals. These projects by scholars have usually involved a single Sanskrit text or a group of texts that relate to the particular interest of the researchers. This has been particularly true in Japan were private data sets were created for a variety of texts. Most of these data have never been made available to a large audience.

An attempt at putting in some of the most important texts was started by a young Korean graduate student at the University of Tokyo. Jong-cheol Lee set up a small input center in India and financed it mainly with his own money. Some support came from the Buddhist Studies Center at University of California, Berkeley. Professor Lee did the input with the desire to create a Sanskrit lexicographical polyglot database which will include mappings among Sanskrit, Tibetan, Chinese and Korean. This is a long term project that will be web based.

As a follow up to the Pali project at Mahidol University, Professor Supachai also input several thousand pages of Sanskrit texts which he plans to make available in the future.

A new project was mounted in 2000 working with a grant from the Fo Guang Shan Educational Foundation. Joining is this effort was the Nagarjuna Center in Kathmandu under the direction of Min Bahadur Sakya. Setting up the input center in Kathmandu, the project group produced a dataset of published editions of Mahayana Sanskrit texts as well as Tantric texts from manuscripts. When completed, the texts were put online by the University of the West in Los Angeles for free public use. The project continues with additional support from Professor

Tsai Yao-ming of Taiwan National University who is working on the dharani texts of Nepal. Miroj Sakya, now a visiting scholar at the University of California, Berkeley works with Professor Alexander von Rospott and Mr. Ralph Moon to formulate the project with best practices and international standards.

Central Asian Languages

Professor Dr. Jost Gippert of the University of Frankfurt established the Thesaurus Indogermanischer Text- und Sprachmaterialien (TITUS) for the purpose of creating a database of Buddhist texts written in Indo-European languages from Central Asia. In the first phase, slides of the manuscripts were prepared, scanned, and stored as graphic images. The second phase called for the input of the text using UNICODE for the various scripts and allowing the display as a screen font.

Chinese Buddhist Canon

It is difficult to establish exactly when input of Chinese Buddhist texts began. In 1986, a group at the Institute of World Religions of the Chinese Academy of Social Science in Beijing formed a "Bureau of the Chinese Buddhist Canon." One of the first and most difficult issues to be dealt with was the lack of a font containing all of the ancient characters of the canons. Several attempts were made to create software that could produce the glyph form for any possible combination of the elements of Chinese characters. While thousands of these combinations were constructed, it did not result in the creation of a usable font. In the 1990s, Prof. Fan Guang-chang reported at one of the international EBTI meetings, that 106 volumes had been completed along with other data of imagery for art and artifacts. He also indicated that there was a project set up to input one of the Ming dynasty editions. The distribution of this data has not yet been documented.

The Zen Texts Project of Hanazono University

One of the earliest and most influential centers for the research on the input of Buddhist texts was the International Research Institute for Zen Buddhism (IRIZ) at Hanazono

University in Kyoto. Under the leadership of Dr. Urs App, IRIZ explored the problems of doing computer input including the "missing" characters that did not exist in any available fonts. Working with Christian Wittern, Dr. App played an important role in helping to raise the consciousness of the scholarly community to the potential of the digital world. As early as 1990, he published the first volume of The Electronic Bodhidharma. It was in many ways the announcement of the arrival of the new technology.

The paper publications were followed in 1995 with the release of Zen Base CD I, which created a digital resource of the study of texts from this important school of Buddhism. It is hard for later generations to understand the range of problems faced by those who began to explore the new technology at a time before there was industrial development of software, large memory capacity, and personal computer hardware. The contributions of scholars such as App and Wittern was essential to the process that unfolded over the past two decades. They, along with other scholars, helped to define the problems of computing for the humanities. The efforts of the pioneers affected the way in which computer engineers did their development of tools and standards.

Prof. C. C. Hsieh of Academia Sinica played a crucial role in helping with the various input projects. In the 1980s, he had headed up the first major input project of a Chinese archive, the Twenty Five Dynastic Histories of China. It was his work that inspired the Buddhist scholars to go forward with the canonic input. The Dynastic History database of 40 million characters proved that a large amount of information in Chinese characters could be put into digital form for search and retrieval.

Koryo Buddhist Canon

The oldest complete set of printing blocks for the Chinese Buddhist canon are found at Hae-in Monastery in South Korea. Carved in the 14th century, the collection is composed of more than 83,000 blocks. Based on the Kaipao Edition from the Northern Sung, prints from these blocks were used to produce the Tokyo edition of the 19th century and later the Taisho

Issaikyo metal type print of the 20th century. Lewis Lancaster received support from the Buddhist lay community in Korea to start the input of the Koryo edition in 1993. Working together with Urs App, Christian Wittern, Sungtaek Cho, an input facility was found at the Shanghai Chemical Research Institute where the computer center had installed the newest technology in the late 1980s. Chinese institutions were having to adjust to new economic models and these included the requirement to seek for funding from contracts outside the campus. In order to accommodate the Buddhist input project, the Institute received permission to insert the traditional character font into their system. A staff was assembled at the institute and nearly 2 million characters (of the total of more than 52 million for the whole of the canon) were put into digital format. At the same time, Ven Chonglin and Ven Hyemuk of Haein Monastery were starting to experiment with the input of the Koryo version and held a summit conference to discuss the way in which the work could be accomplished.

The Berkeley project and that of the Haein Monastery group were joined in 1994 and the work of the input passed over to Seoul. Fund raising efforts resulted in the adoption of the project by Samsung Corporation. Setting up an input laboratory, Samsung employed over 30 full time typists and 6 engineers who spent one year to make a complete input of the whole content of the 83,000 printing blocks at Haein Monastery. In January of 1996, the Samsung work was completed and the first CD ROM was made available.

In that same year, the printing blocks were designed a UNESCO World Heritage. There was still the task of proof reading and this began in April 1997 after a fund raising project supported by a month long ad in the newspaper Joongang Ilbo asking for donations from the general public. In order to make the digital version look like the block print, a whole new font was developed that followed the glyph patterns of the 13th century scribes.It was necessary to create more than 30,000 user defined characters. Known as the Tripitaka Koreana, the project is still on-going under the leadership of Ven Chonglin. As part of the continuing effort, the Institute of the Tripitaka

Koreana in cooperation with Nanzenji in Kyoto has been digitizing images of ancient printing and manuscript examples of the Chinese Buddhist canon.

Chinese Buddhist Electronic Text Association

While the Taisho Issaikyo has been the most used edition for the Northern Sung version of the Chinese Buddhist canon, copyright issues delayed the input. The publisher of the print version, Daizo Shupphansha, Inc. attempted to undertake the initial input as a commercial project. Working with the late Professor Ejima of Tokyo University, four CDs were produced for separate volumes of the printed edition. The recovery cost for production meant a very high cost for each disk and sales did not create enough income to make such a project possible. As a result, the work came to a halt.

Another model was needed to make the digital version affordable and available. An agreement was reached between the publisher and the Chinese Buddhist Electronic Text Assocation (CBETA) of Taiwan. The leaders of the CBETA team were Ven Hui-Min and Mr. Aming Tu. Once the copyright license had been given CBETA set to work in 1998 on an electronic version. Support for the work came from a number of sources, the Chung-Hwa Institute of Buddhist Studies, the Yin Shun Foundation of North America and the Buddhist Bodhi Foundation. As with all the Buddhist canon input projects, it was the donations of the religious community that made such work possible.

This agreement between CBETA and Daizo Shupphansha, Inc. was a milestone in terms of dealing with the intellectual property rights of information available on the internet. The copyright for the content remained with the publisher of the print edition while permission was granted for distribution without charge to users of the internet and CD ROMs. In 1999, the first release was volumes 5-10 of the Taisho. This was followed by an updated release for volumes 1-55 and 85 of the print edition. At this point, CBETA provided the contents of the Northern Sung edition found in the Hae-in Monastery printing blocks with a few additions. Volume 85 contained texts from Dunhung manuscripts. Because CBETA relied in part on existing data, it was possible to move rapidly toward the digital publication.

Mr. Hsiao Chen-kuo, a Buddhist laymen, had been working on the input of the data for some years. Since he had done the work out of religious commitment, he released his data for use with CBETA. Christian Wittern took the input of the Koryo project in Korea and converted it to Big Five code for use in the digital publication. Since the Taisho text is a copy of the Koryo block prints, the data was easily adopted for C BETA. CBETA records a series of names and sources for the input data such as Tseng Kuo-feng and Leo Flamenco.

In 2004, the project was enlarged with the distribution of materials from the Zokuzokyo, texts that do not occur in the core of Chinese canon contained in vols 1-55 of the Taisho. With the CD ROMs and internet versions of the Chinese canon from CBETA, Buddhist studies was finally able to have usable information for digital study of the tradition. While the Tripitaka Koreana had been completed earlier, it was CBETA that overcame the hurdles of introducing the digital canon to a wide audience.

SAT

Work on the input of the Chinese canon has been done in Japan. The group most responsible for this has been Samganikikritam Taisho Tripitakam (SAT). This same project has also been known as the Association of the Computerization of Buddhist Texts (ACBUT). Since the copyright for the print edition of Taisho is held in Japan, an early attempt was made to do the input of the edition in Tokyo. The nature of the Japanese project shifted after the untimely death of Prof. Ejima. Later the effort would be led by Shigeki Moro and Ishii Kosei. Through SAT, it was possible to negotiate the license for CBETA in Taiwan and thus make the Taisho available to the world. Rather than limiting activity to input, SAT began to explore the ways of dealing with the many variant readings in the multiple translations of the Buddhist texts and to research the best practices for using the digital version of the canon.

Hong Kong

In 1999, a separate project in Hong Kong produced a CD ROM with volumes 1-85 of the Taisho content. Because the CD can only be read with one reader that only runs on a version of MS Windows for traditional Chinese characters, the CD did not find a ready audience. Given the easy availability of CBETA on the web, it was not possible to make an impact using complex and limited methods.

Chinese Buddhist Manuscripts

In addition to the inputs of the canonic texts, there was a major digital project at the British Library in London. The International Dunhuang Project (IDP) led by Susan Whitfield has scanned in images of thousands of manuscript pages from the materials collected by the expeditions of Sir Aurel Stein during the early part of the 20th century. In particular, the digital Buddhist Chinese manuscripts from Cave 17 at Dunhuang constitute a major step forward for research. Scholars now have internet access to manuscripts that were previously only available for limited use in the British Library. A major figure in the development of this computer resource was Colin Chinnery. Since the Stein collection of manuscripts is mostly made up of Buddhist materials, this resource in invaluable for future work on the exploration of textual criticism for Chinese canonic readings. Added to the images of the manuscripts is a digital map with the photographs from the Stein archive giving context to the locations of the archaelogical sites that contained the Buddhist materials.

Persistence of Digital Data

One of the great dangers of relying on the digital technology is the fragile nature of the storage of data. Major libraries have not yet solved the question of how to preserve the databases for perpetuity. CD ROMs and DVD disks will only last as long as the layers are kept sealed. It has been estimated that 30 to 40 years is the longest lifespan for these disks. Even when material is stored in super computer centers, there is the question of whether the functional formats of the data will be usable when retrieved after several decades. There will be a great need to have the ability to transfer data from one platform to another over time to keep it current. The cost of maintaining high level security for data and the continual upgrade for the new software and hardware will put pressure on libraries and archives as they seek to fund this long-term commitment. The ACIP group has faced this problem and are backing up the digital material with microfilm which is thought to be useful for a century or more. In terms of longevity, acid free paper is still a very necessary storage option. Scanned images can be printed onto paper and thus will have centuries of potential usefulness. There is probably no one issue that equals the dangers of loss, as scholars and institutions opt to make use of digital information.

The attempt to engage in this work of transference of information in and out of the digital media brings with it a broad range of new problems, which require careful, well-coordinated solutions, without which the work of digitization can quickly turn into a quagmire of incompatible platforms, codes, categorization systems, unnecessarily repeated work and so on. It was with the solution of these sorts of concerns in mind, that the Electronic Buddhist Text Initiative was first convened at a small informal meeting at UC Berkeley in 1992, with 16 persons present. This has been followed by a more or less annual sequence of meetings, each of which marks a clear development in both scope and sophisticated digital projects. The administration of EBTI moved from Berkeley to Dongguk University in Seoul, where it continues to serve the scholarly community..

Buddhist Response to Digital Canonic Developments

Venerable Chao Khun Phra Dhammapitaka (Prayudh Payutto)Bhikkhu Prayudh Payutto has been a senior monk of Thailand responding to the new technology and giving his thoughts about the impact it will have on Buddhism. When Mahidol University was inputting the Siam Edition of the Pali texts, he served as adviser and worked closely with Prof. Supachai in the proofing of the texts. In his appraisal of the situation, he posed the question of whether there is a decision of "a natural humanity living in a natural world, or whether to attempt to make a 'scientific human' for the scientific world." He noted in his public lectures that the data being housed in digital format is far beyond the memory capacity of the mind. With the construction of such large amounts of information, we must rely on the computer in the future to help us deal with the data banks.

From the Buddhist perspective, Bhikkhu Payutto formulates the issue from the point of view of the concept of creating benefit. In this regard, he has suggested that the question of technology for Buddhism will rest on the decision of whether it is "creating benefit" or merely "seeking benefit." This type of speculations from a Buddhist monk indicates that technology is being evaluated within the realm of benefit for "self" and benefit for "others." The implication of his remarks are that seeking of benefit at any cost is quite different from the creation of lasting benefit. Another important point that Bhikkhu Payutto has made is the fact that in the past we have been dependent on the sense organs for information which is processed into perceptions. This process is described in great detail through out the Pali texts. Now, he asks whether we have a new source of knowledge that is from the digital and technological realm. Instruments can extend information collection far beyond what the physical senses are capable of achieving. This new data will challenge all of our previously held opinions and thus, Bhikkhu Payutto, states that Buddhists must decide how to handle this shift of sources for knowledge in terms of the basic doctrines of the tradition.

5

Virtual Archaeology, Knowledge and Communication

When the terms "virtual archaeology" was introduced and popularized (Forte 1997; Forte 2000), most academics reacted to it with extreme caution, lack of understanding, or with hostile polemics, both for terminological reasons and, especially, because of the difficulty (which one could, indeed, sympathize with) of imaging the scientific (and not just the didactic) potential of 3D worlds, both those reconstructed ex novo ("virtual antiquity") and those documenting the current state of archaeological remains ("observed antiquity"). I believe that this diffidence was motivated by the difficulty of imagining the 3D model as an interactive, a multimodal, and-especially-a holistic container of information, a whole greater than the sum of its parts.

Indeed there is no doubt but that a 3D model, be it of a landscape or of a monument, can add information and thus insight to what we already knew, at least if the model is correctly built. This 3D navigable map represents the geo referenced information provided by the model. The 3D geometric model of the cyber map shows by means of different forms and colors the relationships that develop at every multimedia node/ theme within the system: iconography, style, light, color, composition, and space (Forte et al. 2002). In this case the cyber map seeks to demonstrate that information, if associated with conceptual-spatial models, is a better instructional tool than are traditional means (scholarly lectures, papers, textbook descriptions, etc.). That is to say, in a VR system of this kind, the interaction occurs in X,Y,Z coordinates and this leads to the creation of a mental map of the monument which subsequently grows upon contact with the actual monument. The cybermap demonstrates in an eloquent way how the third dimension permits us to build a new cognitive geometry of the cultural artifact, especially if, as in this case, it is associated with narrative and communicative sequences.

The balance sheet of the last twenty years of archaeological research on the application of the third dimension as a research tool is fairly depressing: the use of 3D representations has been completely random and thus has not had a great impact on the development of research methodologies and protocols. Only rarely is adequate time and attention paid to them in university courses and programs of study. There are, of course, a few courageous exceptions, but to the extent that 3D has made it into the curriculum, it has been at the level of short, post-graduate training courses. As for fieldwork, here the picture is much the same: the use of 3D technologies for data capture, analysis, and reconstruction is still considered experimental and is thus still quite rare. In the best of circumstances, 3D is used to represent data collected by hand and in two dimensions and/or integrating spatial information that is either not correct or simply invented.

This leads to a first and complete separation between knowledge acquisition and knowledge communication, a sequence we hold to be the cybernetic vehicle necessary for cultural transmission. If the 3D world constructs its own holistic models based on unreliable or hard-to-test information, then the result in archaeological methodology is a lack of transparency as well as a lack of semiotic super-positioning of the sources of knowledge. To give one example, it is one thing to create a 3D model of a site drawn manually on a plan, and it is quite another to do so on the basis of a corresponding point cloud of data points collected by a laser scanner or by some other digital technology.

The issue is not trivial because the ontology of archaeological information, or the cybernetics of archaeology, refers to all the inter-connective relationships which the datum produces, the code (or the "map," as Bateson 1972, calls it) of transmission, and its transmittability. Because it depends on interrelationships, by its very nature information cannot be neutral with respect to how it is processed and perceived. It follows that the process of knowledge and communication have to be unified and represented by a single vector. Thus, from the first phases of data acquisition in the field, the technical methodologies and technologies we use influence in a decisive way all the subsequent phases of interpretation and communication. In the light of these considerations, what is the relationship between information and representation? How much information does a digital model contain? What sort and how many ontologies ought to be chosen to permit an acceptable transmittability? These and many other questions on related topics take on certain urgency because they relate directly to the loss of information from understanding, learning, and the transmittability of culture.

Indeed, our ability to transmit culture depends on a model which combines on the same axis processes of understanding and communication. Thus, the questions which we pose in a phase of bottom-up knowledge (for example, in an archaeological excavation) will influence the top-down phases of interpretation, or the mental patterns (for example, a comparative analysis and reconstruction of models). From this derives the need to interconnect the top-down processes with the bottom-up in accordance with a reciprocal systemic interaction, for example in a virtual space where both sequences can coexist. If we peremptorily separate knowledge and communication, we risk losing information along the way, reducing the relationships that are constructed between acquisition/input and transmission/output.

Archaeological communication ought to be understood as a process of validation of the entire cognitive process of understanding and not as a simple addendum to research, or as a dispensable compendium of data. But the methodological tradition which we inherit has almost always separated the realm of fieldwork, reports, and publications from the realm of cultural communication, which is too often popularized and marginalized under the vague term "didactic." To the contrary, the grand challenge posed by digital technologies is to integrate the ontologies of data into a single process: digital acquisition, digital processing, digital communication (online and off-line). Every conceivable segmentation of this process leads to a loss of data and of knowledge and to a diminution of the social impact of research: what is not perceived cannot be communicated. Moreover communication often is marginalized precisely because it ought to face the difficult challenge of proposing hypotheses of reconstructing the ancient world, harmonizing the observed and observable data within models that seem to be arbitrary. The lack of scientific communication causes the discipline of archaeology to have less social import than it might otherwise have, causing a sort of cultural solipsism and low level of transmittability.

Once the phase of the technological "wow factor" has passed-i.e., the moment in which the aesthetics of models seemed to have a higher priority than the accuracy and quantity of the information they conveyed--we enter into the current phase in which researchers must raise epistemological questions to enable their discipline advance methodologically. The quantity of models (geometric, epistemological, cultural, spatial, etc.) which digital technologies have been able to produce is impressive and grows at a constantly increasing rate. This phenomenon cannot be culturally digested without suitable methodological and theoretical reflections. It is the purpose of this paper to offer a sketch of a possible starting point for such reflections.

Methodology of Archaeological Research

One of the indisputable results of multidisciplinarity in archaeology is continually to pose new questions about research methodology and the use of applied technologies. It is difficult to construct complex ontologies of data if research does not ask new questions. Information per se does not create knowledge, but it constitutes its precondition in accordance with a process of selection: "selection filters the noise and reveals at the same time the information, channeling it into patterns that will result in understanding" (Taylor 2005: 261). The path from understanding to communication is thus selective regarding information and propaedeutic regarding the dissemination and transmission of culture. To select information we must process it in accordance with a valid sequence of acquisition, modeling, representation, and communication. In this sense it is useful to distinguish between accumulated (i.e., not selected) knowledge and the quality of perceived (selected) information. The indiscriminate accumulation and growth of databases, catalogues, and geometric data (one thinks of the millions of points in point clouds created by laser scanners) present serious problems of information management and of knowledge which concern the relationships between data and perceptions.

In the archaeology of landscapes, for example, the reconstruction of the ancient landscape presents a focal and often unsolved problem precisely because the data are too sketchy and the analysis of the territory does not pose questions appropriate to the study of ecosystems but remains limited solely to human activities. In contrast, if one analyzes the landscape as an organism, relationships and activities come to light which would have otherwise not appear in other contexts. If we do not raise the right research questions, it is obvious that we do not have data adequate to create reconstructive models. So, what happens to the pathway leading from archaeological knowledge to communication? If in the phase of input/research the right questions are not asked, the phase of output/ communication will of necessity be lacunose and will not support an adequate monitoring of the path of understanding, following the progressive transformation of the various ontologies of information.

Bottom-up and Top-down

The activity of archaeological research follows rules of the types bottom-up and top-down. In fieldwork, the activity of understanding starts from the lowest level (bottom-up) insofar as precognitive perception is addressed in the identification of forms, patterns, crop-marks, structures, etc. which come to light in the course of archaeological investigation. The bottom-up process follows rules of "pattern recognition," i.e., it identifies borders, forms, and outlines in such as way as to unite mentally the residual traces on the ground to the point where a (stratigraphic, structural, taxonomic, etc.) map can be created. This activity produces discrete (topographical, excavation, etc.) maps, basically composed of vectors, lines, and polylines which presuppose interpretative actions and logics of perception. In contrast, the process of interpretation, which follows top-down rules, functions from high to low, according to the mental patterns which our cognitive experience uses as elements of comparison.

The bottom-up phase of research, especially in the case of archaeological research, is very delicate because it results in the first set of information (often with destructive consequences for the stratigraphy) and hence is propaedeutic to understanding. It extrapolates from the chaos/noise of the information a cybernetic pattern which becomes fundamental for the top-down phase. Next follows the bottom-up phase of survey which should be as careful as possible and concerned to show and validate all the relationships useful for creation of the mental map.

From this discussion we can infer that archaeological understanding is a process of interaction between bottom-up and top-down rules. The construction of cybernetic maps as a result of this interaction constructs codified information which, in the end, can be transmitted. The transmission then takes place through publication tools that are both linear (books, paper, exhibitions, etc.) and non-linear or reticular (multimedia, Web, VR). In the process of standardization of archaeological data destined to be published, there is no doubt but that a hiatus is created between what we call knowledge (or, the scientific knowledge codified for a few experts) and that which we call communication (information shared by and codified for the public).

The problem with digital artifacts, as has been correctly seen by Settis (Settis 2002), is that starting from the second half of the 1980s, they have been used in attempts to resolve the problem structurally with an exaggerated technological inventiveness which has not led to positive results. Digital artifacts have mainly been created purely with the goal of archiving knowledge (but in a retrograde and only pseudo-standardized way) and not with the aim of the multidisciplinary virtualization of information. Thus, on the one hand researchers have undertaken the creation of enormous databases, but, on the other hand, they have delegated to multimedia the task of transmitting cultural information that has been "popularized" for didactic use. Here, again, we find the two realms of knowledge and communication to be distinct. The multimedia products have too often followed the model of linear media, translating into digital format the semiotic formulae of print media with little added value from the digital per se.

It is clear that at this point that the above-mentioned problem of digital artifacts has generated no little confusion: in what way, then, do we ask of archaeological communication that it provide the information gathered from research? Is a strict line of demarcation really needed between knowledge and communication? To have concrete and far-reaching results from the application of digital technology to archaeology, it is indispensable to launch a new cultural policy and a new policy for scientific research.

The methodology of research ought to offer an important space for discussion to cybernetic archaeology, in the etymological sense of the term. Without adequate epistemological reflection, a methodology incorporating a theory of information cannot exist, nor can an absolute cognitive value of technology. According to Bateson's cybernetics, context does not exist without communication, without an exchange of information. We must thus create new codes, new maps, new itineraries of knowledge. The factor of transmittability of culture will depend in a massive way on digital technologies.

Eureka!

A 3D model, be it individual or belonging to a VR system, ought also to be considered a dynamic process, i.e., dependent on interaction and feedback: in action and in 3D behavior we increase the "difference" in a cybernetic sense, thus we learn more and faster. The exchange between mind and model represents the key moment of interpretation: the image re-projected onto the retina is coded and interpreted by the mind;

and it is in this precise instant that we become aware of it. In the top-down phase, mental processing classifies the interpretation with respect to experience and contextualizes it on the basis of our cultural background. In the dynamic characterization of a 3D model is thus implied, as noted above, an acquisition of a greater amount of information, a structured whole, a whole greater than the sum of its parts.

Learning is a process that is essentially dynamic (i.e., an exchange between the learner and his environment), and interpretation results from the dynamic between interaction and the recognition of information. In this regard we recall a paradigmatic experience: working on the reconstruction of the archaeological landscape of Aksum, we used a panchromatic aerial photograph dating from the 1960s which we superimposed onto the digital terrain model. The same aerial photograph was systematically used by the archaeologists who worked for years on the ground and who had already identified numerous features that could be understood as possible ancient anthropic modifications of the terrain.

Superimposing the photo in texture mapping the DTM, we simulated in real time a flight at low altitude. This simulation, through the dynamics of interaction, allowed the archaeologists to recognize some new anthropic features of the landscape which up to that moment they had not noticed or reported. Whence came this additional information, given the fact that the photograph remained the same? Can we speak of something the archaeologists had simply missed or of their insufficient experience in reading aerial photographs? Such reasons certainly would not be applicable in this case since the archaeologists had been working at Aksum for many years (M. Forte, K. Bard, R. Fattovich, M. Foccillo, A. Manzo, C. Perlingeri 2001). The catalyst was identified as the 3D dynamic visualization, the multiple points of view offered by the simulation, and by the simulation of light and shadow in the virtual flight. Thus the difference in a cybernetic sense was determined by the dynamic nature of the model and by the process of interaction, from the holistic relationships of the model with the landscape and especially with the overlaid elements.

Another example of 3D cybernetic exchange was tried in the creation of a VR system of the Scrovegni Chapel (Forte et al. 2002), where a 3D cybermap was projected with the goal of representing the information and behavior of the VR system, following an interface that was basically aniconic, i.e., the space without the images that characterize and contextualize it. In the case of the Scrovegni Chapel, the pictorial registers of Giotto which make up the monument's palimpsest of images constitute the primary source of literacy and learning both in the real world and in the virtual. If, in contrast to this, we use as metaphors of navigation the geometrical solids of the cybermap, we enter into intra-informational behavior, i.e., we move in cybernetic hyperspace, in relationships that each feature of the map produces. The cybermap seeks to simulate, even if in a completely approximate way, the behavior of the mind which proceeds by means of associations, hypertexts, cross-references, etc.: each element of 3D space is interconnected and transmits the codes of the context to which it belongs.

From what we know about the activities of mirror neurons, the imitative process is a fundamental part of the dynamic of learning and refers to the way in which the mental images we perceive take shape (Rizzolatti et alii, 2001). The consciousness of action elsewhere produces an induced mental effect and from this the beginnings of knowledge arise. The awareness and the consciousness of information are key elements which distinguish the evolution of the human mind from that of the Neanderthals. We might call it the "cognitive big bang," because it revolutionizes thought and from it presumably arises the aesthetic principle which constitutes the artifact. The mind of Homo Sapiens in fact represents in toto all the faculties of knowledge, consciousness and transmittability of information and of codes.

A recent book, The Mind in the Cave (Wilson-Lewis 2002), draws attention to the cognitive revolution brought about by pre-historic cave painting. Wilson-Lewis posits a vigorous aesthetic action in cave painting, aimed at reproducing 3D immersive effects that increase the perceptual feedback of those who are admitted to the rite or to its transmission/re-processing.

The cavern becomes the 3D projection of shamanic vision, the immersive world of experience codified by means of symbols of cultural transmission. The extraordinary examples of Lascaux, Altamira and of other African caves offer the traces of the first cognitive experiments in the translation of artistic codes and symbolic complexes, perhaps the world's first system of the symbolic construction of knowledge and of learning from structured iconic models. The environment of the cave was presumably chosen for its immersiveness, its elite status and for its ability to produce feedback, experiential narrativity, three-dimensional communication, relation affordances (see below for the meaning of this term). Here the relationships are not evoked to demonstrate the supernatural character of the experience but to understand the physical world by means of hyperreality, an informational increase in what is real. Understanding of the world occurs through a process of intermediation, the shaman, and the visionary representation of relationships not yet codified in the real world. The prehistoric pictures thus become the map of the natural world, the catalyst of new forms of knowledge and learning.

CONCLUSIONS

The extraordinary growth of information and digital technologies in archaeology raises urgent new questions about research methodology, knowledge and the dissemination of culture (Forte, 2003). In particular, the technologies of 3D acquisition and representation such as computer vision, photogrammetry, and laser scanning create information that has a complexity unimaginable a few years ago and whose codes of representation still must be defined and investigated. We do not adequately understand the cognitive processes which connect the geometric complexity of models with their representation. The key element on which we construct our codes, our maps, is the perception which first selects what is high-priority information and then transforms it into knowledge.

Thus, we do not know the cybernetic geometry of models and the related autopoetic and self-communicative capacity, but we do know that each model contains a universe of discrete information which, when inserted into a digital ecosystem, is able to develop relationships, retroactions and interactions that were not suspected in advance and which modify our level of eco-informational knowledge. But we know that VR is destined to become a living organism made of artificial life and of spontaneous movement: it is not accidental that the concept of digital biology has already been theorized.

The methodological itinerary connecting knowledge and communication is a univocal process and ought to be inserted into a digital ecosystem, from bottom-up digital input (the methodologies of acquisition and postprocessing) to top-down digital output (the mental patterns and comparative analysis). In archaeology, in the phases of input we include the technologies of 3D documentation and modeling; in the output, the technologies of off-line and online VR (from the Web 3D GIS to virtual communities).

From this point of view it is clear that, if, first, information and, secondly, the process of understanding are maintained within a sequence of integrated digital protocols we have more opportunities not to lose data. In this methodological sequence learning occurs by difference, by means of cybernetic maps defined by transmission codes-something that Bateson describes as deutero-learning, or teaching how to learn to learn.

The digital reconstruction of the past is mainly a simulation process; this simulation represents a possible past and the interaction determines the level of communication and exchange with the space (uncoded), first, and the place (coded), then. The result of the mutual eco-interaction and feedback between users and environment constitutes the virtual heritage process. VR, for now mainly offline, but destined to migrate and settle permanent on the web, constitutes the concluding segment of a process of knowledge-communication, precisely because it is able to produce first difference, then knowledge and communication. Most part of the world seems to be interested mainly towards technological and digital aspects of the Virtual, but this direction is over-technological without a correct evaluation of the relations between mind and environment. We'd like imagine the Virtual like a 3D cyberspace in which artificial organisms and humans interact, move, grow on the basis of rules of the artificial societies and of the relations of the ecosystems; the realm of the Virtual, in technical sense, includes all the 3D worlds where the action/reaction/retroaction is free and in real time.

In network and collaborative environments cyberspaces and information are shared and the experience, subjective and objective, is embodied by avatars, actions, interactions, behaviors, navigations, dialogues, feelings, storytelling. This embodiment constitutes a new way of learning, communication and cultural transmission; in cybernetic terms it is a "mirror effect", we can display our action and mind in someone's embodiment. In this field a new project and virtual museum was created in Rome: "The Virtual Museum of the Ancient Via Flaminia". The "Ancient Via Flaminia" was one of the most important roads of the Roman empire and the project is aimed to reconstruct the ancient landscape with the related archaeological sites, villas, mausoleums, necropolis. In this case, a Multiuser Domain has been created through the Virtools Multiuser Pack and the network of five computers. The system allows users to share and exchange information through a map of reciprocal messages. Messages indicate personal or collective status; for instance the avatar's movement is a personal status while the command to activate a movie is a collective status. If an avatar reaches a status, the software communicates it immediately to the other users attending the session. In this way the system becomes continuously updated creating a common process of knowledge and development.

The goal of ECAI is to advance scholarship and understanding through greater attention to time and space. Our underlying hope is to support cultural heritage diversity, complexity, and preservation. The cultural patrimony (in Dutch the erfgoed) of all humans is our shared cultural history on this planet. Our future is to understand and cherish this complexity.

As an initiative, not an institution, ECAI affiliates work in multiple dimensions. ECAI Central at UC Berkeley has several active initiatives at any one time and work proceeds on at least three levels of information and infrastructure. ECAI projects include those whose primary goal is to collect, catalog, and make available specific cultural information. Research activities include focusing on analyzing, organizing, and improving understanding of specific topics or areas. These often include work that is in the nexus between cultural materials, technical tools, and understanding. Thirdly, ECAI participates in activities to support digital humanities and cultural projects on national and global levels.

ECAI affiliates are working on a wide range of projects and issues. A list of past and present ECAI affiliates is on the ECAI web site. ECAI Central works with some of these projects and coordinates collaboration among them. ECAI coordinates two international conferences a year where affiliates are encouraged to meet and present their work on a wide range of issues. ECAI Central also coordinates workshops and training sessions to assist groups in forming their own teams and projects.

As part of the overall ECAI vision, we see a potential for the development of a network of projects that can begin to encompass the history and development of Buddhism in the context of a religious atlas of Asia and eventually the entire world. Several projects already exist in Vietnam, Korea, Taiwan, and Japan. We invite you to join and support this initiative.

Sanskrit Digital Canon

ECAI, in collaboration with the University of California, Berkeley, and the University of the West, has formed the Sanskrit Web Working Group (SWWG), with a goal of increasing the quantity, uniformity, utility, and longevity of Sanskrit and other Indic texts on the Web. As a first step, the Working Group is developing appropriate standards, practices, and tools, using the Digital Sanskrit Buddhist Canon Website as a test case.

Linking of digital resources into integrated services

Some our ECAI work with the Institute of Museum and Library Science (IMLS) has addressed the issues involved in integrating beyond the individual cultural atlas to a system of data within a time and place context. This requires different types of tools to effectively navigate between the different contextual dimensions. Effective systems will also let users collect the information they are interested in into profiles or portfolios and use them in a variety of visualization modes.

LESSONS LEARNED

Cultural atlas design and development

Design requires the ability to bring together diverse resources from distributed providers to create a seamless product. The challenges increase as the amount and complexity of available information increases. It is difficult to make a system that is easy to navigate and presents a complex view of the cultural information. The skills and expertise required to accomplish this includes significant technical and content knowledge. A team of people is usually needed to bring together all the necessary skills.

Learning methodologies from scholars who have been working on these subjects for many years can save much time and avoid having to recreate or redesign systems. For instance, it is best to catalog your information on the smallest reasonable level of granularity possible. For example, if you have a collection of photographs, information on each image is usually preferable. Cataloging to include metadata on time and location at the smallest possible level of your data is also encouraged. Using WGS80 standard latitude and longitude is suggested. However, you can't make up location and time information if it is not available. Generalized information or ranges are better than nothing. Including documentation on the source of your information and the level of certainty and precision about your information is essential.

Creating a new generation global digital library - Digital Library 2.0...

The next generation digital library will bring together both the user interface tools for transactional use (view, sort, store, manipulate and redisplay) of a wide range of information and behind the scenes integration of massive amounts of data within multiple contextual dimensions. Collaboration of communities is needed in order to bring together the physical infrastructure, integration software, management processes, digital reference works, and interface tools needed for a digital library.

Benefits

The potential benefits of creating these new resources are myriad. It is possible to see new patterns in long know facts. It is possible to return to original source materials such as locations of archaeological finds with similar artifacts to discover trade patterns and to compare this to written and oral traditions of migration data. A new understanding of the development and dispersal of cultures becomes possible.

Future Developments

As a long-term vision, ECAI affiliates have been discussing the possibility of a distributed, Religious Atlas of Asia. This would involve collaboration between working groups to create a network of affiliated projects working toward enabling cross project integration of information.

Initial stages include collecting location and time information for temples, monasteries, shrines, and other religious sites. In parallel, work is proceeding on digital texts to indicate references to places and people. Digitization of inscriptions, through rubbings or other methods, and recovery of damaged materials through high tech methods are adding to the corpus of overall information. Historical image collections need to be digitized and hosted in a fashion that they can be accessed effectively through contextual metadata.

Eventually multiple types of data can be linked together in ways similar to those used in IMLS and NEH funded, ECAI Central projects on contextualizing cultural information. We can begin now to build the community of scholars to create this vision.

6

Worlds Earliest Buddhist Library

BACKGROUND

The Library Cave at Dunhuang in western China is the earliest extant Buddhist Library in the world containing tens of thousands of texts mainly in Chinese and Tibetan, the latter being the earliest extant Tibetan manuscripts in the world. But since its discovery in 1900, it has never been studied as a Buddhist library. In fact most scholarship has concentrated on the small percentage of social-economic documents in the cave rather than the more representative Buddhist manuscripts. One of the problems has been difficulty in accessing all the manuscripts which were dispersed to collections worldwide in the two decades after their discovery.

The International Dunhuang Project (IDP) was established as an international collaboration in 1994 to ensure the conservation, cataloguing, digitisation, research and, above all, greater dissemination of the Dunhuang and other Chinese Central Asian manuscripts. With centres in Beijing, Dunhuang, Kyoto, St. Petersburg, Berlin and Paris and collaborations with over twenty institutions worldwide it now gives free online access to over 150,000 high-quality images of the manuscripts along with transcriptions, translations, research papers and educational pages.

As well as manuscripts, the Dunhuang Buddhist Library also contained some of the earliest printed documents in the world. Just as the new technology of printing increased dissemination of the Dharma in the first millennium, today the new technologies of the web and digitisation are making it possible to allow anyone worldwide access to these important Buddhist documents. This will lead to a new era in the understanding of the history and traditions of Buddhism and its spread from India across the Silk Road to China.

Dunhuang and the Buddhist Library

Buddhist monks and lay believers started moving along the Silk Road from northern India in the first few centuries of our era, taking the Dharma first to the oasis kingdoms of the Taklamakan and then to those of northern China. Within a few hundred years Buddhism was thriving on the Silk Road. Monastery complexes were built in every town and Buddhist cave complexes were excavated from the cliffs at many remote river valleys: places of peace where monks could meditate. Texts also travelled with the monks and merchants and started to be translated into the languages of the Silk Road and Chinese. Chinese monks soon realised they needed to learn more and many hundreds travelled to India to visit the sites of Buddhism, collect texts and study under Indian masters. Other monks from India and Central Asia travelled to China and to sites along the Silk Road. The monasteries along the Silk Road built up libraries, even sending monks to China and India themselves to collect missing sutras and other texts. When returned they often stamped the sutra scrolls with a library stamp.

At Dunhuang, a thriving garrison town on the Silk Road, there were over a dozen monasteries and nunneries, several with libraries. By the ninth century the libraries contained tens of thousands of books. Many manuscripts came from Central China, but there were also palm leaf books from India, pothi from Tibet and many locally produced manuscripts. A cache of manuscripts, most probably belonging to one monastery library, were placed in a small side cave that had originally been built as a memorial chapel for a famous local monk, Hong Bian, Abbot of Dunhuang in the ninth century. His statue was moved out and the cave was filled floor to ceiling with this sacred cache. It also included many hundreds of fine paintings and banners on silk, as well as others on hemp and paper, and some printed documents. In total, the cave contained about 40,000 artefacts. In about AD 1000, for reasons which will probably always remain uncertain, the cave door was plastered and then painted over, hiding the entrance from view. The sacred cache remained safe in the dry desert air, undisturbed for almost a millennium until a Daoist monk, Wang Yuanlu, chanced upon it in 1900. He was renovating the Buddhist sculptures in the main cave and the workmen found the door when they were clearing sand from the corridor outside.

Wang Yuanlu rearranged the contents of the cave and also presented some of the finest paintings and manuscripts to local officials after making his report about the cave discovery. But nothing happened and he continued his work of renovation. In 1907, Aurel Stein, the first of a series of archaeologists arrived. Stein was an Hungarian-born British citizen. A French scholar, Paul Pelliot, arrived in 1908. Both bought a large number of manuscripts and paintings from Wang Yuanlu and shipped them back to their respective countries. In 1909-10 a Chinese government appointed envoy was sent to Dunhuang to remove the remaining Chinese manuscripts from the cave: he left the Tibetan pothi behind. But then Japanese and Russian explorers both went to Dunhuang and were sold more manuscripts by Wang Yuanlu. Stein also made a second visit and acquired a further 600 items.

Although it is very unfortunate that the cave's contents and their original arrangement was not documented and that the materials were dispersed worldwide, at least the vast majority were sent to public institutions where they were conserved, catalogued and made available to scholars. But the turmoil of the twentieth century meant that scholarship was often interrupted and it was not until the latter part of the century that reasonably complete catalogues and microfilms became available and scholarship started on this material.

The Importance of the Dunhuang Library Cave for our Understanding of Buddhism

As the only surviving Buddhist Library from this period, the Dunhuang cave is enormously important for our understanding of Buddhism along the Silk Road and in China.

Because there are multiple copies of certain texts in different languages, editions and translations, it can help us trace the lineage of texts. Many of the texts were acquired in central China and come from the imperial scriptorium. For example, there were large donations of manuscripts from the Chinese emperor to Dunhuang in 704 and 852. As such, they these provide very useful models of the standard editions of texts and translations in use at that time in China. These can be compared against the woodblocks of 1251 in Korea.

In other cases, the Dunhuang manuscripts are useful for providing copies of previously unknown or rare texts and editions. Others provide information on Buddhist practices and the monastic structure in Dunhuang at the time.

Buddhist Research to Date and the Factors Impeding Research

Despite the fact that this was a Buddhist cave library, scholarship in China has tended to concentrate on the small proportion of socio-economic texts in the cave. These were probably there by accident. When paper was scarce it seems that scrolls were recycled - the blank verso was used for a new text. Also, old discarded paper documents were kept, probably to make patches and repairs for Buddhist scrolls as they became damaged through use. We find many patches which contain text from a secular document on the back of Buddhist sutras. This is probably why socio-economic documents were found among the Buddhist texts in the cave.

Although some excellent work has been done by scholars worldwide on Buddhist texts, the socio-economic research has dominated the field. Moreover, the Buddhist research has generally focussed on one manuscript or a group of manuscripts. This is in large part owing to two factors: firstly, the dispersal of the texts and the lack of easy access to them for study; and second, the sheer quantity of the texts, numbers of languages involved and the fact that many contain non-standard characters and require manuscript reading skills. This latter factor means that meaningful research projects on the Buddhist Cave Library will have to be carried out by groups of scholars, rather than individuals. Such scholarship is not traditional in the humanities field and also requires grants to enable the scholars involved to meet to hold regular discussions.

By digitising the manuscripts and making them freely available to all on the internet with search tools and catalogues, IDP is addressing the first problem: that of access. It is also addressing the second problem both by working together with groups of scholars and by developing web tools which will enable scholars to work together remotely.

All IDP's activities have been largely dependant on external funds since it was founded in 1994. It is thanks to the generous support of sponsors and foundations that it has been able to achieve so much.

The Work of the International Dunhuang Project (IDP)

The work of IDP encompasses the following areas: conservation, cataloguing, digitisation, research and education. All are essential to ensure the preservation, dissemination and understanding of the Buddhist Library Cave.

Conservation

Since its inception in 1994, IDP has recognized the importance of the manuscripts in the Library Cave at Dunhuang for Buddhist studies. One of the primary tasks of IDP has been to ensure the long-term preservation of these sacred manuscripts and early printed texts. Although many are in excellent condition, others are very fragmentary due to being handled and used so much by the monks and scholars of the time. They need careful care and attention to ensure they do not disintegrate further. This is a time-consuming and skilled task and requires sharing of skills and techniques among conservators worldwide to ensure that the highest standards are maintained and that new generations of conservators are trained for the future.

IDP organises regular international conservation conferences, arranges staff exchanges, internships and publications. It recently launched a conservation section of its website with a multi-lingual glossary, videos, case studies, research papers and links.

Cataloguing

Publishing catalogues of the manuscripts is essential so that scholars and Buddhists can find the texts they want. IDP aims to make freely available online a basic catalogue of all the Dunhuang material by 2013, subject to funding. This will be fully searchable in several languages and also linked to more detailed scholarly catalogues and to online versions of the Tripitaka. In this way, Buddhist interested in reading different copies of a certain text will be able to find them very quickly and easily. By digitisation, they will also be able to read them immediately.

For example, IDP has been working with an international team of scholars coordinated by Professor Karashima to catalogue the Sanskrit manuscript fragments from the Silk Road in the British Library. Most of these are Buddhist texts dating to the first millennium AD. The material was previously unpublished and uncatalogued and so inaccessible to scholars. IDP will complete conservation and digitisation of almost 6000 fragments in 2009. Professor Karashima and his colleagues worldwide will continue work on the identification, transcriptions and cataloguing of these fragments over the coming years.

Digitisation

Digitisation is being used by IDP to ensure the preservation of the original manuscripts while making them far more accessible to all worldwide. With high quality digital images on the internet, anyone interesting in reading a certain text can do so freely without having to travel long distances or handle the original.

Because of the importance of this material and our respect for it, we are carrying out digitisation to the highest standards. While this is time-consuming and expensive, the resulting archives will last for many years and the level of detail captured by the digitisation process means that even the tiniest detail of any manuscript can be seen. IDP is training people worldwide to carry out the digitisation to the same high standards. Subject to full funding being available for both conservation and digitisation, IDP would be able to complete digitisation of over 95% of the Dunhuang Cave Library within five years. By the end of 2008, 60% of the material will be available.

Research

Once the material is conserved, cataloguing and digitised then it is immediately fully available to everyone worldwide for reading and research. But the internet and IDP can help facilitate research by developing links between scholars, internet links between relevant sites and internet tools for research.

IDP is already working with many scholars worldwide and is planning future projects on groups of Buddhist texts, including Chan texts in Chinese and Tibetan from Dunhuang; dated Buddhist texts from Dunhuang; and Tangut Buddhist texts.

Tools

As well as digitising the manuscripts and catalogues, IDP is also preparing tools to help scholars in their research. For example, we have recently developed software which is now freely accessible which enables scholars to 'cut-out' characters and phrases from the digital images of the manuscripts and store them with related information. This was developed for our own palaeographical research but has many other possible applications.

In 2008-9 we plan to develop an interface where scholars can compare two or more texts and images and which will automatically produce a critical edition of one or more texts, which the scholars will be able to supplement with their own annotations. The annotations can include links to other editions and images of the same text. By such means, we will be able to start compiling the lineages of texts across cultures, languages and time.

Conclusion

IDP has achieved much over the past ten years, making over 100,000 images of Buddhist texts freely available to everyone worldwide along with scholarly and educational resources. Its conservation and digitisation programmes are ensuring the long-term preservation of the manuscripts and artefacts from Dunhuang and elsewhere for future generations. Through its cataloguing, website, publications, lectures and educational programmes it has sought to spread information about Buddhism on the Silk Road to a much wider audience.

It still has many years of work ahead but with new technology will be able to achieve much more than originally anticipated and will, we hope, open up Buddhist studies to a new generation.

Imag(n)ing Shuilu'an: A Multimedia Archival Repository

Imag(n)ing Shuilu'an is a project designed to deliver results across a broad range of goals, both practical and conceptual in addressing the development of a rich, complex multimedia archival repository. The American side of the collaborative project was funded by the Andrew W Mellon foundation and Northwestern University. The Chinese side of the collaborative project was funded by the appropriate government agencies associated with the preservation of Cultural relics in China, at the local, regional and national level. The project produced a complete two-dimensional, high-resolution photographic record of the Shuilu'an temple while conducting experimental three-dimensional acquisition in a variety of formats, methods and procedures. It was designed to bring and disseminate the digital acquisition expertise, techniques and research efforts pioneered at Northwestern University to the Chinese partner institution, the Xi'an Center for Conservation and Restoration of Cultural Relics A network mediated model was created for the development of descriptive metadata associated with the media content.

Lastly it was designed to explore and evaluate the scholarly use of a unified network based interface. This interface enables the exploration of the different acquired data sets in context with the physical relationships of the original objects, and preserves those relationships as they reside in the temple. As such, this project in its entirety can be described as being use-neutral. Use-neutral meaning - Each aspect of the component phases of this project; acquisition, production, preservation and presentation, can be demonstrated to be useful across a broad range of disciplines. This paper will describe each of the developed data sets, and the tools developed to build the metadata and the prototype site to present the unified data set.

The Shuilu'an Temple is a freestanding temple located about 60 kilometers east of Xi'an. The site is composed of a small temple compound with five buildings. The target building, the main Buddha hall, is the only remaining structure on the site with any period art that survived the Cultural Revolution. There are apocryphal stories about why this happened.

Either through specific intervention of local villagers, or the protection of soldiers from a local air base, one of the five buildings on the site has survived into the present intact. The main Buddha hall is a Tang era structure with Ming dynasty (15th century) sculptures completely lining the interior of the structure. Often referred to as "Little Dunhuang", it is more accurately described as "Little Dunhuang in 3-D," as if the mural iconography of the Mogao Grottos were realized in dimensional sculpture.

The entire interior of the temple is encrusted with polychrome terra-cotta sculptures that range in size from one and a half meter freestanding guardian figures on the ground of the northern and southern sides of the temple to bas relief figures a few centimeters high with fine incised detail adhered to the walls. The polychrome paint surface of the sculptures is still largely intact though it is now close to 500 years old. There are around 3500 separate figures representing the many different iterations and forms of the Buddha as well as many scenes of the Buddha's life.

This site is at particular risk due to the fragility of the clay and the age of the structure. In the interior of the temple, some figurines have separated from the walls and collapsed. The complexity and detailed nature of the sculpture means that as one piece falls it affects surrounding areas of the temple. To protect the site, it was not opened to the public until recently, in deference to the fragility of the unfired terra-cotta structures. This leads to the last unique aspect of this site, it is to date, without bibliography.

2D Photography

The foundation of the digitization effort at Shuilu'an Temple is the 2D image as it was both the highest resolution and completely comprehensive. The entirety of the main temple interior was captured photographically generating thousands of images during the project's acquisition phase. These images resulted in three data sets: the 2D High-Resolution Composite Images, Virtual Reality Movies, and imagery for mapping photographic textures on to 3-D models.

2D High-resolution Composite Photography

The composite photography for the Shuilu'an Temple was achieved with a series of 2D images captured on a high-resolution digital camera, which were configured to document the entirety of each surface. All of the images for a texture were captured at the same relative distance from the surface in a large grid layout, which was later assembled in post-production to re-create the texture in its entirety, as a single unified piece.

The camera was positioned so that the lens was directly perpendicular to the portion of the texture in front of it. The camera moved across the wall at intervals, so that each frame overlapped the one preceding it by approximately 50%. Using this technique and then raising the camera by a 50% vertical frame interval from row to row, it was possible to photograph the entire wall in extremely high detail from the same perspective, even close to all surface edges and corners.

With the exceptionally large number of files created during the imaging of the temple, it was extremely important to keep a well-organized and systematic workflow in managing the data. A data manager oversaw the entire process- Starting before any image was captured when he helped determine the shooting marks and rows, continuing through the capture process, the transfer of images to the computer, checking the image quality and data sets, and finally backing them up for dissemination and transport.

Using Photoshop, the stitching process re-assembled the entire photographed texture as it had been sectioned out into small, overlapping blocks during production, back into one coherent piece, representing every photographed detail. The resulting stitched texture is a view of the wall which is impossible to see in real life, as it depicts every point of the texture as it is seen when viewed head-on, with virtually microscopic detail, from the lowest point near the floor, to the highest figure at the ceiling, and everything in between.

Virtual Reality Photography

In addition to the high-resolution 2D composite photography, Virtual Reality movies (or VR's) were created of both the temple interior and selected exterior spaces. Acquisition for each VR began with a series of still photos shot in a 360-degree rotation from a single point at the optical center of the camera. Each individual photo overlapped the adjacent photos by approximately 25%, so that once the images were loaded into the VR processing software, the redundant data in each photo could be automatically overlaid and stitched together to create one continuous panorama.

Each VR was covered in full horizontal 360 degrees (6 captures) with the vertical tilt of the camera set to 0 degrees (parallel to the ground), an upward angle (between 30 and 60 degrees), and a downward angle (between -30 or -60 degrees). Additionally, a single shot was captured with a vertical camera tilt of 90 degrees and -90 degrees. With this selection of angles, spherical panoramas, which give the user both a horizontal and vertical 360-degree perspective, were created.

As the VR is a viewing of a space from a single point, choosing the proper camera placement for each node was critical. Since the most effective panoramas are photographed with the widest lens possible, this means that to get sufficient detail, the camera must be positioned fairly close to the main focal texture of the panorama. When deciding the number of panoramas and location of each node within the Shuilu'an Temple, the photographer evaluated both the details of specific objects throughout that were suited to the presentation form of the individual VR movie, as well as the overall layout and sense of space within the entire temple, in order to most accurately and seamlessly represent the whole of the site.

RealViz Stitcher was used to assemble and render the panoramic TIF files. VR specialists arranged overlapping images into position. The software then automatically stitched the images together by identifying similar or identical lines where each photograph overlapped. This, was rarely an error-free process, and after the panorama was rendered and "unwrapped" into a TIF file, the VR specialist patched the rendered file with sections of the original source images to correct errors such as doubling or non-continuous lines, as well as insert properly exposed doorways and floor shots that exclude the tripod and VR head. Once the TIF was completely corrected, it was then "wrapped" again into the .mov format and viewed as a completed and corrected FLASH format VR file.

Texture Photography for mapping

The images that were used for mapping textures onto the 3-D models were acquired independently from those used for VR panoramas and coverage. The process was linked to the movement of the 3-D optical scanner and was designed to provide as much imagery as possible within the available space, which due to the complexity of the sculptures precluded 360-degree views. The attachment of the bulk of the sculptures to the supporting wall and their fragility meant that total coverage was not possible, like the scanning itself, textures were only captured on the surfaces available form the front of the sculptures and without endangering the objects. At each location point of the scanner nine separate images were acquired from nine separate angles. These images were also independently lit specifically for creating a set of files that when combined on to the mesh would result in

Exif Metadata

The first stage of developing the metadata for the project was in the act of photography itself. The Exif data generated by the digital cameras at the point of acquisition became the first component of the technical metadata. This data remains attached to the images throughout the postproduction process and is made available as a component when viewing the source images.

3D Data

To expand upon the 2D image work, select statuary and relief elements of the Shuilu'an. Temple were digitized as 3 dimensional models. Additionally, the entirety of the main temple was surveyed to create site cross-sections at millimeter accuracy. This work resulted in stand-alone end products and also created a framework for the virtual site coordinate system used to reintroduce spatial context to the acquired assets in the final presentation model.

3D Model Production and Site Survey

Linsinger Kultur of Austria was contracted to carry out the acquisition and initial stages of post-production for the 3D modeling and temple surveying. 3D model development began with the acquisition of data through photogrammetry, a process in which a grid is projected onto a physical object and photographed by a camera positioned at an angle to the projector. For each statue and relief scene, photogrammetry captures were taken from numerous positions, with captures overlapping to allow for alignment. This process was repeated until the entirety of the visible surface of the object was captured from numerous angles. Finally, hi-resolution photographs were also taken of each object for texture mapping. A total of twelve figures and six relief scenes from the North wall were scanned with this method, and 3D models were made of them.

During the acquisition process, Linsinger Kultur used the point data to created 3D meshes by converting all recorded points to a unified coordinate system. Due to the intricacy of the surfaces scanned and their physical integration into the temple wall, objects often contained small areas which could not be reached by the scanning process. These areas lacked point data and had to be modeled by eye in post-production.

Once the meshes were complete, photographic textures were mapped to the models by visually matching landmarks. The textured models were then exported as VRML files which were imported into 3D Studio and optimized for web-delivery. Meshes were welded to form complete, combined textures and then reduced in size. Finally, the models were converted to

Director Shockwave format, and viewer manipulation scripts were applied to allow for navigation of each model.

Spatial Metadata

Traditionally, cultural and archaeological site digitization efforts have resulted in disparate digital artifacts that are exhibited according to attributes of the finished media rather than the logic of the original site. To re-introduce site context to the data, the Imag(n)ing Shuilu'an web interface was designed to expose both the array of digital artifacts and, more importantly, the spatial relationships present in the physical site. To achieve this, a virtual site coordinate system was established based on the temple cross-sections. For the on-site temple survey, an origin point was defined at the lower, exterior, southeast corner of the central temple space, and measurements were indicated in meters. These characteristics served as the basis for the development of the virtual spatial framework.

For the virtual site coordinate system, each digital asset was assigned center point coordinates and bounds for 'depth', 'width', and 'elevation'. The coordinates were relative to the common origin point (0, 0, 0) for the temple model and expressed distance in meters from this point in the x, y, and z planes. The bounds described the distance in each plane from the center point coordinates that the digital object represented in physical space. The coordinates described the center of the bounding box. This spatial metadata was used as the foundation for a spatial browser interface that allows users to navigate a 3D model and floor plan of the Shuilu'an Temple.

Web

Web-Based High-Resolution Image Annotation Tool

The image annotation tool was developed to allow for collaboration between experts working in China and the US. Teams working in the United States and China each brought particular areas of expertise to the process. To connect these groups, the Online Annotator was developed. The software allowed image specialists in Chicago to provide completed media to content specialists in Xi'an over the Internet. The Xi'an team was then able to mark the high-resolution 2D images with annotations and metadata. There were two level of descriptive metadata developed. The fist was associated with the entire composite image of each surface. This was accomplished with a form attached to the image viewer with common fields. The region based annotator could then be used to enter image information about specific details present in the images once they had been enlarged.

The tool lets content experts explore high-resolution photographs in a zooming viewer and attach notes to specific image features. Annotations indicate interpretation of features, translations, and notes on condition and restoration. It is important to note that regions can be adjusted by the user to highlight features at any scale from small scratches to large sections of a scene.

The tool supports the use of multi-language controlled vocabularies to tag image features. Users select terms (in one or more languages) from a categorized tree and drag them into a list of terms attached to an image note. The tool supports user-defined forms for fielded information such as materials, measurements, dynasty, and translations. This could of course be modified on the basis of the experts and the type of mark up requested by different applications. In this particular instance the conservation and restoration specialists at the Xi'an Center provided the controlled vocabulary for these areas of their expertise.

The tool is implemented as a Flash / Actionscript 2 application embedded in the Plone content management system. The system supports easy sharing of annotations among a group of researchers that may be separated geographically. Sharing, full text search, and RSS notification of changes are all provided by this system. The goal of this tool is to put these high resolution images onto the screens of cultural specialists regardless of physical location of the original object or the location of the scholar. In our case post production on the images was conducted on site at Northwestern University, descriptive metadata was added at the Center for Conservation ans Restoration in Xi'an China.

Web-Based Scholarly Database and Viewing Tool

The Shuilu'an digitization project produced high-resolution images, panoramic VR movies, navigable 3D models, architectural floor plan and cross-sections, and descriptive and technical metadata. A rich collection of disparate datasets in two languages. This bilingual web application provides a mechanism for navigating the database and easy-to-use browser for these materials. The goal of developing this prototype interface was to be able to maintain the physical context of the objects, and enable exploring the representations of the actual objects while preserving the existing physical relationships.

The prototype Scholarly Web Interface achieves this by locating all data spatially. Users navigate using a floor plan and 3D model of the temple space. Each artifact and representation is shown as a marker in the space. The user can obtain information about each media item or artifact (thumbnail and description) by holding the mouse pointer over the marker.

Each item page includes tabs for displaying:

- o A viewer (depending on the media type) for images, 3D models, and panoramic VR
- o The metadata tab, showing artifact and technical metadata
- o The related items tab, showing the artifacts that are depicted and items that are spatially related to the item. Each link appears as a thumbnail that can be used to navigate to the item's page.
- o The sources tab, allowing access to the source media that went into making the product.

The Scholarly Database is a Zope 3 web application with the addition of Flash and Director / Shockwave client software. High-resolution images and surface annotations are displayed using the Northwestern University developed zooming image viewer and image preparation software.

Dissemination of Results

As part of the development of this project, a relatively large dataset was developed. In its entirety, it represented about 660 gigabytes of storage. Beyond the development of the work related to the prototype presentation model, the actual data was delivered in its entirety to both the Xi'an Center for Restoration and Artstor, for archival storage and appropriate dissemination. The developed pictorial data will be available for scholarly purposes with in the education community via subscription. One lasting result was the further development of the cooperative relationship associated with the digitization of Cultural relics in China. In May 2007, as part of the final report and delivery of the digital content a conference was called to report on the results.

We were priviledged to take part in the Chinese system of evaluation, which after a fashion, is structured to bring together a set of experts of various disciplines that in effect put the project on trial. After presentations on the results of the project, the experts convene, separate from the participants, and author a declaration on the project. The project was determined by the evaluation committee to be a success and there were many positive suggestions to come out of this activity. One is that progress is under way to publish the photographic results of the project in a large format Wenwu publishing house book in 2008. Another was to pursue ways in which the development of the prototype presentation model might be turned into both a permanent online presence and a potential field tool for future field work.

An interesting aspect of this joint project was the respective ongoing efforts associated with the parallel tracks required for administrative approvals in each of the two participants in this international project. The name of this project, Imag(n)ing Shuilu'an, is only applicable to the Andrew W. Mellon grant to Northwestern University. The project that provided funding for the extensive participation of the Chinese team was titled "Applications of 3-D Scanning and Digital Image Production at the Shuilu'an Temple in Lantian" and involved an equally extensive long term effort at navigating the administrative and logistical components at all levels of the effort.

As an illustration of this collaboration, this paper will conclude with the project timeline as developed by both the

American and the Chinese team for presentation at the concluding conference.

DIGITAL DOCUMENTATION OF BUDDHIST SITES IN TAMIL NADU

Buddhism came to South India during the period of Emperor Ashoka (c. 273-236 BC). The rock edicts of him found in the bordering regions of South India invariably refer to the Buddhist dharma. However, the prevalence of Buddhism in the Tamil country till 3rd-4th century AD is not attested by any material evidences. The reason may be that consistent with pan-Indian usage, perishable materials like wood and brick had been used for the construction of secular as well as religious edifices of the early times. However, the discovery of large number of Buddhist vestiges datable to 5th-6th century AD and onwards at various places in Tamil Nadu and Pondicherry indicate the wide prevalence of Buddhism in this region It appears that Buddhism was a flourishing faith during this period and has been patronized by the local people and the merchants and perhaps the rulers as well.

On the basis of the clue from the inscriptions, details given in the local and foreign texts and place names, a large number of sites yielding Buddhist relics are spotted all over Tamil Nadu and Pondicherry. The relics include stone sculptures and bronzes, excavated remains, inscriptions and paintings The author of the present paper documented all these Buddhist vestiges and also prepared a map of Buddhist sites in Tamil Nadu with inputs such as detail of the location, nature, description, date and status of the relics, excavations, detail photographs, published references, etc. (Please see the Annexure for the List of Buddhist Sites in Tamil Nadu and Pondicherry).

Kavirippumpattinam (110 12' 50" N; 790 52' 50" E) in district Tanjavur, the celebrated capital and port city of the illustrious Cholas of the Cankam age1 is said to have been situated on the confluence of the river Kaviri with the Bay of Bengal. This city was known by several names in ancient period, viz., Pukar, Pumpukar, Kakanti, Campapati, Kavirippumpattinam, etc. Ptolemy (c.1st century AD) refers to this place as "Kaberis Emporion" whereas Periplus of the Erthrian sea as "Camara.

Tamil literature of the first three centuries AD gives a vivid account of this celebrate port city of the Cholas, its harbour, sailors, merchants, merchandise, etc. A poem from the 1st-2nd century AD states that big ships entered the port without slacking their sails and poured out on the beach precious merchandise from different overseas countries and also other ports of India. Flags were fluttering on the mast of the ships heaving in the port of Pukar like huge elephants chafing. It also speaks of the tall light house on the coast summoning the ships to the harbour by the night, yavanar-irukkai (colony of foreign traders), etc.

This metropolis was not only famous for its seafaring activities but also well known in times of yore as a glorious centre of Buddhism. Many texts indicate the existence and perhaps the prosperous condition of the Buddhist establishments at Kavirippumpattinam.

The literature of Cankam period, the Augustan age which produced a bumper crop of Tamil, poetical work, do not make any direct reference to either Buddhist or Jain religions, although some references have been interpreted, often in a far-fetched manner, as an evidence of their presence. The Pattinappalai, one of the Cankam works, refer to a tavappalli at Pukar. If the tavappalli is considered as Buddhist monastery-then it would have been the earliest reference in Tamil literature of Buddhist settlement in Tamil country in general and Kavirippompattinam in particular.

There are literary references to a Buddhist monastery called Intira vikaram in this city. According to the tradition, the construction of these viharas are ascribed to Makentra (Mahendra/ Mahindra), son or brother of Ashoka and also God Indra. This vikaram as referred to in Cilappatikaram of c.5-6th century AD was not constructed by hand or machinery, but was a mind-born institution. It further mentions that Indra caused these sacred seven viharas to be built near the Mahapoti tree, sacred to Buddhist in the city of Pukar. Associating any place or religious edifices with the divine heroes or great kings in order to boost its importance and antiquity is a common tradition in India. Following this tradition the vikarams at Pukar are also ascribed to divine authorship i.e. to Indra and to the great kings like Ashoka or Makentra. There is no probability at all of Ashoka or Makentra having built a stupa or monastery in this area. This narration is tainted by legendary accounts and cannot be relied upon for the purpose of history.

The mentioning of seven vikarams at Kavirippumpattinam is quite interesting. Number seven seems to be a very auspicious number to Buddhist religion. The Manimekalai, composed with the intension of exaltation of Buddhism, is crucial for the study of the various Buddhist establishments at Kavirippumpattinam. It is, in fact significant that Manimekalai, the heroine of the poet-philosopher Cattanar, started as a Buddhist novitiate in Pukar, and is made to visit all the key centres of Buddhism in Tamilakam, Ilam (Ceylon) and South-East Asia. She adopted the robes of a pikkuni under the tutelage of Aravana atikal, the head of the Cankam of Pukar.

The existence of seven Intira vikarams at Pukar is conspicuously mentioned in the epics. The reference to the Intira vihara of Pukar and Mapoti occurs in the Cilappatikaram, when Kovalan narrates a dream to the brahmana named Matalan. After leaving Pukar for Maturai, Kovalan and Kannaki are said to have crossed the outer gate of this city and then passed by the seven vikarams known as Intira vikaram. From this statement in Cilappatikaram, it is clear that this Buddhist establishment was located in the outskirts of the urban area. The epic further states that Macattuvan after hearing of his son Kovalan's unjust execution by the Pandya king disgusted of worldly life and joined the Buddhist Cankam establishments in the Intira vikaram of Pukar.

This vikaram is also frequently mentioned in the Manimekalai. The Intira vikaram seems to be very popular at that time and was considered to be prestigious to compare it with other vikarams. While describing the Cera capital Vanci, Manimekalai mentioned a vikaram, which is said to be as beautiful as the Intira vikaram of Kavirippumpattinam. Interestingly, Cattanar speaks of a small pavilion made of crystal in a park called Upavana. A replica of the Buddha's foot print was worshipped there. The same author asserts that Killivalavan, a Cola king converted the prison into a Buddhist monastery at the request of the nun Manimekalai.

In addition, there existed in the same city, the Cakkaravalakkottam, a Buddhist temple near the burial ground. The shrine was also perhaps known as Cutukattukkottam ("temple in the cremation ground"), on the outskirts of Pukar. It was probably associated with the Kapalikas, a group of ardent Saivas, but later seems to have been converted into a Buddhist one. The Cakkaravalakkottam seems to have been a symbolic representation of the universe as per Buddhist notions. Manimekalai's accounts on Cakkaravalam says that it had the depiction in clay; the Meru hill, with its seven allied hills, four island continents, two thousand islets and the celestials residents in them. It is interesting to note that this description strikingly tallies with the plan of the remains unearthed from a site known as Pantuvasnuvara in Ceylon. The excavator of this site gives the following interpretation. "The plan reminds one of the manner in which the universe was conceived by the people of India and Ceylon in ancient times. The square structure corresponds to the mountain Meru, the ridges to the circles of mountains which are said to encompass it, and the depressions to the oceans in between these circles of mountains. Encircling all it was believed, there was Cakkravala, beyond which the light of the sun and moon does not travel. The central features being buried, the universe must have been here represented as seen from a point very much above the summit of Meru. There is thus reason to conclude that the circular site at Pantuvasnuvara is a representation in miniature of the universe..........the Cakkaravala."

The Cakkaravalakkottam at Kavirippumpattinam seems to be a model of a Vajrayana mantalam. In the same locality, there was a small Buddhist temple called Kuccarakkutikai which is stated to have enshrined Goddess Campapati. The name Kuccarakutikai perhaps denotes a small temple of Gurjara (Gujarat) style. The temple was also known as Mutiyal kottam (temple of elderly goddess). Campapati was considered the tutelary deity of the Buddhist at Kavirippumpattinam. In one of the pillars of the Campapati temple existed the pillar-deity known as Kantirpavai, a divine agent which has the spiritual power of explaining the past and future.

Barring the legendary portions and the miraculous elements, the details supplied by the twin epics about the Buddhist establishments at Pukar are reliable and are useful for the reconstruction of the history of Buddhism of that site.

EPIGRAPHICAL AND ARCHAEOLOGICAL EVIDENCE OF BUDDHISM IN KAVIRIPPUMPATTINAM

Coming to the epigraphical and archaeological evidences, the allegedly earliest epigraphical references to Kavirippumpattinam comes from Barhut, the famous Buddhist centre near Satna in Madhya Pradesh, which flourished during the second and first centuries B.C. The inscription engraved on a railing of the stupa here says that it was the gift of a nun Soma from Kakamti. (kakamtiya somaya bikkhuniya danam).

Kakamti is often identified by scholars with Kakanti, the other name of Kavirippumpattinam, which is said to have mentioned in the Manimekalai. There are few points yet to be settled before accepting this identification unanimously. Firstly there is no archaeological evidence available till date at Kavirippumpattinam to prove the existence of a Buddhist establishment of such an early time. Secondly the name Soma is not generally met with as a proper name in the Tamil land. Thirdly there is a less possibility of contact between the coastal town on the extreme south and the remote Buddhist centre in Central India, in the pre-Christian era.

BUDDHIST MONASTERY

Excavations were carried out by the Archaeological Survey of India in many places at Kavirippumpattinam from 1962 onwards. Interestingly the excavations in a locality known as Pallavaneccuvaram at Kavirippumpattinam yielded an excellent evidence about the existence of Buddhist vihara and temple. The excavations at Kavirippumpattinam revealed that the Buddhist monastic traditions of Tamilakam were to some extent common with those noticed in lower Deccan and Andhra Pradesh. The viharas noticed in Andhra Pradesh usually consisted of elongated wings and each of them contained several cells with a common verandah for each wing. The wings led into a courtyard where the shrine unit was located. It is not clear in the excavation at Kavirippumpattinam whether there was any typical chaitya temple either with the replica of stupa or a statue of the Buddha inside as was common in most of the monasteries found in Andhra Pradesh in the Hinayana and Mahayana stages respectively.

One full wing of the monastery, consisting of nine oblong rooms, each measuring 3.10 x 2.40 mt. was laid bare at Kavirippumpattinam. On the south of this row, at a distance of 2.25 mt. a number of offsets were found in the wall indicating the presence of a common- verandah to the monastery. There was a provision of drainages of waste water which moved through a drain under the monastery unit towards north. The cells are laid in the south-east to north-west direction. The extent courses stand up to a meter or more and the size of the brick was 42 x 24 x 10 cm average. A small bronze figurine of a seated Buddha in dhyana pose and a broken terracotta figurine of a goddess were found in one of the cells. The Buddha is shown on his head with the usniṣa, the cranial protuberance symbolizing Buddhahood, in the form of a flame. The shawl covered only the left shoulder leaving the right bare. Stylistically this figure is datable to the 5th century AD or little latter.

BUDDHAPADA

There was a Buddhapada found away from the vihara to its south. It was tilted upside down at the time of discovery, showing thereby evidence of disturbance of life and desecration of the site temporarily. The pottery associated with this layer is dateable to around 3rd-4th century AD. The Buddhapada was of Palnad lime stone and it has a small receptacle cut between the long toes of the feet and intended for the relic offerings of bone fragments and gold flowers, which were customarily deposited in it, related to the acharyas or the Buddha as the case may be, which it venerated. The buddhapada of similar nature of course without receptacle socket noticed at Nagarjunakonda is dateable to 3rd century AD by its inscription. The buddhapada at Kaveripumpattinam is also seemingly of the Theravada school. The buddhapadapair shows the auspicious symbols such as the purnaghata, svastika and srivatsa, etc. The four important events of the Buddha's life ending with chaitya worship representing mahaparinirvana are also depicted on the slab It is datable to 3rd-4th century AD. The available evidence suggests that the monastery belonged to the fourth-fifth century AD. It went into disuse in 5th century AD, perhaps due to the effects of intrusion of the sea.

It is interesting to mention that in the concluding lines of Abhidhammavatara, Buddhadatta the author of the work mentions, "In the lovely Kaveripattana, crowded with hordes of man and women, not belonging to impure castes, endowed richly with all the requisites of a town .... beautified with many gardens, and in a beautiful and pleasant monastery adorned with a mansion as high as the peak of Kailasa, built by Kanhadasa ....while I was living in an old house there, by me, who am shining with qualities, such as writing beautifully on good topics ....this was composed and propounded extensively." After closing the benedictory lines some later writer has added the colophon: This work named Abhidhammavatara was composed by Buddhadatta Achariya, inhabitant of Urugapuram

The second stage of buddhist activity at Kaveripumpattinam began in the form of a temple or caitya. The caitya or temple excavated on the south of the vihara was itself a best example of early brick architecture in Tamilakam. Notwithstanding mainly the foundation and ground floor pattern of the structure is preserved at present, it reveals about the techniques of the construction in brick, adopted at that time The temple, square on plan, built in panca ratha (five offsets) style stands on a lofty plinth of brick, moulded in jagati, padma, etc. The rectangular or 'L' shaped as well as the small square voids in the foundation, together with the large central squarish void, would seem to suggest that the structures stood in more than one storey height and perhaps the shrine was erected by a astylar corbelling principle with staircases leading to the upper floor from all the three sides except the east, towards which it was obviously facing. The sanctum was perhaps on the top of the central large square void, after spanned the void by corbelling method from four sides and provided with floor of the sanctum on its top. Except the traces of granite members, perhaps used as pillars the entire structure was of brick and stucco. The walls were originally decorated with the moulded bricks and stucco ornamentation. Traces of a few layers of paintings have also been noticed on the stucco pieces recovered in the excavation. There is no clear evidence about the height and number of storeys of the structure. But it could not be less than two or three storeys, as it was not uncommon in brahmanical temples of the age. The temple might have been surmounted by a vimana either on the form of kutakara or curvilinear The available evidence suggests that the temple seems to be later than the vihara and can be dated to the sixth-seventh century AD. The nature of some of the numerals engraved on the stone pillars, the style of the stucco heads of vyalas and dvarapalas etc. found in the site also indicate that they are of 6- 7th century AD.

Melaiyur, located very close to the site, where the Buddhist remains excavated at Kavirippumpattinam had yielded beautiful bronzes including a gilted Maitreya as a treasure trove in 1927. This place was a part and parcel of ancient Kavirippumpattinam. Even today a locality in Kavirippumpattinam is known by the same name. This place is often wrongly located by scholars in the Nakappattinam region. Dressed in royal attire and visualized as a crowned and bejeweled Boticattva, the gilted Maitreya figure has a socket beneath its hallow pedestal that suggest it would have fixed on either to the pedestal or prabha of a bigger image. This image is dated to 8th- 9th century AD. Perhaps the main image, by the side of which the beautiful Maitreya fixed originally is the magnifIcent gilted Buddha seated in front of a richly ornamented throne back, now in the collection of the Museum of Fine Arts in Boston. Originally it was flanked by two Boticattva probably Avalokitesvara and Maitreya.

BUDDHIST SCHOOLS AT KAVIRIPPUMPATTINAM

It is curious to know what sort of Buddhist school or sects existed at Kavirippumpattinam and also the reason for the disappearance of Buddhism there. Alike other parts of Tamilakam, Pukar witnessed all the main sects of Buddhism i.e., Hinayana, Mahayana and Vajrayana. Archaeological and literary sources clearly portrayed the existence of Hinayana tradition of symbolic worship and of Vajrayana deities such as Avalokitecuvara, Tara, Maitreya, etc. Cakkaravalakkonam is a model of a Vajrayana mantala. A circular brick structure containing the skull, jaw and ribs of an animal of bovine species found outside the vihara also perhaps indicates the sacrifice tradition of the Vajrayana sect. It is appropriate to point out here that even human sacrifices were also reported to in the Vajrayana temple of Hariti elsewhere.

THE DECLINE OF BUDDHISM IN KAVIRIPPUMPATTINAM

Buddhism seems almost wiped out of Kavirippumpattinam somewhere in the medieval period. Hardly have we got any traces of Buddhism after 8th-9th century. It is but natural; the reason propounded by the scholars for the vanishing of Buddhism in Tamilakam is also applicable to Kavirippumpattinam. In addition to these there seems to be another reason also for the decline of Buddhism in this coastal city. Say around 5th-6th centuries, Pukar's position as a major commercial and political centre was seriously affected perhaps due to the submergence of part or full of the city for sometime. In the subsequent period the maritime activities of southern Tamil land were shifted to Nakapattinam and it served as a major port city under the Imperial Cholas. The decline of commercial activity at Kavirippumpattinam perhaps forced the trading communities to abandon or lessen their activities in this city. This in turn perhaps brought to a crisis for Buddhism as it was mainly patronized by the mercantile community. Even the material evidence available, also proved that in the Tamil country Buddhist influence was confined mainly to the coastal town and urban centers where the trade activities were more. After Pukar, Nakappattinam being a prominent maritime centre under the Imperial Cholas took the responsibility of fostering the Buddhism and trade.

NAKAPPATTINAM

Nakappattinam (100 47' 18.13" N; 790 50' 32.04" E) was referred as Nikama by Ptolemy, Nagavadana by I-tsing, Pa-tan by Marco Polo, Malifattan by Rashiduddin and Navutapattana in the Kalyani inscriptions of Dhammaceti (1476 AD). It was a centre of trade and also of many religions including Buddhism. The close association of this place with Buddhism is revealed through the diggings in the localities called Velippalayam, Nanayakkara street and Maruntukkottala street in between 1856 to 1934 which have yielded as many as 350 Buddhist bronze images ranging from 9th century to 16th-17th century.

The mass production of bronzes in Nakapattinam indicates that this place was an important centre Buddhism in India and large number of Buddhist bronzes was exported from here to various other Buddhist centres in the country. As a result of maritime contacts between South India and South-east Asian countries, there existed in Nagapattinam a colony of Buddhist and also Buddhist temples (Pallis) and Viharas. During the reign of the Pallava king Narasimhavarman II (c.700-728) a Buddhist temple was constructed at Nakappattinam under the order of a Chinese king for the sake of perhaps the Chinese Buddhist who came to Nakappattinam from China for trade. It was during the reign of this Pallava king that the great Buddhist acharya called Vajrabodhi (661-730) proceeded to China to spread Vajrayana there, It is mentioned that he reached China in 720 AD after visiting Ceylon and Srivijaya and presented a copy of the Buddhist text Mahaprajna to the Chinese king. The Vajrayana that Vajrabodhi took to China is also called as Tantrayana and Mantrayana.

The Sailendras, the rulers of Srivijaya kingdom which comprised of Sumatra, Java and Malaysia peninsula were zealous Buddhists. They founded Buddhist establishments not only in their kingdom, but also in many other nations particularly India. An inscription at Nalanda in Bihar, India records that a Sailendra king Balaputradeva built a monastery there in the 9th century AD and at his request king Devapala of Bengal endowed five villages for its upkeep. Similarly the Larger Leyden copper plates of Rajaraja Cola (985-1014 AD) records that a Budddhist palli (temple) in the Culamanivarma Vihara was erected by the Kitara king (kitaratt-araiyan,) Culamanivarma at Nakapattinam, perhaps for his subjects who settled at Nakapattinam for trade purpose. The record states that Rajaraja granted the revenues of the village of Anaimankalam to the Buddha residing in the surpassingly beautiful Culamanivarma vihara, of high loftiness which belittled the Kanakagiri. It had been built in the name of his father by the glorious Maravijayottunkavarman who was born in the Sailendra family, who was the Lord of the Sri-Vishaya, who was conducting the rule of Kataha ... (and) who was the son of Culamanivarman, at Nakapattinam. The Smaller Leyden copper plates of Kulottunga Chola I (1070-1122) dated to 1090 AD records the exemption of certain taxes to the palliccandam villages of two Buddhist pallis at Nakappattinam at the request of the ambassadors of the king of Kataram. One is called as Rajendracholap Perumpalli and the other is Sailendra Chutamanivarma vihara alias Rajarajapperumpalli both built by the king of Katara (kitarattu araiyan). As stated earlier that the Sailendra Chotamanivarma vihara was constructed by the Srivijaya king Maravijayottunkavarman during the time of Rajaraja Chola I (985-1014) after obtaining permission from the later. Rajendracolap Perumpalli was probably constructed during the time of Rajendra Chola I (1012-1044) or Kulottunga Chola I (Rajendra is one of the title of Kulottunga Chola) before 1090 AD.

Interestingly in the collection of Rockefeller III, there is a Buddha bronze image shown standing on lotus pedestal. The pedestal is engraved with inscription in Tamil character datable to 11th cent. It records that this bronze image used as a procession deity in the Rajendracholap Perumpalli Akkasalaip Perumpalli was made by Nalankunakara Utaiyar of Cirutavur. The Akkasalaip Perumpalli is seems to be either the alternative name of Rajendracholap Perumpalli or a sub-shrine within Rajendracholap Perumpalli. Akkasalai means goldsmith and the Patinen visaiyam is a merchant guild of medieval period in South India. Perhaps the Akkasalaip Perumpalli was patronized by the merchant community.

Da tang xi yu qiou fa gao seng zhuan written by venerable Yi-Jing between 1 and 2 year of TianShou of T'ang dynasty (690-691 AD) mentions about thirty- nine Buddhist monks came to India through the south sea during the T'ang dynasty period and visited Nagappattinam perhaps to see the Buddhist centres there. The Guruparamparai of 12th century records that the Vaishnava Alvar Tirumangai of 8th-9th century robbed the gold image of Buddha from Nakappattinam and used the gold out of it for the construction of Ranganatha temple at Srirangam.

The description of a place called Tuta meaning an "earthern tower" in the flat land of Patan (Nakapattinam) in the Daoyi Zhiluels refers to the existence of a brick tower which had a Chinese inscription. The inscription quoted in the Daoyi Zhilue gives the date of construction of the tower as the eighth moon of the third year of Xianchun (AD. 1267).

It is stated in the Daoyi Zhilue the Chinese people came to Tuta and engraved the inscription in that year. Marco Polo of Venice visited Nakappattinam in the 13th century on his way to China and describes an eastern stupa in the flat land of Pa-tan (Nakappattinam) as follows, "It is surrounded with stones. There is stupa of earth and brick many feet high. It bears the following Chinese inscription: The work was finished in the 8th moon of the third year hien chw'en (1267).

It is related that these characters have been engraved by some Chinese in imitation of inscriptions on stone of those countries; up to the present time they have not been destroyed." The existence of Buddhist edifice constructed by the king of China at Nakapattinam is also attested to by the Kalyani inscription (AD. 1476) of Dhammaceti, the king of Pegu. According to the inscription a group of theras visiting Ceylon, being shipwrecked, travelled on foot to Nakapattinam and there they visited the site of the Patarikarama monastery. They worshipped an image of the Buddha in a cave constructed at the behest of the Maharaja of Cinadesa.

It is well known that a broken brick tower had been standing in Nakapattinam till 1867 when it was pulled down by the Jesuits. It was variously known as the Putuvelikopuram, Old Pagoda, Black Pagoda and Jaina Pagoda. Sir Charles Valentyn (1725) called it as Pagood China (i.e. Chinese Pagoda). The sketch of the monument prepared in 1846 at the instance of Walter Elliot provides clue on the architectonic affiliation of the edifice. It had the appearance of an elongated stepped pyramidal structure. Each storey is demarcated by a prominent moulding serving as a cornice. All the four faces of the storeys were relieved with pilasters and had an opening for a door or window in the middle of each side. This structure is closely similar to the multi-storied brick pagoda of China in character.

BHUTAMANGALAM/ BUDALUR (100 46' 46.67" N; 780 59' 00.68" E)

In the closing passage of the Vinaya Vinicchaya, Buddhadatta mentions, "In the undisturbed town of Bhutamangala, containing all kinds of people which was the navel of the great Chola kingdom and .... in the beautiful and pleasant monastery surrounded by well built outer walls and moat belonging to Venhudasa, brilliant with vanira trees lining the banks of the river .... by me who lived (there) in a mansion which clarifies the mind was composed in honour of Buddhasimha this compilation on the principles of Vinaya taught by Buddhasimha for the sake of my pupils and for the good of the Bhikkus who wanted to learn the Vinaya in a short time without difficulty. It was begun and finished during the reign of the blemishless Acchuta Vikkanta of the Kalabbha kula." Bhutamangala is identified with Bodhimangai mentioned in Periyapuranam and Budalur in Tanjavur district. Alutaiyappillaiyar Tiruvantati, Alutaiyappillaiyar Tiruttokai and Alutaiyappillaiyar Tiruccenbai, all the works on the life of Sambandar speak about his encounter with the Buddhist at Bodhimangai, a citadel of Buddhism. Periyapurnam also referred to Bodhimangai as a stronghold of the Buddhist. The large number of Buddhist vestiges found in Budalur and its surrounding areas attested the facts referred to in the literary sources.

KANCIPURAM (120 50' 03.92" N; 790 43' 59.02" E)

It seems Buddhism had a firm footing in the Pallava realm at many places. The Mattavilasaprahasana of the Pallava king Mahendravarman I (c.580-630 AD)

refers to the existence of many Buddhist vihara at Kancipuram, the capital of the

Pallavas. Yuan Chwang, the Chinese traveller who visited India in between 629-645, mentioned in his chronicle that Kancipuram had more than 100 Buddhist monasteries with above 10,000 brethren, all of the Sthavira school. The deva temples were 80 and the majority belonged to the Digambaras. He further mentions that this country had been frequently visited by Buddha and king Ashoka had erected topes at the various spots where the Buddha had preached and admitted people in to his order. The capital was the birth place of Dharmapala Pusa. Notwithstanding there are cases of bitter attack and slender by the people of other rival sects, Buddhism had a smooth sailing in Tamil Nadu during the Pallava period. In fact Buddha was happily considered by the Hindus as their god and included as an incarnation of Vishnu. The Pallava granta inscription in the Adivaraha cave at Mamallapuram mentions Buddha while enumerating the ten incarnations of Vishnu. The sculpture of standing Buddavatara Vishnu was carved in one of the niches on the walls of the Vaikuntaperumal temple at Kancipuram constructed during the time of Nandivarman II Pallavamalla (731-796 AD). Large number of Buddha images ranging from 7th century to 14th century is found in and around Kancipuram indicate that it remained as an important centre of Buddhism. An impressive figure among them is the large standing Buddha of about 7th century hailed from the premises of the Kamakshi temple.

The other Buddhist site in Tamil Nadu mentioned by Yuan Chwang is Molo-ku-ta or Malakuta which is 3000 li south of Kancipuram. During his visit he saw many remains of old monasteries. Of which very few monasteries were in preservation and there was only a small number of brethren. There were hundreds of deva temples and the professed adherents of the various sects, especially Digambaras were very numerous. Not far from the east side of the capital were the remains of the old monastery built by Ashoka's brother Mahendra (?) with the foundations and dome, the latter alone visible, of a ruined tope on the east side of the remains. The tope has been built by Ashoka to perpetuate the memory of Buddha.

PONDICHERRY REGION

The occurrence of many Buddha images of 10th -13h century AD in and around Pondicherry indicates that this area was flourished as an important centre of Buddhism at least in the period between the 10th to 13th century AD. The noteworthy feature is that almost all the places where the Buddha statues reported have yielded Chinese and South-East Asian potteries datable to 10th-14th century AD. Arikametu, the famous trading station on the east coast of India, yielded many Chinese potteries in addition to the pottery and other materials brought from Italy and other Western countries. The Chinese celadon wares found at Arikametu have the characteristic of the Sung and Yuan Lung Chuan wares and may be ascribed to circa 10th-12th centuries AD. The co-existence of the Chinese/South-East Asian materials and the Buddha images of identical period at Manappattu, Kirmampakkam, Arikametu (Ariyan kuppam), Pondicherry, etc. may suggest a close relation between them. It may not be erroneous to presume that the Buddhist vestiges found in this locality are either made for or influenced by the merchants who came to these trading stations for trade purposes from China/South-East Asian countries and settled there either permanently or for a while.

7

The Initiative, its Developments and its Future Applications

INTRODUCTION

ICOMOS, the International Council of Monuments and Sites, has since its establishment contributed worldwide to foster conservation and protection of cultural heritage. This has been also possible through the dissemination of internationally recognized guidelines and charters dealing with specific heritage issues. These guidelines have focused on specific conservation issues and have enhanced the public communication of the importance of cultural heritage to the wider public.

Several charters have underlined the importance of interpretation in heritage conservation, for example the Nara Document of Authenticity (1994), the Burra Charter (1999), the International Charter on Cultural Tourism (1999) and the Principles for the Conservation of Heritage Sites in China (2002). However no specific document has been dedicated to "define the basic principles of Interpretation and Presentation as essential components of heritage conservation efforts and as a means of enhancing public appreciation and understanding of cultural heritage sites", this is what the Ename Charter aims at. This proposed ICOMOS charter is the result of a more than five years long review process whose conclusion will be hopefully the official approval at the ICOMOS General Assembly in Quebec, Canada this year. I will delineate the beginning of the initiative, which started in connection with public heritage project in Belgium and which had led to the creation of a research center first (The Ename Center for Public Archaeology and Heritage Presentation) and of a specific International Scientific Committee inside ICOMOS (the ICIP, International Committee on Interpretation and Presentation) whose task, among other has been to coordinate the final draft of the Ename Charter. Finally some of the future development and activities related to the Charter such as the Illustrated Ename Charter Project will be discussed.

The Ename 974 Project

The first steps of this initiative were born in Belgium in the 1980s. In a village about 25 km south of the city of Ghent, the provincial capital of East-Flanders a project of archaeological excavation, research and public heritage presentation of a medieval site started through a locally sponsored project, the Ename 974 Project. This innovative initiative was the outcome of the collaboration between the Archaeological Heritage of the Flemish Community of Belgium and the Province of East-Flanders.

The village of Ename include the remains of a Benedictine Abbey, the medieval Saint Laurentius church and a natural reserve.

The project resulted innovative computer-based presentation techniques to explain to the visitor the archaeological site of the medieval Abbey without the use of physical intrusive reconstruction, the site was so transformed into an open-air museum. The medieval church was researched and an interactive application was installed to present its history and developments to the public.

A museum was also opened, hosted in a local historical house, to present the daily life of the Ename community from the early Middle Ages to the present day. It also presents an Archeolab, where visitors can learn about the various scientific methods employed in archaeological and historical research, and e an interactive character-based presentation techniques. This system called the Feast of a Thousand Years, is an interactive storytelling which allow visitors to choose objects connected with an historical character and to put them into understandable context, giving new life and meaning to ancient objects.

The natural reserve is remarkable for its ecological value and can be discovered through organized educational tour.

The project included a holistic view of the local heritage with the implementation of innovative techniques and the inclusion of local community who was actively involved and consulted during the project.

The Ename Center and the Ename Charter Initiative

Over the year the project team organized several workshop and developed new technologies for the public presentation of archaeological and historical sites, this led to the creation in 1998 of a permanent research center based on the site of the project, the Ename Center for Public Archaeology and Heritage Presentation. The founding goal of the Center was to develop and disseminate expertise relating to the public interpretation and sustainable development of archaeological sites, museums, historical monuments and landscapes both in Flanders and at partner sites throughout the world.

During the years a series of seminars and meeting were held in Ename and it became clearer and more central in discussions the need of standards for public interpretation and presentation. In the spring of 2002 an initial draft was formulated by the staff of the Ename Center in consultation with international scholars. Among them there was the former Secretary General of ICOMOS Jean-Louis Luxen who suggested that ICOMOS could be the most appropriate international institution for the formulation of an international charter on interpretation and presentation. This first draft was organized into sections of scientific and professional guideline, planning funding and management; tourism aspects and heritage education. The central theme of the draft and the role of heritage professionals into an integrated strategy of heritage planning. The draft was then circulated to international experts before the conference Heritage, Technology and Local Development held in Ghent in the fall of 2002. Their input was included in a subsequent revision of the charter and discussed in a workshop organized by the US National Park Service in Washington in November 2002. The feedback of the participants to the workshops confirmed the necessity of a new charter on interpretation and presentation. There was also present the executive director of US/ICOMOS, Gustavo Araoz who also suggested that ICOMOS would be the most appropriate institution for such a task

In January 2004 the Executive Committee of ICOMOS confirmed that the review of the now called ICOMOS-Ename Charter would be undertaken by an editorial group of international experts of ICOMOS and members of the Ename Center. The new editorial committee restructured the charter which resulted into seven more general principles dealing with: Understanding and Communication; Evidence; Context and Setting; Authenticity; Sustainability; Inclusiveness; Research Education and Training.

This new draft was reviewed during April-June 2004 by all the ICOMOS International Scientific Committees and other international expert. After this cycle of review a new draft was distributed to all the national committees of ICOMOS, their valuable comments let to the formulation of a new draft (Draft Three, 23 August 2004).

In an Advisory and Executive Meeting held in Bergen, Norway a subsequent review was recommended to give more time to the ICOMOS membership to evaluate the new proposed charter, this took place during winter and sprig 2005.

In May 2005 during the 8th International Symposium of US/ICOMOS, dedicated to the proposed ICOMOS Interpretation Charter was discussed and commented by the participants who also formulated a declaration in support of the charter. Their comments were also included in a subsequent draft., Charter Draft Four (dated 5 July 2005).

With the continuing review and reflection on the Charter the need for more formalised ICOMOS institutional sponsorship was felt this led to the formation of a specialized International Scientific Committee on Interpretation and Presentation, which was officially approved by the ICOMOS Executive Committee during the 15th General Assembly in Xi'an, China in October 2005.

In August 2006, the members of ICIP took over and continued the review process of the proposed ICOMOS Charter on the Interpretation of Cultural Heritage Sites as an official activity of the committee. A revised version of Draft Four (dated 31-07-06) was distributed to all members of the committee for their comments and suggestions. The result of this process which included also additional comments from members of the ICOMOS Advisory Council meeting in Scotland in September 2006, was Draft Five.

During the winter and spring of 2007, Draft Five was distributed once more to all ICOMOS National Committees and International Scientific Committees for another review and further recommendations. The comments received led to the formulation of Draft Six. During this last review cycle it became clear that the text was reaching its final form. After the second annual meeting of ICIP in March 2007 a Proposed Final Version was published (dated 10 April 2007). The Committee then voted and approved the submission of the text to the Executive Committee meeting in Pretoria in October 2007. The Final Proposed Draft was thus officially submitted to the ICOMOS Executive Committee for consideration and decision regarding its presentation for ratification at the 16th ICOMOS General Assembly in Quebec. The text of the Charter was officially endorsed by the ICOMOS Scientific Council by its Advisory Committee as well as by the ICOMOS International Executive Committee. This has opened the way to an Official presentation of the Charter for international ratification which will take place at the next ICOMOS General Assembly, in September 2008 in Quebec, Canada.

The Ename Charter Today

The final draft of the Charter, dated 10 April 2007, is a document which addresses the main activities of heritage interpretation and presentation. The former is defined as "the full range of potential activities intended to heighten public awareness and enhance understanding of cultural heritage site" and the latter as "the carefully planned communication of interpretative content through the arrangement of interpretative information, physical access and interpretative infrastructure at a cultural heritage site".

The seven principles in which it is divided clearly mirrors its objectives and deal with broad interpretative issues.

The first principle, Access and Understanding, refers to both physical and intellectual access, whose aim is to enhance personal experience, create connections with the site and increase public respect and understanding. Moreover, Understanding should be addressed demographically and culturally, taking into consideration the different audiences and also different cultural sensibilities which might require restriction to uses and interpretation on site.

The second principle, Information Sources, refers to the necessity of inclusion in all interpretative programmes of information from scholarly research but also from living cultural traditions. These sources should be accessible to the public and archived for future reference. Finally, alternative historical hypotheses and traditional storytelling should be incorporated through participation of members of associated communities.

The third principle, Context and Setting, refers to the wider social, cultural, historical and natural contexts which should be considered in interpretative programmes. This includes the contributions of different historical periods and cultural groups but also the natural and intangibles elements as well as the cross-cultural significance of a heritage site.

The forth principle, Authenticity, refers to the importance for interpretative structure to respect the traditional social functions and cultural practices of a cultural heritage. So every effort should be made to avoid irreversible alterations to the physical structures and disturbance to the life of local residents.

The firth principle, Sustainability, refers to the potential negative effects of interpretative programmes and infrastructure on the natural and cultural environment of the site. Is stresses on the importance of a rationale planning to ensure effective and regular maintenance of the infrastructures and equitable benefits to all the stakeholders.

The sixth principle, Inclusiveness, refers to the fact that interpretative programmes should be the result of active participation between scholars and heritage professional and stakeholders and associated communities. This means also multidisciplinary approach to research and inclusion of public involvement in expansion and revision of the interpretative programmes, with particular attention to intellectual property and traditional cultural rights issues.

The seventh principle, Research, Evaluation and Training, refers to the necessity of a continuous revision, review and assessment of any interpretative programme which should never be considered the final interpretation of any cultural heritage site. In this process all the stakeholders should be included and training should be considered as a dynamic and continuous activity in formal an informal learning.

CONCLUSIONS

The aim of the Ename Charter is to define basic objectives and principles of site interpretation in relation to authenticity, intellectual integrity, social responsibility, and respect for cultural significance and context. It does not aims to dictate on specific content of each interpretative programme. It recognises that the interpretation of cultural heritage sites can be contentious and should include conflicting perspectives as well as contributions from different historical periods. Its main focus is interpretation at, or in the immediate vicinity of cultural heritage sites, even if its objectives and principles can as well be applied to off-site interpretation. The Charter seeks to encourage a wider public appreciation of cultural heritage sites as places and sources of learning and reflection about the past, as well as valuable resources for sustainable community development and intercultural and intergenerational dialogue. The articulated history of the Charter, the remarkable feedback and discussions generated through this initiative in many international contexts, shows that it is really difficult to approach these themes starting from a top-down approach and, on the contrary, it is absolutely necessary the involvement of the global community of heritage, people, cultures, societies. Results and impact of the Charter depend not just from the institutions or from formal applications, but on the ability of the local communities to include the past in their present and future life.

The Charter has now undergone several review cycle which have adapted its principles to a wider audience in consideration of geographical and cultural differences. However to give it more practical application it was suggested to create an "Illustrated Version" of the Charter and this will be one of the main activities that ICIP will undertake in the next years. This illustrated version could re-approach the issue from a bottom-up perspective, from case studies, real examples, showing problems, opportunities, weaknesses.

The project aims at collecting relevant case studies worldwide which can best express the principles of the Ename Charter. A call has been circulated first among ICIP member and several other calls will be distributed in the next months. The aim is to create a database of projects and initiatives which will be available on-line on ICIP website for consultation and reference. The statistical and qualitative analysis of the database of research and heritage projects involving the Ename Charter, will permit to monitor these activities and to create the premises for validating the results.

The ICIP will also foster the application of the Charter to new interpretative projects and seek for suitable case studies project for the application of its principles of heritage interpretation and presentation.

Heritage can be not crystallized in a standardized form, it is a continuous evolving matter immersed and floating in a fast and uncontrolled process of globalization. Heritage can evolve in new contexts and frameworks, but we have to find a way to understand what happen, to re-elaborate to interpret and communicate these phenomena for the benefit of future generations.

This contribution wishes to extend the philosophy and experience of the Charter to the Vesak community and to put 'this message in a bottle' for gathering new feedback from this important conference, hopefully with new case studies from communities involved in this program. The Charter needs urgently to embrace diverse and multicultural communities and post-modern identities.

In 1999, the General Assembly of the United Nations adopted the resolution to recognize the Vesak Day as an International Day of Recognition of Buddhists and the contribution of the Buddha to the world. Now we need to adopt new methods and guidelines for the public communication of the importance of world heritage to the public: to communicate heritage means to save and transmit heritage to the future generations.

8

Appearance of a World of Buddhism

INTRODUCTION

The transformation of the medium for the transmission of Buddhism has always exerted a decisive influence on the formation of Buddhism in its history. This influence has not been one-sided from the sender to the recipient, but, to some extent, always interactive. Given that Buddhism is a historical product of continuous communication, a history of Buddhism cannot be properly considered without taking into account the transformation of the medium of Buddhism.

The emergence of a huge corpus of Buddhist scriptures in modern world as a result of the development of the media of its transmission, represented by the Pali Tipitaka in London and the Taisho Shinshu Daizokyo in Tokyo, has changed the image of the world of Buddhism, on one hand, and, on the other, has accelerated and multiplied the interaction among Buddhists and Buddhist scholars regardless of the historical order of the transmission of teachings.

In this presentation, I will show a future image of Buddhism on the basis of the construction of a scholarly network in the web dependent on the newly completed digitization of the full Taisho Tripitaka by the SAT project.

The Aim of the SAT Project

Human intelligence has come to express itself through a variety of modes in the course of its development of its inner reality through mutual interaction. With the advent of the digital age, we are presented with a dazzling array of new ways to assimilate, analyze, and transmit this knowledge.

The web service we have started to provide is being administered as one reflection of these new possibilities of expression, with the intent of broadly opening up to the world the fruits of Buddhist wisdom as expressed in the Taish? shinsh? daiz?ky?, a corpus of Buddhist text that has played a central role in the conveyance of 2500 years of Asian religious and philosophical culture down to the present.

While we are making available the Buddhist canonical texts which are originally the objects of religious veneration and belief, it is not our purpose to advocate the position of a certain sectarian doctrine or religious system. Rather, we hope to provide a means of access to the Buddhist scriptures and related academic materials of the highest quality, based on the most accurate historical research available. It is our intention to not merely provide new access to this body of knowledge in a passive manner--rather, we hope to provide a ground for the creation of new wisdom.

This web service, at the most basic level, makes available in digital format the text database of the Taish? shinsh? daiz?ky?. This corpus, over time, will be linked with and embedded in a wide range of lexicons, notes, other language versions, and academic research articles, based on the best philological, historical, and text-critical research available.

We offer this developing package of information starting from the basic assumption that the texts in the database, as well as all appended secondary research materials will adhere to the highest standards of accuracy and criticality, and will be developed from a wide range of perspectives. All available information will be treated objectively as possible, while at the same time being presented within a readily understandable and unified structure.

It is our hope that as a result of our efforts, the fragments of Buddhist wisdom which have come to be seen in diversified and narrowly specialized ways as the result of the process of history and the advancement of academic method, can in this great age of globalization be once again consolidated, and be reproduced in a format that will be beneficial to a wide range of potential users.

This great compilation of the corpus of Buddhist scriptures, which has been carried on the backs of countless persons over the passage through the vicissitudes of history, now continues in its life in a new form, turning into the future with unlimited new possibilities. If this site can serve its purpose in this effort, it will be to the greatest delight of all of us who have been involved in its development.

The Future of Buddhism on the Internet

There is a new era of technological innovation sweeping the world - the Internet's World Wide Web, a powerful communications system and learning environment. The use of the Internet should not be seen as just a new way to disseminate or repackage the Buddha's teachings but potentially as a base for an innovative online Dharma Community that offers alternative social and spiritual values.

The World Wide Web provides the Sangha with a unique resource with which to teach and communicate the Dharma. A student can access information, teachings, Suttas, educational resources, and potentially online teachers from anywhere in the world, anytime of day or night, free of charge, with content personally selected and instantly delivered. This ability for Buddhist organisations to publish information and educational programs relatively cheaply, and then make it available to the end user free of charge, is in line with the Buddhist Dharma tradition of 'ehi passiko', that is, an invitation to come and try it out for oneself.

Technological Innovation

Technology will continue to develop at a rapid rate with the Internet combining with modern appliances and machinery to allow new ways to communicate with, and control, the tools around us. The implications for Buddhist education and information technology systems are immense. With the spreading of the Dharma being a key directive of the Buddha, the Internet as a framework for the dissemination the Buddha's teaching fits well with Buddhist community dynamics. It provides a relatively 'toll free' platform for the community to access a great variety of Buddhist websites including traditional centres and monastery homepages, audio talks from the various traditions popular teachers, as well as many of their publications - all available as free downloads. Other resources available include, online directories, such as BuddhaNet's World Buddhist Directory database with contact details for monasteries and centres covering many different countries world wide, as well as online meditation courses, etc.

The challenge now is can the Sangha, that is, committed communities of Buddhists, use the tools and acquire the skills of the Digital Age? And further, can we find new ways and means of presenting the Buddha's teachings that are relevant to the digital world rather than the traditional methods of sermons and ritual that has little or no appeal to the technocratic generation.

It's not just technical skills that are needed but the motivation of selfless service and compassion - core values of the Buddha Dharma as expressed in the ancient Bodhisattva ideal. It is becoming increasingly self-evident that we have to move from the limitation of individual and national boundaries to a worldview of a shared planet.

If such a notion as an Online Dharma community is to come into being - and realistically it will probably take a generational change - it will either come about when young monks in the scholarly tradition in Buddhist countries go online or more likely, as is happening now, the new generation of Western Buddhists, who are not on the whole conditioned by a particular Buddhist culture, produce more appealing e-Dharma content for its own.

Buddhist Insights and the Internet

In a rapidly changing technological world, where many are stretched and stressed, we need to come to terms with the effects of such stress and pressure on the human psyche. I'm not suggesting that we create some 'virtual utopia' as the

Dharma tells us that there is no certainty and that things are inherently unstable and insecure. The experiential knowing of this Insight allows us to let go and be free of clinging to the known, to go with the flow. This acceptance of change and the ability to work with it is in the words of Alan Watts the "Wisdom of Insecurity".

The Internet gives us many opportunities to promote Buddhist values, understandings and Insights on a global scale. Buddhism has survived materially until now because of the practice of 'Dana', which is a culture of sharing and service, as opposed to the greed culture based on monetary values. This leads to misuse of the technology, as the motivation is merely to make a dollar, as we have seen in the collapse of the 'dotcoms', which views the Internet as a market place to exploit. In contrast to this we have the example to the earlier BBS (Bulletin Board System), which had a culture based on a genuine sharing and learning community offering a largely free service operated by volunteers. This is the way an online Dharma Community will ideally operate - as a focal point, a hub for community sharing and support.

In the spiritual vacuum that predominates in the contemporary world - with its preoccupation with having it all, there is a need to make known the contribution that Buddhist mental culture can offer. The techniques of meditation, for example, can be explained and illustrated very well on the Net through streaming audio and video, with the student being guided by an online teacher. The characteristic of the Internet is its interconnectivity - global interdependence. This is a core Buddhist understanding, a universal truth. Its appreciation leads to the maturity that moves from an ego-self preoccupation to an interconnectivity that empathises with all suffering life.

There will be a new emphasis on lifelong learning, on training and retraining, of development and innovation. This era of all-encompassing change will need to be accompanied by an ability to cope with the pressures caused by the new technologies, without becoming overextended and stressed. So we will need to have the skills to manage our own mental health through the healing practices and Insights that the

Dharma can give us. We are seeing that the psychological and healing side of Buddhism is being utilized by modern Psychotherapy, that there has been a shift from what were predominantly the ritual needs of lay people, to a search for help and support in an increasingly alienated world. So counseling services in the form of interactive multimedia via the net is the way of the future, as is demonstrated by the popular "chat culture" on the Net.

It is to be hoped that the online Sangha would be supported by, or be an extension of the locally based Buddhist establishments, as it evolves into a network of like-minded people - lay and ordained - who come together as an online community - followers of the Buddha - living out the Insight of the Dharma and communicating the Buddha's message of intelligence and compassion in this new Digital World.

eLearning or Electronic Buddhist learning can become a tool for spiritual as well as social development, when access is improved and learning techniques are refined. The reality is that it can never altogether replace face-to-face teachings but has added a new delivery medium that allows for skill-enhancement and easy accessible training. The worldwide Buddhist community will need to develop its own eLearning content with the traditions coming together and pooling their knowledge and skills and researching new ways of presenting the Buddha's Teachings out of compassion for this suffering world.

Information or Knowledge?

It has never been considered that the Buddha's teachings are to be found only in the text, actually in the past the Dharma was transmitted as much through oral teachings. There is a temptation to merely dump data (facts) online rather than exploit the new ways of presenting information that the technology provides. Data and information do not necessarily translate into knowledge.

The temple approach in teaching the Dharma is through sermons with the teacher and the content being unchallenged. The new way is through group learning via discussion. On the

Net its through chat groups where the teacher or moderator acts as a facilitator for an ongoing debate or discussion.

The benefit of Internet learning is that you have access to information, and you also have access to other people, students or experts. It's the combination of the two that provides an extra dimension than most other technologies. In fact what is happening now is that students are looking for resources themselves and then interacting with them. Learning from digitally enhanced animated characters that act as virtual teachers, could be the future of online learning. Experts predict that successful electronic learning computer programs will become more sensitive to human nuances and motivation - software that initiates human interaction.

What of the Future?

While for some it may seem rather futuristic, broadband and interactive technology and communication between high-tech and traditionally, low-tech products, promises an enormous expansion of the potential of the World Wide Web to create a true online community and enhance online learning and the way it is delivered. On the other hand, we have to work with the current limitations until the interactive technology matures. And especially, we will have to come to terms with the realities in developing Buddhist countries that are being left behind in the information revolution.

The traditional temples and bricks and mortar centres will continue to service people needs for the Dharma, yet this can be expanded and enhanced, and may I say made more relevant to the young, if the evolving online Sangha, who need resources in this developmental stage of Buddhism on the Internet, are supported in their aspiration to develop sophisticated digital Dharma, using the latest technology that is available.

The key Information and Communications Technology (ICT) issues and challenges faced by Buddhism on the Internet are to develop high-end courses in eLearning, quality multimedia content and establish training centres for young monks and nuns. This will require the cooperation and sharing of resources by Buddhist organisations, both in terms of technical expertise, training and funding. At BuddhaNet we are moving in that direction in as much as we have initiated a partnership arrangement with Mahachulalongkorn Buddhist University and the International Buddhist College (IBC) by setting up a World Buddhist eLibrary Database, which as it develops, will be a Digital Resource Buddhist Library for all traditions in various languages that can be freely downloaded from the Net as well as a Buddhist eLearning System. The training of the Sangha in information and communications technology skills is of vital importance. So it is also our aim to establish a Multimedia Training Centre at the new home of BuddhaNet at Bodhi Tree Forest Monastery, near Lismore, Northern New South Wales, Australia.

Simply because a teaching is ancient, that doesn't mean it cannot sit comfortably with the new technology. If the Buddha were alive today, he would surely be at ease in the digital world. There is a new generation growing up with the Internet's technologies, who regard it as the natural place to find information, for online learning and even for spiritual and emotional support. Can we hope that it will be a place that one goes to have a meaningful experience of the Buddha's Dharma as well - it's the future!

PROSPECTS FOR THE STUDY OF THE HISTORY OF CHINESE PHILOSOPHY AND THE ISSUE OF THE TRUE, THE GOOD AND THE BEAUTIFUL IN CHINA'S TRADITIONAL PHILOSOPHY

Confronting us now is the problem of prospects for the study of Chinese philosophy, that is, the problem of how to evaluate the traditional philosophy of China.

China is a great country with a long history and cultural tradition. The traditional philosophy of China is rich in content and displays an originality. Because society has moved forward and China has been in a backward position for more than one hundred years, and also because we failed to adopt a scientific attitude toward the study of China's traditional thought and culture, we have been unable, over a long period of time, to acquire a true understanding of the value of China's traditional philosophy or to find out wherein its shortcomings and problems lie. However, things have been changing dramatically in this area in recent years.

In addressing the rally commemorating the one-hundredth anniversary of Marx's death, Comrade Hu Yaobang, General Secretary of the Chinese Communist Party, said: "The mistaken tendency to split Marxism from the cultural achievements of mankind and pit the one against the other must be opposed; we must acquire a standpoint of respecting the knowledge of science and culture." Note that in recent years a very important phenomenon has appeared in China's newspapers and periodicals, namely, large numbers of articles on problems in real life all quoting philosophical remarks made in ancient China.

For example, Guangming ribao [Bright Daily] carried two short articles on February 19 this year. One article was entitled "Remain Tenacious after a Thousand Whettings and Ten Thousand Thrashings." It was a line from Zheng Banqiao's poem "On Bamboo," which the article used to encourage an indomitable behavior among the people. Another article, entitled "King of Wei Killed Those Who Knew him and the Fake King of Wei," dwelt on the suspicious character of Cao. The article quoted from the Chronicle of the Reign of Zhengguan what Emperor Taizong of the Tang Dynasty said to Feng Deyi: "Whether a flowing water is clear or muddy hinges on its source.

An emperor is the source of government and the common people are like the water. If the emperor plays tricks himself and expects his ministers to behave honestly, it is like a muddy source expecting its flow to be clear; it is unreasonable." The same goes for quite a few literary works. Take, for example, "A Wreath at the Foot of a High Mountain," a controversial short story, which describes how a PLA commander criticized a high-ranking cadre's wife. As an admonition, the commander quoted from Du Mu's "Epic of E-Pang Palace" by saying: "People of Qin had no time to lament and were lamented by people after Qin. If the people after Qin lamented but did not take warning, then they would be lamented by those after them."

There are many examples like this which can be found everywhere in newspapers and periodicals. All this has raised a question: Since so many ancient sayings in China still bear great significance for us today and serve as an indispensable guide to our behavior in real life, what value does the traditional philosophy of China have in its entirety? A re-evaluation of China's traditional philosophy seems called for.

If we say that philosophical ideas may embody the problems of the true, the good, and the beautiful, then does not the traditional Chinese philosophy have something valuable or unique in this regard? I think it does, and very remarkably so. We can approach this issue from two aspects, one is the contents of its thinking, another is its attitude toward life, both of which aspects are closely related.

CHINESE PHILOSOPHY AS A THREEFOLD INTEGRATION

Regarding the issue of the true, the good, and the beautiful, traditional Chinese philosophy has had three propositions exerting an extended influence over Chinese thinking: namely, the "integration of heaven with man," which inquires into the unity of the world; the "integration of knowledge with practice," the problem of an ethical norm; and the "integration of feeling with scenery," involving the creation and appreciation of artistic works.

Integration of Heaven with Man: the True

How to define the two concepts of "heaven" and "man" varies with different philosophers. Nevertheless, the "Way of Heaven" refers to the basics of the universe or the universe as a whole. The "way of man" often refers to the society of man or man himself. The relationship between heaven and man has always been the fundamental issue studied by Chinese thinkers.

Sima Qian called his Historical Records a book that "probes into the relations between heaven and man." Dong Zhongshu described what he said as a branch of learning that "studies how man is related to heaven." He Yan, one of the founders of the metaphysics of the Wei and Jin dynasties, called another founder, Wang Bi, a philosopher "qualified to discuss the relations between heaven and man." Tao Hongjing, the true founder of the Maoshan sect of China's Daoism (Taoism), said only Yan Huan, another Daoist leader, understood that "what he had in mind." was the problem "between heaven and man." The "relationship between heaven and man" has been explained by different theories in traditional Chinese philosophy. For example, Zhuangzi required that a "distinction be made between heaven and man," and Zhuangzi theorized that "those who are ignorant of heaven know nothing about man." Furthermore, the question of "relations between heaven and man" often has found expression in the discussion about the relation between "nature" and the "Confucian ethical code." Nevertheless, the mainstream of traditional Chinese philosophy has taken as its main task the demonstration or explanation of how "heaven is integrated with man."

Confucius said more about "human affairs" and less about "the Mandate of Heaven." Nonetheless, he also believed that "what the saint says" is in keeping with "the Mandate of Heaven." Mencius, it can be said, is the philosopher who first proposed the idea of "integration of heaven with man" in a complete sense. For example, he said: "Do with all your heart, know your lot, and understand heaven"; "keep up with heaven and earth above and below." Even though Xunzi advocated that a "distinction be made between heaven and man," his fundamental goal was to "bend the will of Heaven to our use" so that "Heaven" would be integrated with man. Laozi (Lao Tzu) of the Daoist school urged: "Man follows earth, earth follows Heaven, Heaven follows the Way, and the Way follows nature."

Even Zhuangzi who was "ignorant of heaven and knows nothing about man" had this to say: "Heaven and earth live side by side with me, and all things on earth are identified with me." He also said that the superior man can "communicate with heaven, earth, and spirit." Dong Zhongshu preached the idea that "heaven and man respond to each other" and his argument was that the two were integrated. The metaphysics of the Wei and Jin dynasties focused its discussion on the relationship between "nature" and "the Confucian ethical code." Even though Ji Kang (Chi Kang) and Yuan Ji advocated that the "ethical code be overstepped and nature followed," the mainstream of the metaphysics school stressed that the "ethical code" be reconciled with "nature." As Wang Bi embraced the idea that "the intrinsic and the extrinsic are like one," he urged that "the essentials (Nature and the Way of Heaven) be upheld to rule the non-essentials (ethical code and mundane affairs)." In stressing "the intrinsic and the extrinsic are like one," Guo Xiang believed "there is no intrinsic beyond the extrinsic" and therefore concluded that "heaven is the general term for all things on earth."

By the time of the Song Dynasty, the Confucian philosopher Zhou Dunyi noted in more explicit terms: "A saint shares virtue with heaven and earth," and "a saint aspires to heaven." Zhang Zai stated in his West Inscription: "That which blocks heaven and earth is my intrinsic; that which commands heaven and earth is my character." The two Cheng theorized that "the intrinsic and the extrinsic come from the same source" and stated: "In heaven it is destiny, in man it is character, and it is the heart that commands the body. They are actually one and the same." Zhu Xi stated that: "Heaven is man, and man is heaven. The beginning of man is derived from heaven. Since this man is born, heaven rests in him." And he added: "A saint ... is integrated with heaven." Wang Yangming said: "The heart is heaven. Stressing the importance of the heart upholds heaven, earth, and all things." "Man is actually one with heaven, earth and all things." "The heart has no intrinsic but takes the response of heaven, earth, and all things as the intrinsic." Later Wang Fuzhi advanced the idea that man moves along with the vaporization of heaven to explain why heaven is integrated with man. Said he: "Destiny is realized by days and character is formed by days." "There is not a day that heaven stops thinking of destiny, and there is not a day that man does not submit his destiny to heaven."

As far as traditional Chinese philosophy is concerned, the major philosophers, either materialist or idealist, all talked about the problem of "integration of heaven with man." By analyzing their theories, we can roughly arrive at the following conclusions: First, in traditional Chinese philosophy, the concept of "integration of heaven with man" gives expression to the idea of observing things in their entirety. It is a direct description rather than a detailed analysis; we can call it a directly perceived "overall concept." Second, in traditional Chinese philosophy, the basic argument for the idea of "integration of heaven with man" is, "The intrinsic and the extrinsic are like one": unity of the ways of Heaven and man is "both the intrinsic and the extrinsic," the Way of Heaven serving as the intrinsic and the way of man the extrinsic. This can be termed as an "'absolute' concept of unity." Third, traditional Chinese philosophy does not see the "way of man" as something rigid; what is more, it also sees in the "Way of Heaven" liveliness and unending vitality. "Heaven moves along a healthy track, and a gentleman should make unremitting efforts to improve himself." That human society should move forward and man should improve himself is due to the necessity of keeping up with the development of the "Way of Heaven." This can be called the unlimited "concept of development." Fourth, in traditional Chinese philosophy, "Heaven" is object and the "way of man" must be brought in line with the "Way of Heaven." However, "man" is the heart of heaven and earth; he should install a heart for heaven and earth. Without "man," heaven and earth would have no vitality, rationality or morality. This can be called the "humanistic concept" of ethics. The above-mentioned four concepts comprise the total implication of the idea of "integration of heaven with man" in traditional Chinese philosophy.

Integration of Knowledge with Practice: the Good

The problem of "knowledge and practice" is an issue of the theory of knowledge; in traditional Chinese philosophy, however, it poses even more a problem of ethics and morality. If, in traditional Chinese philosophy, a question of the theory of knowledge had not been linked to the question of ethics, it would have been difficult for it to be passed down as a part of traditional philosophy. Therefore the problem of a theory of knowledge is often also the problem of ethics. This is why the philosophers advocated that man not only should seek "knowledge" but must also pay special attention to "conduct" (practice).

What is the "good"? The criterion for the "good" can vary, but, according to traditional Chinese philosophy, unity of "knowledge" and "practice" must be regarded as a prerequisite. From the history of Chinese philosophy we can come across many different explanations about the relationship between knowledge and conduct. In History Classic [Chapter 1, "On Destiny"] it was said long ago that "it is not difficult to know but difficult to put it in practice." Later the two Cheng advocated: "Knowledge precedes practice." Zhu Xi was of the opinion that "knowledge and practice each give rise to the other." Wang Fuzhi theorized that "practice precedes knowledge," and Sun Zhongshan advanced the idea that "to know about a thing is more difficult than to do it," and so forth. Taking things as a whole, however, the concept of an "integration of knowledge with practice" actually has run through traditional Chinese philosophy from beginning to end.

Starting from the time of Confucius, the "agreement of one's words with one's deeds" has always been used as an ethical criterion to differentiate a gentleman from a villain. Confucius said: "A gentleman feels it a shame not to be able to match his words with actions." Mencius stressed "intuitive knowledge" and "intuitive ability." Even though he regarded the four factors including the "sense of pity" as inherent, he thought it necessary to "foster and enhance" benevolence, righteousness, rite, and wisdom, which had already become moral codes. As they could be acquired only through moral practice, he advocated that "a noble spirit be cultivated." Zhuangzi stressed "practice" as the purpose of seeking "knowledge"; at the same time, he also admitted the guidance "knowledge" provided for "practice." He said: "One who practices it knows it. One who knows it is a saint." As a saint, therefore, one must "integrate knowledge with practice."

By the Song Dynasty, the Confucian philosopher Cheng Yi, regardless of his opinion that "knowledge precedes practice," argued in terms of morality and self-cultivation that "one who knows but cannot practice is one who does not truly know." Therefore Huang Zongxi noted: "Mr. Cheng already had the idea of integrating knowledge with practice" (Academic Files of the Song and Yuan dynasties, Volume 75). Zhu Xi inherited Cheng Yi's theory that "knowledge precedes practice," but he stressed in particular that "knowledge and practice are mutually dependent" and "efforts on knowledge and practice should be pushed forward side by side." He reasoned: "In terms of sequence, knowledge precedes; in terms of importance, practice is more important." Therefore some people described Cheng and Zhu's as "a theory of integration of knowledge with practice with emphasis on the latter." Even though "knowledge" is the foundation of "practice," "knowledge is shallow when knowledge has just been acquired and yet to be put into practice." "When one personally experiences it, his knowledge will be deeper, different from what he knew before." That Zhu Xi stressed "practice" resulted because he basically regarded "knowledge" and "practice" as an issue of morality. This is why he remarked: "Wherever the good is, one must practice it. Having practiced it for a long time, it will become identified with oneself. Having identified with it, it will become a part of oneself. Failing to practice it, the good remains the good, and oneself remains oneself; they have nothing to do with each other."

Traditional Chinese philosophy often advocated "practicing the Way (Dao)." This idea perhaps had a twofold implication: One was to "take the Way as the intrinsic," another to practice the "intrinsic way," namely, to earnestly practice the "intrinsic way" one advocated. Therefore this is not merely an issue of understanding. As for Wang Yangming's theory of "integration of knowledge with practice," naturally we all know about it; however, our understanding about it seems not to be totally correct. By quoting his remark, "practice begins once an idea is struck upon," people often describe him as "ascribing practice to knowledge" and "taking knowledge to be practice." In fact, Wang Yangming did not equate "knowledge" with "practice" completely. The remark that "practice begins once an idea is struck upon" was made in the context of morality and self-cultivation. Immediately after that, he added: "If the idea is no good, we have to overcome it. We have to overcome it thoroughly and thoroughly so that the no-good idea will not lay hidden in our hearts." He also said: "A close and solid knowledge is where practice lies, and a conscious and precise practice is where knowledge lies. Efforts on knowledge and practice were originally inseparable. Only scholars in later ages split them into two and lost the essence of knowledge and practice."

In regard to the relations between knowledge and practice, Wang explained clearly: "Knowledge gives the idea to practice, and practice is the efforts made of knowledge. Knowledge is the beginning of practice and practice is the end result of knowledge." From the angle of the theory of knowledge, Wang Yangming could be suspected of "including practice in knowledge." In the perspective of morality and self-cultivation, however, emphasis on "integration of knowledge with practice" had a positive significance.

By the time between the Ming and Qing dynasties, Wang Fuzhi advanced the idea that "practice precedes knowledge" and "practice can also gain knowledge." However, he still stressed "integration of knowledge with practice" when addressing the issue of ethics. He opined that "knowledge and practice complementing each other is use and the two progressing alongside is achievement." He criticized Wang Yangming's idea of "integration of knowledge with practice" and called Wang "ignorant of the fact that they each have their own use and complement each other." Nevertheless, Wang Fuzhi, too, was an advocator of "integration of knowledge with practice." He said:

In calling someone engaged in pursuing knowledge and practice we mean he devotes himself to the pursuit of knowledge and makes every effort to practice. Because of his devotion and efforts, achievements can be made and divided. Since achievements can be made and divided, an order of succession can be established. Since an order of succession can be established, the antecedent and the subsequent can complement each other. From knowledge one knows what is being practiced, and from practice one practices what is being known. Thus it can be said the two progress alongside and therefore make achievements."

That knowledge and practice can progress alongside arises because the two, in the final analysis, are a moral issue. According to Wang Fuzhi's opinion: "A wise man is one who knows the rites. A man of ritual is one who practices knowledge. In practicing knowledge, all rituals will be properly performed; in knowing the rites all essentials will go to the mind. Thus one will improve oneself with each passing day and there will be no end to it." A saint "combines his intelligence with sincerity. He practices what he knows and what he practices becomes his knowledge." This is how traditional Chinese philosophy envisages that a man should behave himself.

Now prevailing in the study of traditional Chinese philosophy now is a viewpoint which asserts that "since the Song and Ming dynasties the neo-Confucianists, when discussing knowledge and practice, often mixed up this issue of theory of knowledge with the issue of ethics." It insists that this is where the limitations and mistakes of Chinese ancient philosophers lay. In this regard two questions deserve to be discussed.

First, neo-Confucianists since the Song and Ming dynasties, as a matter of fact, did not regard knowledge and practice merely as an issue of the theory of knowledge. They thought the issue important precisely because it was related to morality and self-cultivation. The final purpose of their discussion of relations between knowledge and practice was to improve moral cultivation. Therefore it is out of the question to assert that the neo-Confucians confused the issue of the theory of knowledge with that of morality. Second, as an issue of morality and self-cultivation, the theory of integration of knowledge with practice and the viewpoint of unity between knowledge and practice cannot be said to be without positive significance. Ethically, knowledge and practice cannot be separated into two ends; what is necessary is that "knowledge be integrated with practice." The remark made by Wang Yangming that "knowledge is the purpose of practice and practice is the work of knowledge; knowledge is the beginning of practice and practice is the end result of knowledge" can be seen as the best summary the Chinese ancient philosophers ever made about this issue.

Integration of Feeling with Scenery: the Beautiful

This is an aesthetic issue which Wang Guowei made a thorough discussion in his Random Talks about Poetry. He said: "Realm is the top quality in poetry writing. Having realm, a poem is naturally of a high quality and carries famous lines."

What does "realm" mean? Wang explained that "realm does not refer to scenery alone. Delight, anger, sorrow, and joy are also a realm in man's heart. Therefore a poem that can depict true scenery and true feelings can be said to have realm. Otherwise it should be said to have no realm." Obviously the term "realm" refers not only to scenery but to "sentiments" as well. In Jialing Manuscripts Discussing Poetry Ye Jiaying made a very perceptive explanation about Wang Guowei's "realm theory." According to Ye:

The generation of realm depends entirely on our sense of perception. The existence of realm depends entirely on what our sense of perception can reach. Therefore the outside world cannot be called realm before we can reproduce it through the function of our perception sense. Judging by such a conclusion, the theory of realm as advocated by Wang, as a matter of fact, can be traced to the same origin as the theory of interest by Canglang and the theory of romantic charm by Yuan Tingzhi.

Bu Yentu, after Wang Guowei, also said in his Questions and Answers on the Methods of Painting: "Landscape painting is no more than portraying feeling and scenery, and feeling and scenery is realm." This is why Wang Guowei remarked: "When people in the past discussed poetry, they divided the verses into those describing scenery and those depicting feeling. They did not know all verses describing scenery depict feeling." Obviously, Wang Guowei regarded as top-grade creative writings literary pieces that "integrate feeling with scenery." However, this aesthetic viewpoint of "integration of feeling with scenery" did not start with Wang Guowei.

Generally speaking, it was in the period of the Wei and Jin dynasties that the theory of China's literature and art truly became independent as a branch of learning, and by that time the idea of "integrating feeling with theory" already emerged. In Introduction to the Grades of Poetry Zhong Rong states:

The four-characters-to-a-line poems, they can be useful if they imply more in fewer words and model on works of literary excellence. However, the problem is they often involve a lot of words but connote little contents. Therefore few people learn to write them. The five-characters-to-a-line poems occupy the primary position in writing and stand out as the most savory among a variety of genres, thus winning the praise of being popular. Isn't it because they are the most detailed and truthful in narrating events, conjuring images, expressing feelings, and portraying things? Therefore there are three approaches to writing poetry: First, implication; second, comparison; third, narration. The idea that there is more to the poem than the words state is what we call implication. Citing things to indicate one's intention is comparison. A direct account of the happening, thus embodying the idea, is narration. Take the three approaches into consideration and choose the most appropriate, enhancing it with charm and force and polishing it with color so that those who read it will find unlimited savor and those who listen to it will be stirred. This will be a poem of the top grade.

A "masterpiece," a "superb work," should "express feelings and portray things." This was the forerunner of the idea of "integration of feeling with scenery." Xie Zhen, one of the later seven scholars of the Ming Dynasty, said in Four Seas Poetic Discussions: "Writing poetry rests on feeling and scenery. Neither can work without the other or conflict with the other." He also said: "poetry is the tool for the portrayal of feeling and scenery. Feeling melts inside, running deep and long; scenery shines on the outside, stretching far and wide." In Poetic Discussions from the Ginger Studio, Wang Fuzhi put it in an even clearer way: "In name feeling and scenery are two things, but in fact they are inseparable."

Those skillful in writing poems have unlimited chances to hit upon good ones. In an ingenious piece there is "scenery in feeling and feeling in scenery." "Feeling is generated from amid scenery and scenery is generated from amid feeling. This is why we say scenery is the scenery of feeling, and feeling is the feeling of scenery." "Once feeling is integrated with scenery, witty expressions are readily available." This last sentence perhaps constitutes the basic proposition for China's traditional theory of art and literature, manifesting its basic view on "beauty." In the traditional thinking in China, what is beautiful has always been linked to what is good. "The substantial is called the beautiful" refers to a spiritual realm in which one has a noble enjoyment. Having listened to the music of "Wu" (nothing, e.g. the silence that follows sound), Confucius commented: "It has all the beautiful but not all the good," and after listening to the music of "Shao" (few), he remarked: "It has all the good and also all the beautiful." Only music that "has all the good and also all the beautiful" can be regarded as the highest and most ideal music. This applies to music and should apply to other arts as well. An art that "has all the good and also all the beautiful" is designed to elevate man's spiritual realm and help him derive therefrom the highest enjoyment of beauty. Because of this, the creator of artistic and literary works must be one who has "realm" and his works must "integrate feeling with scenery."

THE STUDY OF CHINESE PHILOSOPHY AND THE REASON FOR BEING HUMAN

With regard to the true, the good, and the beautiful, why does traditional Chinese philosophy consistently pursue the three "integrations"? In my opinion, it is because the basic spirit of Chinese philosophy is to teach how one should behave like a man. To be a "man" one must have set for oneself a demand, must have an ideal realm of the true, the good, and the beautiful. One who has attained such an ideal realm in which "heaven is integrated with man," "knowledge is integrated with practice" and "feeling is integrated with scenery" is a saint. Therefore the prospects for traditional Chinese philosophy lie in bringing this demand to be a "man" in line with the need of the modernization program and thus realizing it. One's ideal may find expression in an immense variety of ways; nevertheless, one must have an ideal and noble spiritual realm. The three integrations advocated by traditional Chinese philosophy are in fact a unified realm for one to be a "man." They cannot be separated, at least theoretically.

The proposition of "integration of heaven with man," though designed to illustrate the relations between man and the entire universe, was made in view of man as center of the universe. The Golden Mean states: "Honesty is the Way of Heaven; to be honest is the way of man." "An honest man who hits the target without difficulty, arrives at the right idea without brain-racking, and conforms to the Way without hurry is a saint." The role of a saint is to "foster a heart for heaven and earth, create a life for living creatures, carry forward peak learnings for posterity, and open up peace for thousands of generations to come." Therefore a "man" (mainly, the saint) must behave in accord with the requirements of the Way of Heaven and should assume it his responsibility to fulfill them. Being alive in the world, one must not take a passive attitude; rather, one should "make unremitting efforts to improve oneself" so as to embody the evolution of the immense universe. In this way, one will set oneself a demand, find a reason for one's being, and foster a noble spiritual realm. Since one has set a demand for oneself and has a reason for one's being, the most important thing is for one to "integrate his knowledge with his practice." One must have an ethical standpoint unifying the two. The three programs and the eight items listed in the Great Learnings tell us the exact reason for this. It says:

The Way of the great learning lies in shedding light on the bright principles, being close to the people, and stopping at nothing but the utmost good. Those in ancient times who wanted to shed light on the bright principles for the world had to first bring order to their own kingdoms. To bring order to their kingdoms they had to first bring their own houses to order. To bring their houses to order they had to first cultivate their own moral character. To cultivate their own moral character they had to first set their minds straight. To set their minds straight they had to first foster a sincere desire. To foster a sincere desire they had to first carry knowledge to the utmost degree. To carry knowledge to the utmost degree they had to first inquire into the properties of things. Having inquired into the properties of things, they were able to carry knowledge to the utmost degree. Having carried knowledge to the utmost degree, they were able to foster a sincere desire. Having fostered a sincere desire, they were able to set their minds straight. Having set their minds straight, they were able to cultivate their own moral character. Having cultivated their own moral character, they were able to bring their houses to order. Having brought their houses to order, they were able to bring order to their kingdoms. Having brought order to their kingdoms, the whole world would be at peace.

"Knowledge" must be integrated with "practice." From "inquiring into the properties of things to carry knowledge to the utmost degree" to "bringing order to their kingdoms and peace to the world" is a process of cognition and, more important, a process of moral practice. Man must have an ideal. The highest ideal is to "achieve peace" and thus enable human society to attain a realm of "Great Harmony." The basic demand of a society of "great harmony" is that everyone should set on himself a demand, find a reason for his "being," and "not do to others what he does not wish done to himself." Said Confucius: "My way is consistent; it is nothing more than honesty and forbearance." Leading a life in this world, one should behave like a "man" and must enjoy the pleasure of "being a man" and appreciate the creation of the universe.

In order to have a genuine appreciation of the creation of the universe, one should have the ability to display man's creativity through the reproduction of "the creation of the universe." One should display the spiritual realm of man, the why and how for a man to exist as a man: this makes it possible to render a writing into a "masterpiece," a painting into a "superb work," and music into the "sound of nature." Therefore art requires "integration of feeling with scenery" so that "feeling is generated amid scenery and scenery is generated amid feeling."

In the realm of creation one reaches a situation in which the true, the good, and the beautiful are integrated; there lies the meaning of life and the man's highest ideal. Confucius professed: "At the age of seventy, I can do everything as my heart pleases without violating the rule." What he described was probably such a realm in which all one did and said was in harmony with the universe, human society, others, and oneself--both body and mind, inside and without. This realm of life is, of course, that of the saint.

Traditional Chinese philosophy still bears existential value precisely because it tells us the reason for being a man. To be a man is by no means easy,and it is even more difficult to have harmony with nature, society, other people, and oneself in both body and mind, inside and outside. But is this not necessary for today's world? Therefore we cannot underestimate traditional Chinese philosophy and ignore its proper value. Precisely because traditional Chinese philosophy tells us only the reason for being a man, it is inappropriate to set undue demands upon it in other regards, and it should come as no surprise to us that it is inadequate in certain areas. For example, it does not emphasize issues of logic and the theory of knowledge, nor provide a well-conceived demonstration of the structure of its own theory; we should not be overcritical of this. Under such circumstances, can we further develop traditional Chinese philosophy while engaged in studying its value? We should and we can. Note that, aside from the Book of Change, the pre-Qin Dynasty Confucians, seldom touched upon problems of ontology. Under the impact of Buddhism, however, neo-Confucians of the Song and Ming dynasties founded a very significant theory of ontology which made great progress and became neo-Confucianism. As the mainstream of China's traditional philosophy, thinking and culture, the Confucian philosophy has sustained today an even heavier impact than in the past. Having made a profound criticism of it, we are now reexamining its value. Is it inconceivable that we can develop it again, or impossible under the new impact to establish a new logic and theory of knowledge proper to it? Traditional Chinese philosophy should have a third phase development because "one must have a reason for being a man." Whether or not it can be developed depends on whether or not it can establish for itself a new system of logic and theory of knowledge. "Man can enhance the Way, not the Way can enhance man." The outcome depends upon our efforts.

9

System of Traditional Buddhistic Philosophy

Aristotle's Categories outlined the philosophical categories of ancient Greece, putting forward and thoroughly analyzing ten categories. Hegel's Logik outlined contemporary Western philosophical categories in a comparatively complete categorical system. Did China's traditional philosophy (China's ancient philosophy) have a categorical system? Why and how should we study the question of traditional Chinese philosophy's concepts and categories? This essay attempts to contribute to the discussion of these questions.

THE SIGNIFICANCE OF STUDYING THE CATEGORICAL SYSTEM OF TRADITIONAL BUDDHISTIC PHILOSOPHY

The study of the categorical system of traditional Chinese philosophy has its general and particular significance. Its general significance can be expounded in at least the following three aspects:

First, while the study of the history of philosophy necessarily requires the study of the historical function of philosophers and philosophical schools, the ultimate value of such a study is to reveal the necessary logic that determined the specific development of certain philosophical thinking in history. For instance, what is the necessary logic of the development of the pre-Qin philosophical thinking from Confucius to Mencius to Xunzi? A scientific history of philosophy with Marxism as its guiding thought should reveal not only the developmental causes of philosophical thought but also the inner logic of the growth of such thought. Since philosophy is a science of the most general laws of nature, society and human thought presented in the form of abstractions, the development of the content of philosophical thought is therefore a history of the continuous advancement of concepts and categories and of their continuous clarification, enrichment and growth. We should study how concepts and categories were advanced in the history of philosophy, how their contents became clearer, richer and more systematic, and how the categorical system became more complicated, more comprehensive and more systematic; we should conduct a concrete analysis of the development of concepts and categories. This will enable us to discover the laws governing the development of philosophical thought and reveal its inner logic.

Second, when we say that the history of philosophy is one of the struggle between materialism and idealism we do not mean to imply that this struggle and the development of man's cognition are two separate processes. It was the one and same process through which man's knowledge of the world has been developing in the struggle between materialism and idealism which manifests the law of the development of man's knowledge. As the process of knowledge calls for the use of concepts and categories, every stage of development in the history of philosophy is marked by differing explanations of certain basic concepts and categories out of which emerged materialism and idealism.

In the history of Chinese philosophy, for example, the struggle between materialism and idealism before the Qin Dynasty generally centered around the differing explanations of the Heavenly way and the human way, name and content, knowledge and conduct, and the variable and the constant. During the Wei and Jin Dynasties it centered around such pairs of concepts as being and non-being, essence and function, word and idea, ethical code and spontaneity. During the Song and Ming Dynasties it focused on principle and force, mind and matter, mind and nature, subject and object. A study of the development of concepts and categories is a key to the exposure of the law governing the struggle between materialism and idealism. What is more, this study will enable us to understand the necessity of the emergence of certain concepts and categories in the history of cognition and to overcome the shortcomings of maintaining an oversimplified negative attitude toward idealism which can be found in the past studies of the history of philosophy. Wang Bi was an idealist philosopher, but it was he who advanced some categories such as essence and function, the one and the many, word and idea "which help us recognize and master the focal point in the web of natural phenomena." Despite his incorrect presentation of these categories, his advancement of them marked a step forward in man's knowledge, which deserves recognition for its position in the history of philosophy. Only after Wang Bi first posed the concepts of "taking nonbeing as essence" and "forget the words having grasped the concept" did there appear Ouyang Jian's later theory of "The Word Expresses the Concept" (Yan jin yi lun) and Pei Wei's "On the Exaltation of Being" (Chong you lun). Therefore the study of the concepts and categories in the history of philosophy and their development constitutes an indispensable link in correctly appraising materialism and idealism in the history of philosophy.

Third, Engels believed that the study of philosophies of the past was the only way to temper one's theoretical thinking. A scientific history of philosophy can certainly play such a role, and a scientific history of man's knowledge essentially would be the history of the development of concepts and categories. Since concepts and categories in the history of philosophy reflect man's deepening knowledge, when we study its development we are rethinking in our own thought the process of man's coming to know the world. Of course we discard the accidental and secondary factors and grasp the essential, normative content. This process of rethinking inevitably deepens our own thought. In our study of the development of concepts and categories, we not only relive the process of mankind using concepts and categories to understand the world, but invariably use certain methods to revisualize them. That method can only be one of making a theoretical analysis of the contents of the concepts and categories and the relationships between them and the logical relationships in their development. Such a process of analysis itself is a kind of theoretical thinking. In this sense, this study can help us improve our ability for theoretical thinking.

The above-mentioned three points give only the general significance of studying philosophical concepts and categories, for that significance exists in the study of the history of any philosophy (e.g., the Western or Indian). However, the study of the study of the categories of traditional Chinese philosophy and its history of development has also its particular significance; namely, it will enable us to understand the characteristics and level of development of traditional Chinese philosophy. Western philosophy has its own categorical system; its characteristics and the different levels of development of its philosophical thinking at different historical stages are reflected in the development from Aristotle's Categories to Hegel's Logik.

The categories used in the primitive Indian Buddhism and the categories of the Kunya and Bhava sects of Mahayana, more or less in succession and each with its striking features, represent the fairly high level Indian Buddhism attained in logical thought and categorical analysis. Traditional Chinese philosophy has its own concepts and categories which gradually formed a fairly comprehensive system. Because of this it will not do just to take them in terms of the concepts and categories of Western philosophy, nor will it do to take them in terms of the Marxist philosophical concepts and categories.

Except for a few concepts taken from Indian Buddhism, the concepts and categories which have taken form in the long history of Chinese philosophy basically developed independently, hence their striking features. For example, the Heavenly way (Tian dao) and the human way (ren dao) as a pair of categories were very important in the history of Chinese philosophy.

Therefore traditional Chinese philosophy not only paid considerable attention to the study of the relationship between the Heaven and man, but paid special attention to the study of the relationships between man and man (society). Another example is the pair of categories ti and yong which contain the meanings of not only noumenon and phenomenon, but also base and function, whole and part, and abstract and concrete.

Such series of pairs of concepts and categories reflect not only the characteristics of traditional Chinese philosophy, but also the level of theoretical thinking at a certain stage of historical development. To make a not completely apt comparison: traditional Chinese medicine certainly has its own particular tradition with its own particular theoretical system, particular medical terms and concepts. Despite the fact that we have not found clear scientific explanations for some of the theories and achievements, since it does achieve good results in medical treatment it must reflect certain aspects of objective reality and contain fairly profound truths. Since concepts and categories are necessary conditions for the formation of knowledge and play a pivotal role in linking the subjective to the objective, definite concepts and categories reflect definite achievements made by man in recognizing certain aspects of objective reality through his theoretical practice; hence, different concepts and categories mark different depths of man's cognition. Therefore, when we study the concepts and categories at different stages of the development of traditional Chinese philosophy, we can see the level of theoretical thinking at the different stages of development of Chinese history.

In the history of Chinese philosophy, there are three periods during which schools made major contributions to the formation of the categorical system of traditional Chinese philosophy, namely, the various pre-Qin schools, the metaphysical school (Xuanxue) of the Wei and Jin, and the Neo-Confucianism (Lixue) of the Song and Ming Dynasties. When we compare the categorical system of traditional Chinese philosophy in the three stages with those of the Western philosophy, we are impressed by its distinct features and fairly high level. This comparison between the categorical system of traditional Chinese philosophy and those of other countries, nations and regions constitutes an important subject in comparative philosophy.

HOW TO STUDY THE CONCEPTS AND CATEGORIES OF TRADITIONAL BUDDHISTIC PHILOSOPHY

Fundamentally speaking, the study of the concepts and categories of traditional Chinese philosophy requires the scientific analytical method of Marxism. Merely to pose the concepts and categories used in the history of Chinese philosophy is contrary to the goal of our study. For that will not uncover the laws governing the development of philosophical thought, nor will it help us better to understand the laws of the struggle between materialism and idealism, or to improve our theoretical thinking; in particular, we will be unable to recognize the characteristics and level of traditional Chinese philosophy. To achieve our goal, it is necessary to use the scientific analytical method of Marxism to: 1) analyze the meaning of the concepts and categories, 2) investigate the development of those meanings, 3) analyze the systems of concepts and categories of philosophers or philosophical schools, and 4) study the similarities and differences between the concepts and categories of Chinese and foreign philosophies. It is only on the basis of such an analysis that it is possible to advance the study of the history of Chinese philosophy along a scientific path.

Analysis of the Meaning of Concepts and Categories

The advancement of one or of a pair of concepts (categories) marks the level of man's understanding of the world, yet it is up to us to make an analysis of the meaning of such a concept or pair of concepts. When ancient philosophers advanced a new concept they did not have as clear and scientific an understanding of its meaning as we do today; this is particularly true of the concepts they used to explain the origin of the world. For instance, Laozi (Lao Tzu) was the first man to advance the "way" (dao) as the paramount category in his philosophical system. This concept of the "way" he advanced as an antithesis to the contemporary concept of "respecting Heaven." By taking the "way" as the origin of the world, Laozi (Lao Tzu) certainly raised the level of ancient Chinese philosophical thinking. But what was the meaning of the "way"? Laozi (Lao Tzu) himself found it difficult to give a clear definition. He said: "I do not know its name; I call it Dao. If forced to give it a name, I shall call it Great." Therefore he used quite a number of adjectives to describe the "way," such as "soundless and formless," "eluding and vague," and "deep and obscure." Obviously, with the limitations of the objective conditions and their level of knowledge, the ancient philosophers found it difficult to give lucid definitions of the concept of the origin of the world.

Thus it is necessary for us to investigate the meaning of the concept of the "way" in the light of the book Laozi (Lao Tzu).1 The term "spontaneity" (ziran) was widely used by ancient Chinese philosophers but each had his own definition. It was Laozi (Lao Tzu), too, who was the first to use "spontaneity" as a philosophical concept, by which he generally meant non-activity. Wang Chong of the Han Dynasty continued this usage when he wrote: "The Heavenly way is spontaneous non-activity." By the time of the Wei and Jin Dynasties, the proponents of non-activity such as Wang Bi and Xiahou Xuan practically took "spontaneity" for the "way"--that is, the primal stuff of the universe. Xiahou Xuan wrote: "Heaven and earth operate with spontaneity and the sage functions following spontaneity. Spontaneity is the way, which originally had no name and Laozi (Lao Tzu) was forced to give it a name."

Even the same philosopher had different definitions for "spontaneity." We can use Guo Xiang's definitions of "spontaneity" as an example for analysis. He identified at least five connotations for "spontaneity." First, the actions of Heaven and man are "spontaneous." In his Annotations of Zhuangzi (the chapter, The Great Teacher) he wrote: "He who knows the deeds of both Heaven and man is a sage, means knowing the deeds of Heaven and man is spontaneity." Thus, Guo Xiang looked not only at the natural phenomena but also at man's deeds as in a sense spontaneous; in what sense could this be so? Second, "working for oneself" (ziwei) is "spontaneity." Guo Xiang said: "To say that matter is spontaneous means non-activity." He also wrote: "We value this non-activity and matter's working for itself." Then why is "working for itself" a kind of "non-activity"? Third, "being self-willed" is "spontaneity." Guo Xiang held that "working for oneself" is "spontaneity," but "working for oneself" does not mean acting wilfully, but "acting by one's nature," namely, "acting in accordance with one's nature, that is spontaneity, thus called nature (xing)." "According to spontaneity" means "according to one's nature," that is, neither making others succumb to oneself nor allowing oneself succumb to another. Fourth, "inevitability" is "spontaneity." Guo Xiang wrote: "Knowing the reality of destiny one will not seek what lies beyond it, but just to fulfill one's nature." One who "knows his destiny" will not ask for what cannot be done--this is called "spontaneity." Destiny here means "inevitability." Fifth, "chance is spontaneity." Guo Xiang wrote: "Things are all spontaneous, acting without knowing why or how it should be so." By not knowing the reason of action, "spontaneity" implies "chance." Therefore, when the philosophers were trying to explain "self-generation" they often employed such terms as "suddenly" or "abruptly"--all meaning that things exist without reason, the causality being beyond explanation.

According to Guo Xiang, "spontaneity" has the above-mentioned five inter-connected meanings, of which the last two are most important, that is, "spontaneity" has the meaning of both "inevitability" and "chance." Actually, they are a pair of antagonistic concepts and, from the dialectical point of view, are mutually connected and transform themselves into each other, with inevitability manifesting itself through chance. Guo Xiang used the term "spontaneity" to explain both "inevitability" and "change," precisely because he saw the relationship of mutual dependence between them: that a matter so exists is "inevitable" in one respect because "things emerge by themselves abruptly." In Guo Xiang's philosophical system, things must have these two aspects. From this analysis of Guo Xiang's definition of the concept of "spontaneity" we can see the general characteristics and level of the philosophy of Guo Xiang.

Analysis of the Development of the Meanings of Concepts and Categories

Not only do the meanings of concepts and categories differ from one philosopher to another, at different times they also differ in meaning. Nevertheless, if philosophical thoughts follow one another, it is always possible to discover the relationship of succession between these concepts and categories. The study of their development is extremely important for understanding the laws of the development of man's knowledge. In the following, we will analyze the growth of the concept of qi (often translated as material force, ether, or fluid--tr.) in traditional Chinese philosophy. Some thinkers as early as the Spring and Autumn period already discussed the impact of qi on man. For example, the Zuo Zhuan mentioned "the six qi" in the medical theory recorded in the first year of the reign of Duke Zhao of Lu (B.C. 541). By the Warring States period, qi became a general concept. People not only believed that the body of man was made of qi, but some believed that the spirit of man also was made of qi. In "White Heart," "Inner Function" and "Mechanism of the Heart" chapters of the book Guanzi, it was said: "As for essence (jing), it is the essence of qi"; "the qi of all things changes and thus becomes life"; "when qi goes to the ground, grains grow; when it goes into the heavens, there emerge the constellations; when it floats in the air, it becomes ghosts and spirits; when it goes into man's chest, the man becomes a sage," and "therefore when there is qi, there is life; when there is no qi, there is death," etc. According to these thinkers, among the "qi" there is an "essential qi," the life-giver. When such an "essential qi" enters the body of a man, he becomes wise and turns into a sage.

During the Warring States period this unscientific theory of "essential qi" was used to explain man's spirit. If we considered it materialist, it would be a materialist viewpoint with grave defects which, under certain circumstances, were used by idealists and turned into a component part of their system. It could also be utilized by the supernaturalists who transformed it into a basis for advocating "life without end."' We know that Mencius also talked about qi, and posed a sort of qi called the "qi of vastness" (hao ran zhi qi). The "White Heart" chapter of the book Guanzi mentions the "essential qi" that can give man wisdom and "this qi should not be checked by strength but should be accommodated by power (de)" which is to say, qi itself possesses an intelligence which should be consolidated by moral power. And in the theory of Mencius, his "qi of vastness is "obtained through accentuating righteousness." Obviously, qi in Mencius' theory has already become spiritual.

By the Han Dynasty, Dong Zhongshu went a step further and moralized and mystified qi which became the manifestation of the will and power of God. Dong Zhongshu held that qi had the power of meting out punishment and award, that there were good and vicious qi and that qi had emotions such as happiness, anger, grief and joy. So qi, though still retaining material appearance, already lost its material substance. Later, during the Han period, there were all sorts of superstitious explanations of qi which were indeed the outgrowth of the viewpoint of Dong Zhongshu.

From the historical data of the pre-Qin period and the Han Dynasty, we can see that the concept of qi is closely linked with questions of spirit and form, and thus has much to do with the question of the preservation of health, which often was deemed a means to becoming a deity. In Zhuangzi the "true man"(zhenren), the "spiritual man" (shenren) and others were often described as "with the spirit guarding the form to achieve longevity," "drinking dew and breathing the wind instead of eating grain," "unifying their nature and preserving their qi." They made their spirit integrate with their form so that they could accomplish the goal of "keeping their form perfect and replenishing their spirit to be merged into one with Heaven and earth."

The Lü Shi Chun Qiu includes numerous discussions of the "preservation of good health" and considers that to "achieve longevity," qi "should be made to flow constantly within the body," and "with essential qi renewed daily, the vicious qi will go and a full life span will be reached; this is called truth." In Huai Nan Zi the preservation of qi, of form and of nature are the same thing; moreover all are linked together with qi. The writers of both of these two books were influenced by the "theory of essential qi," in "White Heart" and other philosophical works. They all thought that "spirit" (jingshen) is also a kind of qi, or "essential qi which can reside or leave the body and that when spirit and body are at one, there will be long life."

Meanwhile, some philosophers of the pre-Qin and Han periods held a materialist view of qi and considered it to be the matter that constitutes the world. Xunzi held that everything in the universe, including man, was made of qi. He wrote: "Water and fire have qi but no life, plants have life but no senses, birds and beasts have senses but know not righteousness and man has qi, life, senses and also righteousness." The chapter "On Spirit" of the book Huai Nan Zi says that the universe was originally a murky body of original qi without any shape and that later the interaction of the positive and negative forces gave birth to everything, so "the dirty qi became worms and the pure essential qi became human beings." Wang Chong put it with even greater clarity.

He wrote: "The merging of the qi of Heaven and earth gave birth to everything," and that was the result of the movement of qi. He said: "When Heaven moves, it gives qi, . . . qi comes out and it gives birth to things." In order to oppose Dong Zhongshu's idealist view of qi, Wang Chong particularly pointed out that qi has no will, no aim. He said: "qi is void of ambition, purpose or scheme"; "qi is like smoke and cloud, how can it listen to man's request"? Nevertheless, like the book Huai Nan Zi, Wang Chong took the spirit of man (or the phenomenon of life) as "essential qi." He said: "Man lives because he has essential qi; when man dies, the essential qi vanishes." An analysis of the contents of the concept qi in the history of ancient Chinese philosophy reveals clearly the development of this concept. The three doctrines, or rather definitions, mentioned above, however, were all merged into the thought of Daoism (Taoism) toward the end of the Eastern Han Dynasty, which we will not discuss here.

Analysis of the Systems of Concepts and Categories of Philosophers (or Philosophical Schools)

Historically major philosophers, in establishing their philosophical systems, have invariably used a series of concepts and categories. Thus the study of the relationships between these concepts and categories is necessary for us to make a thorough analysis of their theoretical systems. The level a philosopher's thought reaches often can be judged by how richly and systematically his concepts and categories reflect the essential relationships between the objects they are meant to reflect. Divergent views in the study of a past philosopher (or philosophical school) sometimes arise from the lack of a comprehensive, systematic study of the system of concepts and categories of that philosopher or school. For example, if we merely take into account Guo Xiang's concepts of "being" and "nonbeing" and their relationship, we might conclude that he was a materialist. But the reason why Guo Xiang's philosophy was the zenith of the Wei and Jin metaphysical school was not that he put forth a view different from that of Wang Bi's on the relationship between "being" and "nonbeing," but that he had a fairly complete philosophical system, an analysis of which reveals that it comprises the following four groups of basic concepts. (Though there are other important concepts in Guo's philosophical system, we will not deal with them here.)

"Being" and "nonbeing": The central topic of discussion among the Wei and Jin metaphysicians was the question of "origin and outcome, being and nonbeing." The philosophy of Guo Xiang might be considered to originate from the discussion on this topic. Guo believed that "being" (the "being of everything") is the only thing that exists; it is constantly present; although being undergoes infinite changes and transformations, it cannot in any instance become nonbeing," and "we say the Heaven and earth constantly exist because there is no time they have not existed." As for "nonbeing," he held that the creator above "being," or "the nonbeing" serving as noumenon, is non-existence, that is, "nothing." Thus he said: "Nonbeing is simply nonbeing, it cannot produce being," and "I venture to ask whether there is a creator or not? If not, how can he create things"? Therefore, from the very beginning, Guo Xiang denied the existence of a "creator" above the being of "everything," or a "nonbeing" which is the antithesis of "being" which as the primal body serves as the basis for the existence of being. However, Guo Xiang's philosophy did not stop here, but went further.

"Nature" and "destiny": Since the existence of things is not based on "nonbeing" as the primal body, then is there an inherent cause for the existence of things? According to Guo Xiang one cannot say that the being of "everything" is groundless. Since things exist, their very existence is the basis for their existence.

Specifically, the basis of their existence is their own "nature": "Everything has its own nature and every nature has its limit." The "nature" Guo Xiang meant is "the reason that things are what they are" which has the sense of "necessity." Thus he said: "Each gets what he deserves by nature; there is no avoiding it nor adding more." He also said: "Things have their own nature, so the wise stays wise till his last day while the dull goes on being dull till his death, neither able to change halfway." As for "destiny" Guo Xiang defined it as "inevitability"; as he put it "destiny means things all act spontaneously without anything acting on them," and "being aware of the impossible." Obviously, his "nature" and "destiny" are two concepts he employed to prove the point that "being" alone exists and that "nonbeing" as creator or primal body is absolutely non-existent.

"Self-generated" and "self-sufficient": The "nature" of things is the basis for their existence, but how does this "nature" originate? Is its emergence with some purpose, or condition? Guo Xiang said: "Things exist by themselves without a source; this is the way of Heaven" and "the emergence of things is just out of their own accord." If the "nature" of a thing is not "self-generated," then it must be given by others or intentionally produced by a creator. Yet this thing becoming this thing and that thing becoming that thing is not something else making this or that thing emerge and exist, nor even making itself emerge and exist; therefore "self-generation" can only be produced "unexpectedly," "abruptly" and "spontaneously" by itself. Were there any reason or purpose for the emergence and existence of a thing, it would inevitably lead to the admission of the existence of an initiator.

Then what is the relation between one "self-generated" thing and another "self-generated" thing? Guo Xiang held that everything is "self-generated" and its existence is "entirely in keeping with its own nature" and therefore is "self-sufficient" (wudai). On the one hand, "self-sufficiency" is possible because "things produce themselves"; "things produce themselves without relying on anything else." On the other hand, anything can be "self-sufficient" as long as it "conforms with its own nature," and "is content with its own nature," "for when satisfied with its own nature, a giant roc does not despise the sparrow and the sparrow does not covet the heavenly lake and both are quite satisfied. Thus, big or small, all live in complacence." So, to insist on the premise that one must recognize that it is "self-generated" and "self-sufficient."

"Self-transformation" and "mutual indispensability": To support the concepts of "self-generated" and "self-sufficient" requires the solution of another question. Suppose everything exists by itself, this being this and that being that with one differing from another, then are not all the things related? Suppose all the things are relative, then are not they limited? Suppose they are limited, then are not they "insufficient" (you dai)? To answer this question, Guo Xiang advanced the concept of self-transformation" (duhua). By self-transformation," he meant that everything emerges and generates independently, hence "self-sufficiency" is absolute. If we try to seek the cause and basis of the emergence and generation of things, ostensibly we can pursue this question infinitely, but ultimately we can come only to the conclusion of "self-sufficiency." Thus he said: "If we try to find out what a thing relies on and what is the cause of its creation, there will be no end and finally we will come to self-sufficiency and the working of self-transformation will be obvious." In his "Annotations on (Zhuangzi's) Qi Wu Lun" Guo Xiang cited an absolute example. He said that the bodily form, the shadow and the penumbra are all beings of absolute independence, for "thus throughout the realm of things, there is nothing, not even the penumbra, which is not "self-transformed."

If one thing does not exist independently, then everything else is not independent, which will inevitably lead to the existence of a primal body (or creator) above "everything," serving as the basis of their existence and inevitably recognized as "a cause of creation and generation." Although things exist independently and self-sufficiently, as long as everything fully realizes its "nature," brings it into full play and "the wise stays wise till his last day and the dull goes on being dull till his death," then the ideal realm will be achieved where "Heaven and earth are not so long-lived but live along with me, and things in the world are not divergent, but the same as me." Relating this way to every other thing has the greatest function; that is, "the greatest function of mutual indispensability is the perfection of self-transformation." Seen from another angle, everything is indispensable as long as it exists. Guo Xiang said: "A man, though only seven feet tall, possesses the five constant virtues; thus this mere body is provided with everything in the universe. Therefore none of the things in the world can be dispensed for one day. With one thing lacking, the living will not have means to live; with one law lacking, the living cannot fulfill their natural life-span." Thus, everything existent is rational, inevitable and not mutually exclusive. This view appears to contradict the doctrine of "self-transformation," but it does not. According to Guo Xiang, everything that exists is rational, inevitable and not mutually exclusive precisely because, as the condition for the existence of everything else, everything fully and absolutely brings its "nature" into full play, creates itself and generates self-sufficiently.

From this analysis of Guo Xiang's system of philosophical categories, we can see that his philosophy finally arrives at the doctrine of "self-transformation," and the concept of "exalted being" (chongyou) is merely a bridge to "self-transformation." What is more, in Guo Xiang's system, only after the establishment of the doctrine on "self-transformation" can one support "sublime being" and a relatively thorough refutation of a "nonbeing" above everything as the basis of the latter's existence.

If we want to know whether a philosopher is a materialist or idealist, or the characteristic of his philosophy, its ideological relations with its predecessors and successors and its place in history, we must first make an analysis of his categorical system.

Analysis of the Similarities and Differences Between the Concepts and Categories of Chinese and Foreign Philosophies

A comparison between the categorical systems of Chinese and foreign philosophies will undoubtedly enable us to have a better understanding of the characteristics and level of traditional Chinese philosophy. Because of the breadth of this topic and the limited study conducted by this author, we can make only a rather superficial comparison here between Wei and Jin metaphysics and the Buddhist doctrine of Prajna introduced into China in that period.

The central theme of Wei and Jin metaphysics is the question of "being and nonbeing, origin and outcome." Therefore "being" and "nonbeing" are two basic categories in the Wei and Jin metaphysics. The Buddhist Prajna doctrine also discussed the question of "being" and "nonbeing" (or the "void," kong), hence Dao-an said: "Of the twelve books, Vaipuliya is most copious and its doctrine on the void of being and non-being is similar to the teachings of Laozi (Lao Tzu) and Zhuangzi, thus the doctrine of Mahayana has been easy to spread in China." The concept of the "void" (or "nonbeing") of the Buddhist Prajna school is actually different from the "nonbeing" advocated by Wang Bi and other Chinese metaphysicians, despite their apparent similarity. The Buddhist concept of original nonbeing, or Tathata in Sanskrit, has the meaning that "all the different dharmas are in their original nature void and empty" and that all things have no original actual forms. Wang Bi and other metaphysicians also talked about "original nonbeing" by which, however, they meant that everything "is based on nonbeing as its origin."

Although the two concepts of "original nonbeing" cannot be considered to be entirely different, they do have vast differences in meaning. In Wei and Jin metaphysics, Wang Bi's thought succeeded the doctrines of Laozi (Lao Tzu). In his philosophical system, the category "nonbeing" is one and the same thing as "the way" or "principle"; as he said: "The extreme of greatness is nothing but the way! . . . though it is important that it has nonbeing as its phenomenon, yet it cannot do without nonbeing as its noumenon"; "nothing exists without principle, everything operates according to its own law." Obviously, the "nonbeing" used by Wang Bi is not the "void" or "non-existence," but the "substance" of a thing. The "original nonbeing" of the Buddhist Prajna doctrine on the void only means that "all the different dharmas are in their original nature void and empty."

They held that everything is void of nature, but created through the association of hetupratyaya. From this one can see that the Buddhist Prajna School in its discourse on the void refers not to "substance," but to "non-existence." As for the content of "being," the Wei and Jin metaphysicians usually referred to "universal being," namely, all sorts of actually existing things whereas, on the other hand, in the translation of Buddhist scripts, terms denoting different meanings of "being" (existence) were all translated into the term "being."

After its introduction into China, Buddhism first attached itself to Daoist necromancy during the Eastern Han Dynasty and then to Wei and Jin metaphysics. The various schools of the Prajna doctrine formed by Chinese monks during the Eastern Jin period generally still used metaphysical thought to explain the teachings of Prajna until the arrival in China of Kumarajiva whose translations of Modhyamikasatra, Satasastra and Dvadasa-mikaya sastra of the Mahaprajnapramitasastra provided Chinese Buddhist with the material for understanding the true meaning of Buddhism Monk Zhao's On No Real Non-Existence is more or less close to the original meaning of "neither being nor nonbeing" of the Buddhist Prajna doctrine.

A comparison and analysis of the Chinese and foreign philosophical concepts and categories can thus show their characteristics and level of development as well as the impact of foreign culture on indigenous traditional culture and the process of a foreign culture being assimilated and becoming a component of the culture of the country (nation, or region) into which the foreign culture was introduced.

A TENTATIVE THEORY OF THE CATEGORICAL SYSTEM OF TRADITIONAL BUDDHISTIC PHILOSOPHY

The term category has myriad definitions in the history of philosophy in the West. Aristotle in his Categories treated it as the basic mode of being and put forward ten categories such as substance, quantity, quality, relation, place, time, state, action and passion. And Kant described his twelve categories as principles related to cognition or as the precondition for constituting experience. Lenin said: "Categories are stages of distinguishing, i.e., of cognizing the world, focal points in the web, which assist in cognizing and mastering it."2 A Dictionary of Philosophy published in the Soviet Union defines category as "the basic concept that reflects the most general and most essential character, aspect and relationship of the various phenomena and knowledge of reality.

"Category" then is generally explained from the two aspects of the existence and knowledge of reality: from the aspect of existence it is defined as "the basic mode of existence" or "the most general and most essential character, aspect and relationship of the phenomena of reality"; from the aspect of knowledge it is defined as the "precondition for constituting experience" or "focal points in the web, which assist in cognizing and mastering it." The necessary precondition for knowledge is certainly the reflection and manifestation of the "basic mode of existence" while the "basic mode of existence" is meaningful only in the process of man's knowledge. From what we listed above, we can see the relationship between "category" and "concept": a category is a basic concept whereas a concept is not necessarily a category. Thus, what we are discussing here is what are the categories or basic concepts of traditional Chinese philosophy. If, using the basic concepts of classic Chinese philosophers, we can form a system which shows how traditional Chinese philosophy identified and explained "the basic mode of existence" and which reveal the line of development of the traditional Chinese philosophical thinking, then we have proven that traditional Chinese philosophy does have a categorical system. This is presented first in the following diagram (see next page) and further explained below.

In this diagram, twenty pairs of basic concepts make up the categorical system of traditional Chinese philosophy. This is certainly a very preliminary proposition. However, despite its many possible defects, it is intended to initiate discussion and study on this question. Here the author would like to explain some points:

This diagram is divided into three major parts. Part I is intended to indicate what basic concepts are used in traditional Chinese philosophy on the question of the existence of the world; Part II is meant to show what basic concepts are used to present the form of being; and Part III is meant to show what basic concepts are used to denote the existence and knowledge of man. The relationship between "Heaven" (or the Heavenly way) and "man" (or the way of man) has always been a central theme for discussion in traditional Chinese philosophy and it is around this question that the struggle between materialism and idealism has been waged in the history of Chinese philosophy.

Zi Can was the first Chinese philosopher to make a proposition on the relationship between the two when he wrote: "The way of Heaven is remote, whereas the way of man is near." Confucius attached importance to the "mandate of the Heaven" but he gave even greater attention to the "affairs of man." Although he mentioned that he "began to know the mandate of Heaven as the age of fifty," he seldom discussed this question. "The master was seldom heard discussing the question of nature and the Heavenly way," reports the Analects which, however, extensively records Confucius' sayings on the question of the "way of man."

Mencius talked about "obeying nature, and knowing fate and Heaven," and the Doctrine of the Mean says: "Sincerity is the way of Heaven; knowing sincerity is the way of man." Xunzi said: "Grasp the way of Heaven and man. Laozi (Lao Tzu), the founder of Daoism (Taoism) said: "The Heavenly way is spontaneous non-activity," and he played down the importance of "humanness and righteousness" (the way of man). And Zhuangzi "was misguided by Heaven and ignorant of man" Dong Zhongshu, the Confucian master of the Han Dynasty, described his research as a study of "the relationship between Heaven and man." Sima Quan who was much influenced by Daoist thinking said that his Historical Records were works of "investigations into the relationship between Heaven and man and the changes past and present." The Wei and Jin metaphysicians concentrated on the question of "spontaneity" (the way of Heaven) and "ethics" (the way of man). Hence, He Yan said: "Only with people like Wang Bi, can you discuss the question of the relationship between Heaven and man."

The Song Neo-Confucians of both the School of Principle (Lixue) and School of Mind (Xinxue) strongly believed: "The supreme ultimate (the principle of Heaven) is simply an utterly excellent and supremely good normative principle"; the supreme ultimate is an appellation for "all that is good in heaven and on earth, and among men and things." The "principles of Heaven" and the "desires of man" are still a question of the relationship between Heaven and man. Even Wang Fuzhi still made this a focal point in his philosophical discourse. He held that "Rites, no matter how pure they are, are merely expressions of the principles of Heaven inevitably to be found in the desires of man," and that "the desire of man, when reaching superb altruism is the perfection of the principle of Heaven." Thus, traditional Chinese philosophy proceeded from the discussion of the pair of categories: (the way of) Heaven and (the way of) man, an indication of the main attention and particular content of traditional Chinese philosophy.

This diagram shows the development of the categories of traditional Chinese philosophy and their relationships. Proceeding from the study of the relationship between Heaven and man, traditional Chinese philosophy branches out into two parts: Daoism (Taoism) and Confucianism. Laozi (Lao Tzu) advanced the relationship between the "way" and "all things." He said: "The way creates one, one creates two, two create three and three create all things." He also said: "All things in the world are produced by being and being is produced by nonbeing," therefore the relationship between the "way" and the "way" and the "thing" is also represented by the pair of categories "being" and "nonbeing."

The Confucian School however proposed the categories the "way" and the "instrument" in the Commentary on the Book of Changes, which says: "That which shapes and is above is called the way and that which shapes and is below is called the instrument," and adds: "Change contains the supreme ultimate which produces two extremes," and "the alternation of yin and yang is called the way"; thus the relationship between the way and the instrument is reflected in the categories of the supreme ultimate and yin and yang.

The Han Dynasty witnessed some development in philosophical thought, but it seems that practically no new and influential philosophical categories were advanced. The Wei and Jin metaphysics upheld three philosophical classes, Laozi (Lao Tzu), Zhuangzi and Zhou Yi, which brought a gradual merging of Daoism (Taoism) with the Confucianism of the Zhou Yi system. This established the theory of a primal body as the origin of the universe, a theory with Laozi (Lao Tzu)'s and Zhuangzi's thought as the framework. The Wei and Jin metaphysicians used categories such as "essence" and "function," "stem and branch," the "one" and the "many" to illustrate "nonbeing" (the primal) and "being" (everything or the various manifestations of this substance). They used "spontaneity" (essence) and "ethics" (function) to present the relationship between the "originality of the universe" (primal body) and "human social relations" (the various social positions and codes), and used the pair of categories "idea" and "word" to explain questions on understanding the substance of the universe. From the Wei and Jin Dynasties and the Northern and Southern Dynasties, onward, traditional Chinese philosophical thought, under the impact of Buddhism introduced from India, evolved into the Neo-Confucianism of the Song Dynasty.

If the Wei and Jin metaphysical doctrine on substance has the thought of Laozi (Lao Tzu) and Zhuangzi as the framework, then Neo-Confucianism of the Song-Ming period alternately were based on an objective idealism (represented by Zhu Xi), a subjective idealism (represented by Wang Yangming) and a fairly high level materialism (represented by Wang Fuzhi). The philosophical categories of this period succeeded Wei and Jin metaphysics and also absorbed Tang Buddhist thought in the Sui and Tang periods. Thus, there was a confluence of the thinking of Confucianism, Daoism (Taoism) and Buddhism within a Confucian framework.

The most basic philosophical categories of the time became "principle" and qi, "mind" and "matter"; the question of "mind" and "nature" grew into the question of whether "mind is principle" or "nature is principle." Categories such as "subject" and "object," "investigation of things" and "fulfillment of principle" were used in the discussion of the question of knowledge and the categories "Heavenly principle" and "human desire" were used to discuss social issues.

Lenin in his On the Question of Dialectics wrote:

"Circles" in philosophy: (is a chronology of persons essential? No!) Ancient: from Democritus to Plato and the dialectics of Heraclitus.

Modern: Holbach--Hegel (via Berkeley, Hume, Kant). Hegel--Feuerbach--Marx.

In his Conspectus of Hegel's Book "Lectures on the History of Philosophy," he wrote: "Comparison of the history of philosophy with a circle . . . a circle on the great circle (a spiral) of the development of human though in general."4 Hegel's comparison of the history of philosophy with a circle, as pointed out by Lenin, is a penetrating reflection of the law of development of the philosophical thought. This is of tremendous importance in our study of the development of traditional Chinese philosophic thought.

From the above diagram, we can see that the development of traditional Chinese philosophy is roughly made up of three spiraling circles: The first covers the period prior to the Qin Dynasty; the Confucian School, including Confucius, Mencius and Zhuangzi (or the Commentary on the Book of Changes); Daoism (Taoism) including Laozi (Lao Tzu), the School of Shuxia (i.e., the "White Heart" and other works) and Zhuangzi; with the Han Dynasty forming a transitional period. The second circle was the period of the Wei and Jin Dynasties represented by Wang Bi--Xiang Xiu--Guo Xiang (or Wang Bi--Guo-Xiang--Seng Zhao). Buddhism was in vogue from the Northern and Southern Dynasties through the Sui and Tang Dynasties and after a period of development, Buddhism in China grew into several sects such as the Huayan (Avatamsaka) Sect and the Chan (Zen) Sect. The third circle covers the Song and Ming Dynasties represented by Zhang Zai--Zhu Xi--Wang Fuzhi.

In the second column of the diagram only three pairs of categories are listed, of which the most fundamental is the pair "quiescence" and "movement," whose manifestation is the pair "constant" and "variable," though in fact "positive" and "negative" are also peculiar manifestations of "quiescence" and "movement." Although many philosophers of traditional Chinese philosophy discussed the question of "quiescence" and "movement," little discussion on the question of "time" and "space" was conducted among Chinese philosophers (except for the pre-Qin philosophers of the School of Names and philosophers of the later Mohist School). Philosophical propositions in traditional Chinese philosophy seem not to have been restricted by time or space and they paid little attention to the question whether movement took place in time and space. That is why we have not included the categories "time" and "space" in our diagram.

The question of man (the way of man) was much discussed in traditional Chinese philosophy which was especially characterized by the study of the question of "morals" (ethics). Therefore careful consideration should be given to what should be included in the categorical system of traditional Chinese philosophy. In this diagram (column III) five pairs of categories (in fact not all of them are related to the way of man) seem to be sufficient as basic concepts. "Spirit" and "form," or the relationship between spirit and body, are used for the study of the phenomena of the human life. This was discussed from pre-Qin days onward, with materialists and idealists holding different views. The question of "nature" and "emotion" might be looked at as the key ethical issue. There have been divergent views on the question of "nature" ever since the pre-Qin days, such as "man is born good by nature," "man is born evil by nature," "man is born with a mixed nature both good and evil," "man is born neither good nor evil by nature," and "man is born good or evil by nature, all depending on the specific man," etc.

On the question of nature and emotion, there were views that "nature is good whereas emotion is bad," "nature is quiescent and emotion is active," etc. The Wei and Jin metaphysicians paid considerable attention to this question, but concentrated on a discussion of the difference and similarity between the sage and the ordinary man. The Song and Ming Neo-Confucians divided nature into "the universal nature" and the "humoral nature," with the former stemming from the "principle of Heaven" and the latter from man's inherent emotion and desire or from the qi that makes up the body. Hence, this is still a question of nature and emotion and the importance of ethical education is to "maintain the principle of Heaven and suppress human desire." The question of "knowledge" and "action" also occupies a very important position in traditional Chinese philosophy. Most of the past Chinese philosophers upheld both "acknowledge" and "action" and thought the latter was even more important. The categories "name" and "actuality" were always contained in traditional Chinese philosophy and the categories "subject" and "object" were borrowed from Buddhism, but all four are related to the question of knowledge. Therefore column III of the diagram contains categories involving existence and knowledge.

DISCUSSION

As the categorical system of traditional Chinese philosophy is a rather broad and complicated issue, it calls for an earnest and extensive discussion. The following are only preliminary views on some of the questions:

Should the categories in the categorical system be in pairs?

This question should be discussed in two aspects. On the one hand, in the history of philosophy, the philosophical categories used by a philosopher may not be in pairs. For example, the concept "spontaneity" used by Laozi (Lao Tzu) seems not to have its opposite in the book Laozi (Lao Tzu). The concept qi used as the most general concept in the "White Heart" chapter of Guanzi did not seem to have its opposite either. However, taking the development of traditional Chinese philosophy as a whole, the categories are in pairs. For example, the concept "spontaneity" is paired with "ethics" and "principle" with qi. On the other hand, everything is contradictory, with two contradictory aspects, of which one does not exist without the other. Therefore, the categories which reflect the essential relationships of things must be in pairs of opposites. Some of the philosophical concepts and categories of traditional Chinese philosophy indeed seem to have no pairs of opposites, such as the "mean." We certainly cannot say there is a "counter-mean." Yet an analysis of the meaning of the mean may possibly lead to the solution of this question. Confucius advanced his "doctrine of the mean" to oppose "excess"; he said: "Excess amounts to insufficiency." Thus, the "mean" has the sense of "middle" or "correct." Therefore it would be sufficient to have the concepts of the "positive" and the "negative" in traditional Chinese philosophy since "mean" is included in the meaning of "positive."

Not all the categorical systems used by Western philosophers necessarily reflect the unity of opposites. Among the ten categories used by Aristotle, some can be paired up as opposites such as "quality" and "quantity," but "substance" has no specific opposite, though the other nine categories might be considered to be the opposites of "substance." The twelve categories used by Kant and the categories of the categorical system of Hegel's Logik are mostly pairs of opposites. Though divergent in their views on the categorical system, all Marxist philosophers agree that categories are in pairs, for instance, essence and phenomenon, content and form, necessity and chance, possibility and actuality, etc. Marxist philosophy holds that categories must be pairs of opposites; this is certainly a correct view and reflects the reality of things. Thus when we today study the categorical system of traditional Chinese philosophy and try to make it more systematically and scientifically reflect the characteristics and level of traditional Chinese philosophy, we should try to find out the law of unity of opposites in its categorical system.

How many categories should the categorical system of traditional Chinese philosophy contain in order to be sufficient to indicate "the basic pattern of being" or "the basic concepts that reflect the most fundamental characteristics, aspects and relationships of the phenomena and knowledge of the reality"?

The twenty pairs of opposite basic concepts of the categorical system of traditional Chinese philosophy are merely a tentative proposition. They indicate mostly what the "world" and "man" are; for example, the existence of the "world" comprises "principle" and qi and the existence of "man" comprises "spirit" and "form." The categories used by Western philosophers, however, generally show the mode of existence and the "principles of knowledge." The contemporary categories of Marxist philosophy as a whole also show the characteristics and aspects of being and do not include the most basic concepts such as "mind" and "thing" in the categorical system. By this criterion, some of the categories listed above should not be included in the categorical system of traditional Chinese philosophy and some other concepts should be added. However, the way we have indicated the system of traditional Chinese philosophy might be just one approach, for the various categories listed in the diagram do indicate the "basic mode of existence" so far as their contents are concerned, and are also "focal points in the web" of man's knowledge. Would not, then, our way seem to be better suited to reflect the characteristics and level of traditional Chinese philosophy? Of course it would be even better if we could use less basic concepts to indicate traditional Chinese philosophy, such as the diagram on the next page.

Can "the categorical system of traditional Chinese philosophy" reflect its characteristics and level?

This is a major question because serious research and thorough discussion is needed to ascertain the characteristics of traditional Chinese philosophy and its level. Could we venture to say that our diagram of the categorical system more or less reflects the characteristics and level of traditional Chinese philosophy?

Apparently, traditional Chinese philosophy paid special attention to the study of the basic mode of existence and the existence of man and the relationships between things; that is, the identity of things, hence the multitude of concepts such as the "Heaven and man combine as one," the "knowledge and action combine as one," "essence and function are like one," "nonbeing originates in being," the "spirit and form combine as one," and "mind and matter are not two." Although traditional Chinese philosophy did not devote much discussion to such concepts as time and space, cause and effect which are not included in our diagram, yet as a categorical system, traditional Chinese philosophy already attained a fairly high level as compared with ancient Western and Indian philosophy in that it covered a vast scope, with basic concepts all in pairs and the development of the meaning of its concepts reflecting the world with increasing depth.

The categorical system of traditional Chinese philosophy has not been widely discussed and is a fairly new topic. Here, the author has ventured to propose some preliminary propositions with the aim of arousing interest in the discussion of this topic in the hope that the study of the history of Chinese philosophy, under the guidance of Marxism, will advance even more scientifically.

NEW PROGRESS

In recent years study of the history of Chinese philosophy has been in full swing in China. The Society of the History of Chinese Philosophy has been set up and has in publication two journals entitled Studies of the History of Chinese Philosophy and Chinese Philosophy dedicated to publishing research results in this area. A number of books specializing in the subject have come off press and dozens of seminars have been held to discuss special issues. Thus a variety of different views in regard to Chinese philosophers ranging from Confucius to Sun Yat-sen have come forth. All this signals the new progress made in the study of the history of Chinese philosophy. However, I do not propose to discuss here the concrete issues; rather, I would like to talk about the prevailing trends in the study as these probably can give a better picture of the new progress made in this area and points to new prospects which will open up in the studies. In light of this, I would like to address myself to four mutually related issues.

THE HISTORY OF CHINESE BUDDHISTIC PHILOSOPHY AS THE HISTORY OF KNOWLEDGE OF THE CHINESE NATION

There had been in the past a theory which moved from the classical conclusion that the history of philosophy was an historical account of the struggle between materialism and idealism to the study of the history of philosophy as the development of man's knowledge and the laws governing the development of theoretic thinking. However, the many years of practice in taking the history of philosophy merely as an historical account of the struggle between materialism and idealism not only gave rise to such drawbacks as oversimplification and indiscriminate labeling, but also failed to identify any concepts that bore the nature of regularity. How should we resolve this problem? The discussion of "how to evaluate idealism" and "the object of the study of history of philosophy" had failed to lead us out of the dilemma. Under such circumstances people began to turn their attention to studying how philosophy as theoretical thinking developed in history rather than becoming unduly entangled in the class background of a certain philosopher and his place in history.

A philosophical idea that once played a role in the development of man's knowledge naturally had a place in history. But excessive discussion about the relative superiority or inferiority of materialism and idealism is unnecessary, for which of the two is better can be fully determined by the effect they each produced on the development of man's knowledge. The study of the history of Chinese philosophy, in particular, used to stress the role played by a certain philosopher or philosophical school in history and how they were related to the ongoing class struggle and political struggle at that time.

Of course, studies of this sort are also important, though strictly speaking they are the problem that the historical study of philosophy is designed to resolve eventually. The final purpose of such a historical study is to reveal the logical inevitability of the development of theoretic thinking as it occurred in history. In the pre-Qin Dynasty philosophy, for example, was there any inevitability for the ideas of Confucius to develop through Mencius to that of Xunzi? At present more and more people who study the history of Chinese philosophy as a history of knowledge. For example, a multi-volume book entitled History of the Development of Chinese Philosophy is now being compiled under the auspices of Professor Ren Jiyu, who asserted that the book was intended to deal with the developmental history of the Chinese nation's knowledge. The History of Chinese Philosophy compiled with the joint efforts of Wuhan and Zhongshan universities also applied this idea as its guiding thought. In the preface, Xiao Jiefu (Hsiao Che-fu) of Wuhan University remarked: "The history of philosophy is the history of how the contradictions of philosophical knowledge have developed; it is man's understanding about the general laws governing nature, society and movements of thinking manifested in the form of theoretic thinking."

Chen Junmin of Shaanxi Teachers University wrote that the "study of the history of philosophy is in essence a science that inquires into the dialectic movement of man's philosophical understanding." In the article "On the Scope, Target, and Task of the History of Chinese Philosophy" Zhang Dainian observed: "The history of philosophy is the history of knowledge in its totality." "It is the history of how man's knowledge develops, that is, a process in which the relative truths developed by mankind accumulate and increase, and the new ones replace the old." To find out in its totality the law that governs the development of Chinese philosophy, Chinese philosophical circles have also turned their attention to Hegel's idea of "likening the history of philosophy to cycles." In the preface to his newly published History of Chinese Philosophy: New Version, Feng Youlan made a special reference to this issue.

Two seminars were held in Beijing, one on "The Philosophy of the Han and Tang Dynasties," was convened by the editorial department of Study of the History of Chinese Philosophy, the other on "Philosophy of the Han Dynasty" was under the auspices of the editorial department of Chinese Philosophy. At both meetings I suggested as a clue to the development of traditional Chinese philosophy in its totality that it is formed by a large spiral cycle constituted in turn of three smaller spiral developmental cycles. The first cycle was pre-Qin Dynasty philosophy. With Confucius as the starting point, it moved on through Mencius and Xunzi to the Book of Change (also through other masters of the School of Logicians) and thus formed the first cycle in the history of Chinese philosophy. The second cycle was the philosophy of the Wei and Jin dynasties and the Northern and Southern dynasties. Starting from the idea of "valuing nil" advocated by Wang Bi and He Yan, it developed through "esteeming substance" upheld by Xiang Xiu and Guo Xiang, to Seng Pi's "doctrine of non-vacuum" which was "neither something nor nothing." The third cycle began with Zhang Zai and moved on through Zhu Xi to Wang Fuzhi.

In the midst of the three cycles were the study of the Confucian classics of the two Han dynasties and Buddhist studies during the Sui and Tang dynasties, indicating the transition from one cycle to another. The three cycles of spiral movements made up the large cycle of traditional Chinese philosophy. Namely, from the philosophy of the pre-Qin period and the two Han dynasties with Confucianism as its main body, it moved on to the metaphysics of the Wei-Jin period and the Sui and Tang dynasties built on the framework of Lao-Zhuang theories.

Gradually it assimilated Buddhism (the Hua Yan sect, the Chan sect) and finally developed into the neo-Confucianism of the Song and Ming dynasties, a new school of Confucianism that had absorbed ideas of both the Buddhist and the Daoist schools which it developed at an even higher plane. This pattern of development, it seems, gives expression to the true feature of traditional Chinese philosophy; it shows the place of Confucianism in traditional Chinese philosophy and also the profound influence which Buddhist and Daoist ideas exerted over the philosophy.

THE CONCEPT AND CATEGORY OF TRADITIONAL CHINESE BUDDHISTIC PHILOSOPHY

If we intend to study the history of philosophy as the history of man's knowledge and reveal the law of the development of theoretic thinking in history, we must probe the issue of concept and category. As theoretic thinking, philosophy is unavoidably manifested through a series of concepts and categories and philosophical propositions formed by concepts and categories. This applies to philosophies in general and is particularly significant in the study of concepts of traditional Chinese philosophy. As Hegel said: "As cultural difference is generally formed on the basis of differences of ideological categories, it is even more so by difference of philosophy." Therefore the study of the concepts and categories of traditional Chinese philosophy and the history of its development will help us understand the characteristics of China's traditional philosophy and the level of its development.

Except for having absorbed some concepts from the Buddhism of India, philosophical studies in China had in the main developed independently prior to modern times and thus maintained a very distinctive character. Precisely because traditional Chinese philosophy has a set of concepts and categories of its own and has gradually formed itself into a complete system it is inappropriate to apply to it concepts and categories of Western philosophy in an oversimplified way; nor is it possible to equate them simply with the concepts and categories of Marxist philosophy. For example, the concept of "shen" in traditional Chinese philosophy has several implications. It may refer to god and ghosts, the meaning that was probably meant by Confucius when he said: "Worship god as if god were there." "Shen" may also mean "spirit" or "soul." This was what Xunzi implied when he said "'Shen' (spirit or soul) is engendered when matter takes shape." Nevertheless, in traditional Chinese philosophy "shen" has an even deeper layer of meaning, that is, "a subtle change." This idea stood out in the Record of Changes, which said: "When there is no telling whether it is yin or yang, it is called 'shen.'" Even though "shen" implies a variety of ideas, the implications are related to each other. Another example is "ti," the opposite of "yong" in traditional Chinese philosophy. It also has a lot of implications; it implies not only "substance" and "support" but also "whole" and "abstract." The multiplex and mutually related implications embodied in one concept give expression to the special features of traditional Chinese philosophy and its level of development.

Since traditional Chinese philosophy has its special conceptual categories, is it true that it has a special category system? I have discussed this issue in my article "On the Problems of a Category System of Traditional Chinese Philosophy," which, on the basis of the historical development of Chinese philosophy, delineated the system of its categories. According to the article, this system is made up by 20 or 12 pairs of categories. Among them the most important pair comprises "the Way of Heaven" and "the way of man." This problem of "Heaven" and "man" remains the core issue of traditional Chinese philosophy. Starting from Confucius' theory of "the Way of Heaven and life," it moved on through Mencius' idea of "do with all one's heart, understand one's lot, and know about Heaven"; the concept "honesty is the Way of Heaven and to be honest is the way of man" stated in The Doctrine of the Mean, the idea to "establish the Way of Heaven" and "establish the way of man" as advocated by Record of Changes; down to Dong Zhongshu, the great Confucian of the Han Dynasty, who described his studies as a learning that probed into "what links man with Heaven."

Even Sima Qian, much influenced by Daoist ideas, called his Historical Records a book designed as "an inquiry into what is between Heaven and man and a probe into the changes in the past and present." He Yan, a founder of the metaphysics of the Wei and Jin dynasties, described Wang Bi, another founder of metaphysics, as "one who is qualified to talk about what is between Heaven and man." Even Tao Hongjing, a Daoist master during the Northern and Southern dynasties, was also of the opinion that Daoism (Taoism) studied "what is between Heaven and man." By the time of the Song Dynasty, the Confucians discussed such issues as "the separation of reason and Way," "the heart of Way," "the heart of man," "Heaven's reason," "man's desire," and so on, which were all developments of the issue of "Heaven" and "man." Therefore an understanding about the relations between "Heaven" and "man" means having a grip on the basic issue of traditional Chinese philosophy.

Judging by how things stand at present, articles dwelling on conceptual categories of Chinese philosophy in its totality are increasing. Aside from my article, there were "Unfold the Study of Conceptual Categories Inherent in Chinese Philosophy" by Professor Zhang Dainian [Studies of the History of Chinese Philosophy, January 1982], "Unfold the Study of Categories in the History of Chinese Philosophy" by Fang Keli [People's Daily, September 3, 1982], "A Preliminary Discussion of Methodology in the History of Chinese Philosophy" by Xiao Jiefu (Hsiao Che-fu) [Journal of Wuhan University, no. 3, 1982], and others. However, there are even more papers and publications dwelling on the category systems of certain philosophers, or a certain pair of philosophic categories. For example, in the article "Study of Zhu Xi's Thinking" Zhang Liwen made a special study of the relations among different categories of Zhu Xi's philosophy. In his book entitled The Viewpoint on Knowledge and Practice in the History of Chinese Philosophy Fang Keli analyzed knowledge and practice as a pair of categories in the perspective of historical development. The journal Study of the History of Chinese Philosophy began a special column in every issue to publish various studies of categories in traditional Chinese philosophy. In particular we should mention Pang Pu's "On `San (Three)'," in which in the perspective of "can's" various implications he discussed the unique position of "three" in Chinese culture and the special philosophical significance of triaism. It appears the study of traditional Chinese philosophy can take a further step forward only after such research into the categories of Chinese philosophy and its system.

THE COMPARISON AND ANALYSIS OF TRADITIONAL CHINESE AND FOREIGN PHILOSOPHIES

Toward the end of October 1980, a "Symposium on the Comparative Study of Chinese and Foreign Philosophies" was held in Guilin. The conference failed to produce any results; however, the issue it brought up began to arouse the attention of us all. As a matter of fact, the study of conceptual categories of Chinese philosophy naturally would have led to such a question, but special features of the conceptual categories of Chinese philosophy can be identified only through comparison with foreign philosophy. That little attention has been paid to the similarities and differences between Chinese and foreign philosophies is due to a variety of factors. As far as the study of history of philosophy itself is concerned, however, one of the most important reasons was the total neglect of the special characteristics of traditional Chinese philosophy. We tried either to explain it in light of Western philosophy or mechanically to apply Marxist jargon to it. Thus it became unnecessary to study the similarities and differences between Chinese and foreign philosophies. Thus far not many studies have been conducted in this regard and studies generally have been done on some individual topics. For example, the Department of Philosophy of People's University held a discussion to compare and analyze Zhu Xi's idea of "Taiji" [the great ultimate] and the "absolute spirit" advocated by Hegel.

An interesting phenomenon which has emerged in the course of comparing Chinese and foreign philosophies is that a number of people, including some natural scientists, have analyzed the Chinese theory of "vitality" and found that it contains more grains of truth and thus is superior to the Western theory of the "atom."

According to them, the concept of "vitality" as theorized in China has not only the implication of "basic particle" but also that of "field"; in other words, it has a "dual character of both wave and particle." Professor He Zuoxiu of the Institute of Theoretic Physics under the Chinese Academy of Sciences published in Chinese Science an article entitled "The Materialist Theory of Vitality" in which he said: "Vitality is a matter of continuity. It is close to 'field' as discussed in modern science." "The theory of vitality is the forerunner of the contemporary theory of the quantum field." The theory of "vitality" as discussed in Chinese philosophy has special value in holding that the interaction among different things comes as a result of the effect of "vital energy."

But while this thesis probably contains some grains of truth, it appears also to have certain drawbacks, namely, it lumps together all different phenomena under "vital energy" or the "effect of vital energy" instead of focusing attention on analyzing the phenomena. The "theory of the atom" which prevailed in ancient Greece required that the smallest, indivisible particles be found and called "atoms." While this was, of course, incorrect, in terms of method it called for analysis of concrete matter which cannot be but as an advantage for Western philosophy. As far as the method of thinking is concerned, traditional Chinese philosophy seems to have laid more emphasis on the relations among things and the unity of their many aspects. On the contrary, Western philosophers in ancient times were probably more concerned about the distinction between different things and stressed the analysis of their various aspects.

As attention has been paid to the comparison of Chinese and Western philosophies, the comparison between Chinese and foreign religions also has drawn more attention than before. More studies have been carried out on Daoism (Taoism), the religion of the Chinese nation.

There are institutions for Daoist studies, for example, the Institute of Religion under Sichuan University specializes in the study of Daoism (Taoism). Special courses on Daoism (Taoism) are now being offered in universities, special teams have been set up to compile An Outline of Daoist Collections, and articles have been published comparing Daoism (Taoism) with Buddhism. The January issue of Philosophical Studies in 1981 carried an article under the title of "A Preliminary Discussion of the Early Daoist Theory of Life, Death, Spirit, and Body"; which, based on historical data, this analysis of these specific concepts in Daoism (Taoism) and Buddhism revealed the special features of Daoism (Taoism) as a religion.

In the perspective of a comparison of Chinese and foreign philosophies, two important questions have been raised. First, in view of the different development in Chinese and Western societies, some have asked very perceptively whether there is a "mode of Asian thinking."

Did not some major propositions of traditional Chinese philosophy express the characteristics of the Chinese mode of thinking? Over the last few years quite a few articles have addressed such propositions as the "integration of Heaven with man," "identification of the intrinsic with the extrinsic," "integration of knowledge with practice," and "feeling and scenery in perfect harmony."

Do not all these propositions embody a search for "unity," and is this the basic characteristic of the mode of thinking in traditional Chinese philosophy? If such be the case can we predict that once its lack of logical analysis and demonstration has been rectified Chinese philosophy will develop more along this search for unity? The second question raised is where the national spirit of Chinese culture lies. The answer to such a question can be found only through the comparison of Chinese with foreign philosophies.

THE METHOD EMPLOYED BY TRADITIONAL CHINESE PHILOSOPHY IN ESTABLISHING A SYSTEM

At the "Symposium on Philosophy of the Han and Tang dynasties" and the "Discussion of Philosophy of the Han Dynasty" held in 1983 the method of establishing a philosophical system was raised and Jin Chunfeng was the first to address this issue. He said philosophers of the Han Dynasty generally used the method of positivism to establish the philosophical system; the Wei and Jin people used a different method, but he was not sure how to define it; the method used by neo-Confucians of the Song and Ming dynasties can be called the method of ethical rationalism. At an enlarged session of the editorial committee on Study of the History of Chinese Philosophy held in 1981 I proposed that this question be chosen as a topic for solicited contributions. Philosophy has two aspects, the "contents" and the "method." Not only the "contents" but the "method" as well reflect a philosophy's level of theoretic thinking. During the period from the pre-Qin Dynasty to the Wei and Jin dynasties traditional Chinese philosophy comprised two major systems, Confucianism and Daoism (Taoism). These two schools were significantly different not only in their contents, but also in terms of the methods they used in establishing their systems.

To put it briefly, the method used by the Confucians was basically that of experience, namely, to use experience in demonstration of things transcending experience or other experience. By the method of experience we mean that the rationality of a philosophical idea can be proved through experience. Confucius said: "To draw a simile from something close can be called the method of benevolence." Mencius remarked: "Categorize and list things that are similar." Xunzi also noted: "Things of the same category do not conflict; they are of the same rationality even after a long time." The Record of Changes mentioned "draw close experience from your own person and distant experience from things," "make a divination to observe nature," "observe astronomic phenomena above and study geographical features below" to illustrate the principles of its thinking. Dong Zhongshu put forward the idea that "things that can be counted are of the second number and things that cannot be counted are of the second category," and with this he demonstrated that "things can be combined by the category and Heaven becomes one with man."

By the time of the metaphysics school in the Wei and Jin dynasties, the method underwent a change. In fact, metaphysics was built on the framework of Lao-Zhuang's thinking, and therefore the method it used in establishing its philosophical system can be called "dialectical thinking," which is characterized by demonstrating the rationality of things existing in experience with things transcending experience. Wang Bi said: "Forget words when the idea is grasped"; Guo Xiang said: "place words within the framework of the idea"; and Ji Kang (Chi Kang) remarked: "Words cannot express the idea completely"--they all meant the same thing.

Wang Bi cited "implements originate from the Way" to demonstrate that "ministers are subordinated to the king." Guo Xiang tried to prove the "fairyland" did not exist "beyond the real world" ("to take a journey to the outside world in order to enhance the inner world" "inside and outside are mutually obscure.") The method of "dialectical thinking" was used in all these.

Neo-Confucianism of the Song and Ming dynasties was a combination of the two schools and an improvement on them. Their method perhaps can be called "introspection of ethical rationality." Regardless of whether it was "character is rationality" advocated by Cheng Yi and Zhu Xi or "heart is rationality" upheld by Lu Jiuyuan and Wang Yangming, they all took "rationality [taiji], a priori morality, as the basic contents. Zhu Xi said: "Taiji is a principle of the extremely good. Every man has a taiji, and every thing has a taiji." Lu Jiuyuan remarked: "Those who know before others know this reason, and those who become aware before others are aware of this reason. For this reason one loves one's close relative and respects one's older brother."

In either "the Way questioning the learning" or "respecting virtue and character," one can perceive the "reason of Heaven" in its totality through a moral introspection.

Why was this question raised? Because at that time we were thinking about Engels' remark: "Theoretic thinking is merely an ability endowed by nature and should be developed and trained. To train it, there has been no other method up to now except studying philosophies of the past." Theoretic thinking calls for the formulation of a number of philosophic concepts and the formation, on the basis of philosophic concepts, of a series of philosophic propositions. In order to form the concepts and propositions of a philosophical system as well as the system itself it is imperative to use a certain method, which itself must be a certain kind of abstract thinking. The abstract thinking one exercises in the course of establishing one's philosophical system certainly will train and improve one's level of theoretic thinking. If we can reveal the different methods employed by the various philosophers and philosophical schools in history and make a clear analysis of them they will be an important help in analyzing the philosophers and philosophical schools under study. In addition, practice is no different from telling people a method for training and improving their level of theoretic thinking, and is therefore very significant.

Judging from the problems mentioned above, we seem to be able to perceive such a trend of development; namely, people may raise the question: What are the prospects of traditional Chinese philosophy, or in other words, does the continued existence of Chinese philosophy in its entirety have any value? If this question is raised and the proper conditions are available, then a comprehensive and systematic analysis can be made of Chinese philosophy in today's perspective. But at present quite a few people continuously maintain a negative attitude toward traditional Chinese philosophy as a whole. Whatever the circumstances, they regard traditional Chinese philosophy as a product of old times, an ideology of feudal and even slave society. Nevertheless, certain ideas of the philosophy are continuously quoted in everyday life. We can see that a great many articles, especially writings on "spiritual civilization," often quote passages from books of ancient China or historical stories in ancient times which were mostly the embodiment of traditional Chinese philosophical thinking.

Why are there such a contradictory phenomena? Is the concept of "value" involved here? Where does the basic spirit of traditional Chinese philosophy lie? Does this spirit still have value in today's world? Following the disclosure of the law of how traditional Chinese philosophy developed, the study of this problem will, in my opinion, show increasingly clearly that it works continuously toward the solution of a major problem, namely the value of the "'Way of' Heaven" and the "'way of' man" and their relations.

This problem should be resolved through the continuous elevation of man's spiritual realm, a concept in Chinese philosophy which requires that man should transcend "oneself" and identify with the "Way of Heaven." Having attained such a realm in which "Heaven is integrated with man" and "man succeeds alongside the Way," an individual could become a saint and society a "world of Great Harmony." As to how or whether it would be possible to realize such an ideal, there were, of course, different views due to the difference in historical conditions and environments. Nevertheless, philosophers in Chinese history tended to take as their motto the epigram that "Heaven moves along a healthy track, and a gentleman should make unremitting efforts to improve himself." How things will develop is hard to predict; we are not prophets, nor do we believe in prophecy. But if things always develop according to law, can we predict its future development by studying and analyzing its previous experience; can the development of philosophy be forecast to help us know what will happen with Chinese philosophy in the future? I think it is possible.

Is there the possibility for Confucianism to have a third-phase development? In saying this we mean to regard the school of thought advocated by Confucius, Mencius, and Xunzi during the Spring and Autumn period and the Warring States as the first-phase development of Confucianism. After the Han Dynasty Buddhism spread to China. Under the impact of Buddhist ideas, a Confucian school of idealist philosophy emerged during the Song and Ming dynasties. It greatly pushed forward the Confucian doctrines and constituted the second phase development of Confucianism. Over the last century,

Western Civilization has found its way into China. Especially around the time of the "May Fourth" [1919] Movement Marxism was also disseminated into our country, having an even bigger and more serious impact upon China's traditional thought and culture. Under such circumstances, is it possible for Confucianism to have a third-phase development? Can it be brought back to life? Can it still have a role to play in China and the world? In my opinion, it is perhaps too early to conduct an all-round discussion of this issue. However, to raise questions and opinions from certain angles in an attempt to push the inquiry forward may prove helpful.

In discussing whether it is possible for Confucianism to have a third phase development we must, first of all, acquire a clear understanding about the basic spirit of Confucianism. Regarding this basic spirit there have been in the past, and may be in the future, a variety of different views. The existence of different views is not necessarily a bad thing; it may help deepen the study of this issue. In clarifying the basic spirit, I think attention should be paid to two parts: the thoughts that have been constantly effective in the entire course of the development of Confucianism, and the thoughts that still have vitality today. By combing the two for consideration we may perhaps discover whether a third-phase development of Confucianism is possible from a certain aspect.

Running through the entire course of the development of Confucianism are two basic elements which still bear a major significance for us today: one is idealism and the other humanism; the two are connected.

Confucianism is a kind of idealism. Starting from Confucius, this school of thought has cherished the ideal of having a society in which "right principles prevail" and has made every effort to materialize the ideal in the real world. Despite its acknowledgment of the unattainability of such a goal, it still insists that one should foster the ideal and dedicate oneself to realizing it in the spirit of "Doing the impossible." Therefore when Zigong asked Confucius: "What if one can generously give to the people and provide relief to them?Can that be called benevolence?" Confucius answered: "One who behaves with benevolence must be a saint! Even Yao and Shun fell short of that." Evidently, Confucius did not regard the society of Yao and Shun's time as man's highest ideal. What then should we see as an ideal society? According to the Confucians, an ideal society is an ideal, which has the possibility, but not the necessity, of being realized. Despite the fact that an ideal society has never been realized before, it is a matter of fundamental importance, a problem of one's attitude toward life, whether or not one should seek to realize it. The Confucians' belief is that one should ceaselessly seek after it. This is why people at that time criticized Confucians as "being ignorant of world affairs."

Though it is not necessary that an ideal society be realized in the real world, as far as the Confucian philosophers are concerned, it can be realized in their minds. Why was the West Inscription by Zhang Zai so highly respected by later Confucians? Because it embodied the Confucian spirit of seeking to realize an ideal society, plus the fact that Zhang Zai had already built in his mind the ideal society. True, it was important whether the ideal society in which "the people are my brothers and I share my things with them," as Zhang Zai conceived, could be realized in the real world, but more important was whether one could have a world outlook in pursuing an ideal society. Therefore the last sentence of West Inscription says: I carry on my pursuit when alive, and rest at ease when I die." While one lives, one has a duty to fulfill. The duty is to exert oneself for the realization of the ideal "world of commonweal." It can be said that this is an attitude of "concerning oneself only about cultivation instead of gains." Whoever holds such an attitude toward life has a clear conscience. Today we need more than ever such an attitude.

Confucianism is a kind of idealism for which humanism is a prerequisite. Why is it that man must have an ideal and seek to build an ideal society?According to the Confucians, man is the most important factor in the world because he can "formulate ethics for the universe, provide sustenance for the people, carry forward consummate learnings into posterity, and win peace for thousands of generations to come." Confucius said: "Man can enhance the Way and not the reverse." The "Way" or the "Way of Nature" is an objective existence, but it needs to be enhanced and carried forward by man; it has to be effected by man through practice. How can man embody the "Way of Nature"? If, as the Confucians envisaged, man can understand how "Heaven is integrated with man," "knowledge is integrated with practice," and "feeling is integrated with scenery," man can then attain the loftiest realm of being a man. In other words, man can congeal in his heart the ideal of the true, the good and the beautiful.

The integration of Heaven with man, knowledge with practice and feeling with scenery are the three basic propositions the Chinese traditional philosophy about the true, the good and the beautiful; they are the ideal realms the Confucian school has been trying to attain. Why is it that Confucianism is in pursuit of the three integrations? In my opinion, Confucianism is nothing more than a teaching regarding how to behave oneself, namely, one should set a demand upon oneself and hold oneself responsible to the world and the nation. This is a very common question, but involves a task extremely difficult to fulfill. Whoever has attained such an ideal realm of the true, the good and the beautiful is a saint.

Although the proposition of integrating Heaven with man is designed to illustrate the relations between man and the entire universe, it begins with man as the center of the universe. Zhongyong (The Golden Mean) stated: "Being honest is the Way of Heaven. Striving to be honest is the Way of man. An honest man hits the right Way without difficulty and understands it without deliberation. One who conforms oneself on the Way of Heaven without qualm is a saint." Therefore a saint not only behaves in conformity with the requirements of the Way of Heaven, but also assumes as his responsibility the fulfillment of such requirements. In living a life in this world, one should not behave passively; rather, one should "make unremitting efforts to improve oneself" in order to embody the ceaseless flow and evolution of nature. In this way, man will set a demand upon himself; he will find a reason for his existence and foster a lofty ideal. In this light the most important thing is for one to "integrate one's understanding with one's behavior" so that one can have an unified viewpoint on understanding and behavior in terms of morality and self-cultivation. The three programs and eight articles outlined in Da Xue (The Great Learning) tell us exactly what this is about.

It is said in Da Xue: The Way of the great learning lies in shedding light on the bright principles, being close to the people, and stopping at nothing but the utmost good. Those in ancient times who wanted to shed light on the bright principles for the world had to first bring order to their own kingdoms. To bring order to their kingdoms they had to first bring their own houses to order. To bring their houses to order they had to first cultivate their own moral character. To cultivate their own moral character they had to first set their minds straight. To set their minds straight they had to first foster a sincere desire. To foster a sincere desire they had to first carry knowledge to the utmost degree. To carry knowledge to the utmost degree they had to first inquire into the properties of things. Having inquired into the properties of things, they were able to carry knowledge to the utmost degree. Having carried knowledge to the utmost degree, they were able to foster a sincere desire. Having fostered a sincere desire, they were able to set their minds straight. Having set their minds straight, they were able to cultivate their own moral character. Having cultivated their own moral character, they were able to bring their houses to order. Having brought their houses to order, they were able to bring order to their kingdoms. Having brought order to their kingdoms, the whole world would be at peace.

This is a process of knowledge, but still more a process of moral practice. Many must have an ideal, and the highest ideal is to "achieve peace" so that human society can attain a realm of "Great Harmony." In turn, the world of "Great Harmony" requires that everyone should set for himself the requirement of being a man, a reason for being a man, and "not do to others what one does not wish done to oneself." Noted Confucius: "To implement my principle is nothing more than being honest and just." Whether the ideal society of "Great Harmony" can be attained or not remains, of course, a question. But a Confucian must have such a goal and find pleasure in pursuing it. To lead one's existence in the world and be a man, one must find pleasure in doing so and appreciate the creation of the universe. To have a true appreciation of Nature one must be able to display creativity and man's spiritual realm in reproducing the "creation of the universe."

One must be able to show why man should be a man, to create poetry and prose "masterpieces," paintings of "superb workmanship," and music like "the sounds of nature." This is why art requires that "feeling be integrated with scenery." Wang Fuzhi observed: "In name feeling and scenery are two things, but in reality they are inseparable. Those gifted in writing poetry are capable of unlimited wit. A witty line naturally has feeling in the midst of scenery and scenery in the midst of feeling." "Once feeling is integrated with scenery, a witty remark is ready at hand." When one enters the realm of creation, it will be a realm in which the true, the good and the beautiful are integrated with one another. This is precisely where the meaning of life and the highest ideal of mankind lie. Confucius described himself as "doing things at will without violating rules at the age of seventy." Probably it was the ideal realm as mentioned above. Indeed, it must be the realm of a saint when whatever one says and does is in harmony with the entire universe, society, and one's own frame of mind.

That the continued existence of Confucianism still has a value is due perhaps to the sole fact that it provides a reason for being a man. It is most difficult for one to be a man, still more to maintain a harmony between oneself and nature, society and others, or between one's inner and outer sides in body and soul. Is such a requirement unnecessary in today's world? Confucianism only tells us the reason for being a man. We should not set demands on it in other aspects, and it should come as no surprise that it suffers from some inadequacies.

THE PROBLEM OF HARMONIOUS COMMUNITIES IN ANCIENT CHINA

Why did the ancient Chinese philosophers pursue these three unities? In my opinion, Chinese philosophy does not engage in investigating the external world, but is concerned rather with pursuing internal human values. In other words, traditional Chinese philosophy teaches people how to be human by making demands upon themselves, i.e., to cherish an ideal form of human life. Sagehood is defined by the attainment of the three unities. Beginning with Confucius, Chinese philosophers have always aspired to the creation of harmonious societies, and have attempted to bring them into being. Even when unsure of the outcome of their efforts, they still consider the endeavor to be obligatory. Thus it was said of Confucius that he "knew the impossibility [of the task] and yet continued to do it." The ideal societies they sought are characterized by harmony; for example, the Confucian description of a society of "great harmony" in the Li Yün chapter of the Book of Rites, and the "small country with a small population" in Chapter 80 of the Daoist classic Dao De Jing (Tao Te Ching). Such communities exhibit a concordance between man and Heaven, a unity of knowledge and action, and an intermingling of sentiment and scenery.

But these ideals may not be realized in the actual world. Whether we should pursue the ideal of harmony is a matter of attitude. Ancient Chinese philosophers believed that some of their ideals might only be realized in their minds. Why was Zhang Zai's "West inscriptions" so highly esteemed by later thinkers? I think it is because the essay reveals the spirit of an ideal harmonious society. The essay begins: "People are my compatriots; things, my fellow-beings," and ends "Living is following my nature; death, my tranquility." When alive, one must fulfill the responsibility of realizing the ideal of "great harmony." Thus one can enjoy serenity without feeling shame to the end of one's life.

This search for an ideal harmonious society differs from Western humanism, though it can be looked at as humanism of a Chinese type. According to the ancient Chinese thinkers, only human beings are the most important link between Heaven and Earth. Sages are capable of "establishing the mind of Heaven and Earth, determining the destiny of human lives, restoring discontinued traditions of learning from the past, and commencing a period of supreme peace for one's descendants. "Hence the Confucian notion that men can expand the Way, rather than the other way around. Although the Way of Heaven is an objective Being, it needs human embodiment. According to ancient Chinese thought, a man can embody the Way when he understands the unity of Heaven and man, practices the unity of knowledge and action, and creatively reveals the unity of sentiment and scenery. Conceiving of the loftiest possible realm of humanity, one may concentrate on the above-described ideal in one's mind in order to actualize it. Such a realm harmonizes individual words and deeds with all human societies and even extends this harmony to the whole universe. In traditional Chinese philosophy, the major role of human beings is to "be human" in pursuing the ideal of a harmonious society. As the central element in nature and the community, man assumes a great responsibility.

In brief, the Chinese mentality may be characterized by the pursuit of harmony and unity. Most distinguished Chinese philosophers viewed reality positively and endeavored to transform the conflict-ridden societies in which they lived into harmonious communities. Although their ideals and doctrines did not bring about actual political changes, Chinese rulers used philosophical ideas as window dressing. For instance, the ideals of great harmony and supreme peace degenerated into emperors' reign-titles, and rulers called themselves the emperor or empress of Supreme Peace. Peasant revolts throughout history used "supreme peace" as a catchword for their righteous cause. At the end of the Eastern Han dynasty (25-220), the Yellow Turban Rebellion used the slogan "The Way of Supreme Peace" to organize farmers; Song dynasty (960-1279) peasant-revolts were aimed at "destroying all inequality in order to achieve supreme peace"; in modern times, the peasant-rebellion led by Hong Xiuquan (Hung Hsiu-ch'uan) was known as the "Supreme Peace Army" (Taiping Jun) belonging to the "Heavenly Kingdom of Supreme Peace" (Tai-ping Tianguo).

Despite its preeminence in the Chinese mind, the ideal of attaining supreme peace has never been actualized. At most, the illusion of "supreme peace and a prosperous world" was realized during short periods of history. Chinese traditional idealism is basically fantasy. Past sages might have promulgated the ideal of "governing the country and bringing peace to the world" with true sincerity, but since its actualization is impossible, their intentions have to be looked at as little more than idealized feudalism.

We can observe that Chinese thought has always been characterized by a search for unity. From its earliest beginnings, Chinese philosophy stressed the unity of two concepts, or the mutual relationship between several concepts. In the Book of Changes, Qian and Kun (later yin and yang represent concepts of duality in unity, the "Great Principle" chapter in the Book of Rites was based on the system of "five elements" related through dualistic unities. Once Heaven and man were looked upon as dualistic philosophical concepts, Chinese philosophy began to place more emphasis on the unity of Heaven and man. This way of thinking is rational in its stress on harmony and unity, and in its objection to excess and insufficiency.

Under certain conditions, this ideal is beneficial to social stability and social development, as well as to the investigation of the actual relationships between objects. Social development requires a period of relative stability, while thought-cultures benefit significantly by mutual assimilation and confluence. History has alternating periods of maintaining the status quo and reformation. Since the Qin and Han dynasties (221 B.C.-A.D. 220), China has been in a state of great unity. Situations of fragmentation or division were always temporary. The Han people and the minority nationalities formed a unified country while at the same time assimilating foreign cultures. Based also on the concept of unity, Chinese medicine stresses an organic connection between man and his environment, between the human body and human spirit, between the organs of the body, as well as between various remedies. Qi (vitality) was used to explain the unity of things and the reason behind their mutual influence. There is a similarity here to the findings of modern physics.

Despite the contributions of Chinese philosophy, we cannot overlook the shortcomings in this national way of thinking. An overemphasis upon harmony and unity resulted in the prolonged stagnation of feudal society, the slow growth of capitalism, exaggerated national pride and a lack of progressive thinking. Chinese traditional philosophy lacks a systematic epistemology and a tradition of logic. Theoretical thinking in Chinese philosophy has not undergone analysis, and is rich in terms of the cognition of essences, similar to some of the conclusions of modern science. But without the necessary analysis and argument, it cannot develop into modern science. Because of the excessive attention paid to mutual relationships and unity and the total disregard of advanced anatomy, the traditional Chinese failed to mature along the path taken by modern science in the West. We must reform our traditional ways of thinking, applying logical discourse and scientific epistemology to the concepts of relationship, unity and cosmic harmony. We should stress specific analysis, avoid the long-recognized shortcomings in our philosophy, and make good use of the tenets of Western philosophy, in order to establish a school of scientific philosophy with Chinese traits. (Translated by Yuk Wong).

Bibliography

Adikaram, E. W.: *Early History of Buddhism in Ceylon,* Buddhist Cultural Centre, Dehiwala, 1994.

Aronson, Harvey B.: *Love and Sympathy in Theravada Buddhism,* Motilal Banarsidass, Delhi, 1980.

Auboyer, Jeannine: *Buddha: A Pictorial History of His Life and Legacy,* Crossroad, New York, 1983.

Beal, Samuel: *Buddhist Records of the Western World,* Paragon, London, 1885.

Behl, Benoy K.: *The Ajanta Caves: Artistic Wonder of Ancient Buddhist India,* Harry N. Abrams, New York, 1998.

Brown, R.L.: *The Dvaravati Wheels of the Law and the Indianization of South East Asia*, E.J. Brill, Leiden, 1996.

Buddhadasa, Bhikkhu: *Teaching Dhamma by Pictures,* Social Science Association Press of Thailand, Bangkok, 1968.

Chakravarti, Uma: *The Social Dimensions of Early Buddhism,* Oxford University Press, Delhi, 1987.

Cummings, Mary: *The Lives of the Buddha in the Art and Literature of Asia,* University of Michigan, Ann Arbor, 1982.

Grousset, Rene: *In the Footsteps of the Buddha,* Routledge and Kegan Paul, London, 1932.

Haldar, J. R.: *Early Buddhist Mythology,* Manohar, New Delhi, 1977.

Horner, I. B.: *The Living Thoughts of Gautama the Buddha,* Cassell, London, 1948.

Ireland, John D.: *The Itivuttaka: The Buddha's Sayings,* Buddhist Publication Society, Kandy, 1991.

Ireland, John D.: *The Udana: Inspired Utterances of the Buddha,* Buddhist Publication Society, Kandy, 1990.

Jayatilleke, K. N.: *The Message of the Buddha,* Free Press, New York, 1974.

John Powers: *The Yogacara School of Buddhism: A Bibliography,* Scarecrow Press, Lanham, 1991.

McDermott, James P.: *Karma and Rebirth in Classical Indian Traditions,* University of California Press, Berkeley, 1980.

Miksic, John: *Borobudur: Golden Tales of the Buddha,* Shambala, Boston, 1990.

Nakamura, Hajime: *Gautama Buddha,* Buddhist Books International, Los Angeles, 1977.

Pal, Pratapaditya: *Light of Asia: Buddha Sakyamuni in Asian Art,* County Museum of Art, Los Angeles, 1984.

Robinson, James B.: *Buddha's Lions: The Lives of the Eighty-Four Siddhas,* Dharma, Berkeley, 1980.

Seneviratna, Anuradha: *King Ashoka and Buddhism,* Buddhist Publication Society, Kandy, 1994.

Sharma, R. C.: *Buddhist Art: Mathura School,* Wiley Eastern Limited, New Delhi, 1995.

Snellgrove, David L.: *The Image of the Buddha,* Kodansha International, Tokyo, 1978.

Wagle, Narendra: *Society at the Time of Buddha,* Humanities Press, New York, 1967.

Wray, Elizabeth: *The Ten Lives of the Buddha,* Weatherhill, New York, 1972.

Yang, C. K.: *Religion in Chinese Society,* University of California Press, Berkeley, 1961.

Yushin Yoo: *Books on Buddhism: An Annotated Subject Guide,* Scarecrow Press, Metuchen, 1976).

Zürcher, Erik: *Buddhism, Its Origin and Spread in Words, Maps, and Pictures,* E. J. Brill, Leiden, 1959.

Zwalf, W.: *Buddhism: Art and Faith,* British Museum Publications, London, 1985.

Index

❑❑❑